T0305808

Cooperatives as a Catalyst for Sustainability
Lessons Learned from Asian Models

ASIA-PACIFIC BUSINESS SERIES   (ISSN: 1793-3137)

Series Editor
Léo-Paul Dana
Professor
Dalhousie University, Canada

Published

Vol. 12   *Cooperatives as a Catalyst for Sustainability: Lessons Learned from Asian Models*
edited by Léo-Paul Dana, Naman Sharma, Sneha Kumari, K K Tripathy, B P Pillai & R Jayalakshmi

Vol. 11   *Organising Entrepreneurship and MSMEs Across India*
edited by Léo-Paul Dana, Naman Sharma & Satya Ranjan Acharya

Vol. 10   *Guanxi and Business (Third Edition)*
by Yadong Luo

Vol. 9   *Asian Models of Entrepreneurship: From the Indian Union and Nepal to the Japanese Archipelago: Context, Policy and Practice (Second Edition)*
by Léo-Paul Dana

Vol. 8   *Catalyst for Change: Chinese Business in Asia*
edited by Thomas Menkhoff, Hans-Dieter Evers, Chay Yue Wah & Hoon Chang Yau

Vol. 7   *From Adam Smith to Michael Porter: Evolution of Competitiveness Theory (Extended Edition)*
by Dong-Sung Cho & Hwy-Chang Moon

Vol. 6   *Islamic Banking and Finance in South-East Asia: Its Development and Future (Third Edition)*
by Angelo M. Venardos

Vol. 5   *Guanxi and Business (Second Edition)*
by Yadong Luo

Vol. 4   *Asian Models of Entrepreneurship — From the Indian Union and the Kingdom of Nepal to the Japanese Archipelago: Context, Policy and Practice*
by Léo-Paul Dana

Vol. 3   *Islamic Banking and Finance in South-East Asia: Its Development and Future (Second Edition)*
by Angelo M. Venardos

The complete list of the published volumes in the series can also be found at
http://www.worldscientific.com/series/apbs

Cooperatives as a Catalyst for Sustainability

Lessons Learned from Asian Models

Edited by

Léo-Paul Dana
ICD Business School, Paris, France & Dalhousie University, Canada

Naman Sharma
Indian Institute of Foreign Trade, India

Sneha Kumari
Symbiosis International Deemed University, India

K K Tripathy
Government of India, India

B P Pillai
Agricultural Co-operative Staff Training Institute, India

R Jayalakshmi
Vaikunth Mehta National Institute of Cooperative Management, India

World Scientific

NEW JERSEY · LONDON · SINGAPORE · BEIJING · SHANGHAI · HONG KONG · TAIPEI · CHENNAI · TOKYO

Published by

World Scientific Publishing Co. Pte. Ltd.

5 Toh Tuck Link, Singapore 596224

USA office: 27 Warren Street, Suite 401-402, Hackensack, NJ 07601

UK office: 57 Shelton Street, Covent Garden, London WC2H 9HE

Library of Congress Cataloging-in-Publication Data
Names: Dana, Léo-Paul, editor.
Title: Cooperatives as a catalyst for sustainability : lessons learned from Asian models /
    edited by Léo-Paul Dana, Dalhousie University, Canada [and 5 others]
Description: Hackensack, NJ : World Scientific, [2023] | Series: Asia-Pacific business series,
    1793-3137 ; 12 | Includes bibliographical references and index.
Identifiers: LCCN 2022017128 | ISBN 9789811253782 (hardcover) |
    ISBN 9789811253799 (ebook) | ISBN 9789811253805 (ebook other)
Subjects: LCSH: Cooperative societies--Asia. | Community development--Asia. |
    Sustainable development--Asia.
Classification: LCC HD1491.A3 .C663 2023 | DDC 334.95--dc23/eng/20220602
LC record available at https://lccn.loc.gov/2022017128

British Library Cataloguing-in-Publication Data
A catalogue record for this book is available from the British Library.

For any available supplementary material, please visit
https://www.worldscientific.com/worldscibooks/10.1142/12764#t=suppl

Desk Editors: Balasubramanian Shanmugam/Lai Ann

Typeset by Stallion Press
Email: enquiries@stallionpress.com

Printed in Singapore

This book is dedicated to Michelle Brandstrup.

https://doi.org/10.1142/9789811253799_fmatter

About the Editors

Léo-Paul Dana is Professor at ICD Business School, Paris, France and holds titles of Professor at Dalhousie University and Visiting Professor at Kingston University. He is also associated with the Chaire ETI at Sorbonne Business School. A graduate of McGill University and HEC-Montreal, he has served as Marie Curie Fellow at Princeton University and Visiting Professor at INSEAD. He has published extensively in a variety of journals including *Entrepreneurship: Theory & Practice, International Business Review, International Small Business Journal, Journal of Business Research, Journal of Small Business Management, Journal of World Business, Small Business Economics,* and *Technological Forecasting & Social Change.*

Naman Sharma is currently affiliated with the Indian Institute of Foreign Trade, Kolkata, India, as an Assistant Professor, and has nearly five years of academic experience. Dr. Sharma also has substantial research experience and his research has been published in ABDC-ranked/Scopus-indexed journals and other reputable publishers, such as the Emerald Publishing Group. He has also authored four books with publishers of international repute, such as IGI-Global, and is a serving guest editor for various journals.

Sneha Kumari is an Assistant Professor at Symbiosis School of Economics, Symbiosis International (Deemed University). Prior to that, she was an Assistant Professor at Vaikunth Mehta National Institute of Cooperative Management, a National Institute of Ministry of Cooperation,

Government of India. She completed her graduation (I.C.A.R. fellowship) in agriculture from Jawaharlal Nehru Agriculture College. She holds a degree in Agribusiness Management from Chaudhary Charan Singh Haryana Agriculture University (I.C.A.R.) and PGDBA in Human Resource Management, PGDBA in Marketing Management from Symbiosis International University. She has also qualified ICAR SRF and completed her PhD as JRF. She is associated with different institutes for various educational and research-related project assignments. She has published around 50 research papers in peer-reviewed journals, including those published by ABDC, Scopus, and Emerald, and has published two books with Emerald. She is a reviewer for several peer-reviewed journals.

K.K. Tripathy is an officer of Indian Economic Service (IES), Government of India. Prior to joining the IES, he worked as Executive Magistrate in Government of Odisha after getting into Odisha Administrative Service in 1998. He did his PhD from Department of Management Studies at Indian Institute of Technology Delhi on micro-finance management and its impact on rural livelihoods, master's in Economics from Ravenshaw College of Utkal University, and Bachelor of Law (LLB) from MS Law College of Utkal University. He is presently posted as Officer on Special Duty in Ministry of Cooperation, Government of India. During the past 23 years of public service, he has served in the Ministry of Chemicals & Fertilizers, Ministry of Education, Ministry of Agriculture and Farmers Welfare, Ministry of Rural Development, Ministry of Food Processing Industries, Planning Commission, and United Nations Development Programme. He has published around 75 research articles, papers, book chapters etc.

B.P. Pillai is the former Director of the Agricultural Co-operative Staff Training Institute, an autonomous institution under Government of Kerala. He has been in teaching and training for more than four decades. He has consulting experience with Cooperative Banks of Kerala for strategy formulation and policy making. He has expertise in financial management, cooperative law, and business management.

R. Jayalakshmi has more than 30 years of academic experience. She has worked as faculty in different training institutes, and is currently working at Vaikunth Mehta National Institute of Cooperative Management, a National Institute of Ministry of Cooperation, Government of India, Pune. She also has very rich experience in cooperative training, research, and teaching. She has published several books on cooperatives. She is the placement director and is responsible for the development of management skills for student teaching and placement.

About the Contributors

Anil Kumar Angrish completed his Ph.D. from University Business School, Panjab University, Chandigarh. He is presently Associate Professor (Finance and Accounting) in the Department of Pharmaceutical Management, NIPER SAS Nagar (Mohali). Dr. Angrish has teaching and research experience of more than 20 years. He has authored/co-authored about 60 publications in reputed journals (e.g., *Research Bulletin*), news papers (e.g., *Business Line*), magazines, and books. He has conducted studies for the WTO Cell, Union Ministry of Health and Family Welfare, Competition Commission of India (CCI), and the Department of Pharmaceuticals. His write-ups (article, debate, and comments) have appeared in the Hindu Business Line, Financial World, Financial Express, and Business Standard. He has reviewed two manuscripts for Pearson Education and Tata McGraw.

In the past 20 years, he has been associated with more than seventy (70) institutional and outside committees, including Investment Committee, Patent Licensing Committee, IPR Committee, and Agreement Handling Committee. He has served as Internal Audit Officer, Deputy Registrar (Finance and Accounts), Associate Dean (Student Affairs), and Officiating Registrar of NIPER SAS Nagar. He is also Member of the Standing Committee of Punjab Biotechnology Incubator (now part of Punjab State Biotech Corporation). As organiser/co-organiser, he has coordinated about ten seminars, conferences, symposiums, and workshops. He has been invited as a speaker by more than 50 institutions/organisations such as Ludhiana Stock Exchange, TIMT (Yamunanagar), Doordarshan

Chandigarh, Department of Gandhian Studies, Panjab University (Chandigarh), Bhaskaracharya College of Applied Sciences (University of Delhi), Kurukshetra University, Punjab Institute of Cooperative Training, and Rajiv Gandhi National Institute of Youth Development, Regional Centre (Chandigarh) to lecture on topics such as Special Economic Zones (SEZs), IPR Pricing, Goods and Services Tax (GST), and Corporate Governance. He has guided more than 130 MBA students on major research projects.

Anindita Baidya works as Senior Manager in the Cooperative Training group in the National Dairy Development Board. She has 25 years of experience in training and capacity building of stakeholders of people's organisations.

Sanjeev K. Bansal is professionally qualified and has teaching, research, administrative, and industrial experience. A Gold Medallist in M.Com. from Panjab University, Dr. Bansal has also passed the Final Examination for CA, CS, and CMA. Apart from teaching at U.G. and P.G. levels at various institutions, he has also worked in Bharat Sanchar Nigam Ltd. (A Govt. Telecom Company) for more than seven years as Accounts Officer. While at IKG Punjab Technical University, Kapurthala, he acted as a Special Member of the Board of Studies (Commerce) and also as Deputy Controller of Exam at PIT Khunimajra. Dr. Bansal has also acted as a Paper Setter for a few universities. He has conducted viva voce for B.Com., BBA M.Com., and MBA examinations at various institutions affiliated to IKG PTU, Kapurthala, and other institutions affiliated to Panjab University, Chandigarh, and Punjabi University, Patiala. Now, he guides a number of students pursuing Ph.D. and M.Phil. degrees, a few of whom have earned their respective degrees under his supervision. He has published more than 31 articles/research papers in various journals of repute. He has also participated and presented papers in a number of national and international conferences. His areas of interest include Corporate Accounting, Management Accounting, Cost Accounting, Income Tax and Business Ethics, CSR, and Corporate Governance. In the recent past, Dr. Bansal co-edited a book entitled *Business and Management: Some Emerging Issues* published by MITRAM, Kolkata. Very recently, an article co-authored by him was published in *The Management Accountant*, a journal published by the Institute of Cost Accountants of India, Kolkata (India).

Nisha Bharti has been working as an Assistant Professor and Head of the Department of Agribusiness Management at Symbiosis Institute of International Business, Symbiosis International University, Pune, since 2013. She is a Fellow (Doctorate) in Rural Management from the Institute of Rural Management, Anand (IRMA). She holds a Post Graduate degree in Agriculture from Indira Gandhi Agricultural University, Raipur. She worked as visiting faculty with various institutes like Gokhale Institute of Politics and Economics and VAMNICOM. She has industry experience of working with an organisation, PRADAN, for two years. She has published more than 25 papers in various top-ranked journals, including ABDC. She is a Reviewer and Editorial Board Member in several top-ranked journals. She was awarded Best Professor in Rural Management (Regional round, Pune) by the Dewang Mehta Foundation in 2017. She is also a recipient of the Award of Prof. Indira Parikh Women in Education Leaders from World Education Congress in 2017.

Madhuri Chaure is a graduate in Agriculture and Masters in Agricultural Economics from Dr. Panjabrao Deshmukh Krishi Vidyapeeth, Akola. She further pursued her Ph.D. in the field of Agricultural Economics from Mahatma Phule krishi Vidyapeeth, Rahuri. She has five years of work experience in the field of agriculture and cooperative research. She is currently working as an Assistant Professor at Dr. D.Y. Patil Vidyapeeth's Global Business School and Research Centre, Pune. Her research includes trends in agricultural production, agricultural marketing, agricultural inputs, cooperative training, credit cooperatives and consumer cooperatives etc.

Neha Christie is a Ph.D. Scholar and professional with nine years of experience in academic research institutes and non-profit organisations. Her areas of interest are Collectives, Institution Building, Social Capital, Democracy, Leadership Development, and Rural Livelihood.

A. Allan Degen is an Emeritus Professor at Ben-Gurion University of the Negev, Beer Sheva, Israel. After receiving his Ph.D. at Tel Aviv University,

Israel, he joined Ben-Gurion University (1980), where he was Head of the Desert Animal Adaptations and Husbandry Unit (1985–2015) and Chairman of the Wyler Department of Dryland Agriculture (2001–2004 and 2013–2015). He was the incumbent of the Bennie Slome Chair for Desert Livestock Production (2004–2015) and served as the co-Editor-in-Chief of the Israel Journal of Zoology (1999–2007). Allan has studied the livelihood of ethnic groups in different countries and, is conducting research on Negev Bedouin in Israel. He has authored or co-authored 24 books or chapters and over 250 publications in peer-reviewed journals.

Lily Degen received her Doctor of Professional Studies (Supervision in Clinical Psychology) from Middlesex University, England, in 2017, and her M.A. in Clinical from Bar-Ilan University, Israel, in 1995. She has been working as a Clinical Psychologist and Supervisor in the field of mental health with children, adolescents, and adults. Lily's areas of specialisation include Depression, issues of Grief and Mourning, and Difficulties in Commitment, and her practice focuses on Psychodynamic Psychotherapy and Supervision.

Yogesh Desale is currently Assistant Professor in the Faculty of Commerce and Management at Vishwakarma University, Pune. He has done his education in MCM (Computers). He has over 12 years of experience in Information Technology, including subject knowledge and practical experience. He has done received certifications to enhance learning and to get current industry exposure in MCP, MCTS, and MCSA certified professional from Microsoft. He has attended a wide range of seminars, FDPs, and workshops at the national and international level. He is also the recipient of a special appreciation award (2012–2013) from VIM. He has published a number of papers in referred journals and book chapters in books published by reputed international publishers.

Ashok Kumar Gupta is heading the Cooperative Training group in the National Dairy Development Board, based at Anand, Gujarat. He has the 32 years of experience in the development sector and academics, especially in the fields of Natural/Human Resource Management and Producer-Centric Institution Building Processes, and in building learning ecosystems for different stakeholders of the developmental sector, especially dairy.

Subhanwesha Mahapatra works as Senior Manager in the Cooperative Training group in the National Dairy Development Board and brings in 17 years of experience in Personnel Relations, Human Resource Development, and Quality Management Systems.

Darshnaben Mahida is a Ph.D. Scholar with a high track record of publications in the area of Dairy Cooperatives, Agriculture Science, Finance, Business Management, and Rural Development.

Satarupa Modak completed a Ph.D. from Uttar Banga Krishi Viswavidyalaya, West Bengal, in 2019, was involved in a three-month PG internship programme at MANAGE, Hyderabad, in 2017; qualified for ASRB-NET in 2016; completed an M.Sc. (Agricultural Extension) from Anand Agricultural University, Gujarat, in 2014; and completed a B.Sc. (Agri) from Central Agricultural University, Imphal, in 2012. She worked as Watershed Development Team Member of IWMP, a project of the State level Nodal agency, for six months in the year 2014; as Senior Research Fellow in the PDASMASS/PDFMD project of ICAR at the State D.I lab for 10 months during 2014–2015; as Research Officer in the NGO Centre for Research Innovation and Science Policy (CRISP) & Agricultural Extension in South-east Asia (AESA) network for another six months during 2019–2020; and is currently working as Assistant Professor, Department of Agricultural Extension, MSSSOA, CUTM. Dr. Satarupa has published 11 research papers, three book chapters, two magazine articles, and a discussion paper, and also has experience in guiding three master's students so far.

Triptesh Mondal has completed his M.Sc. (Agri.) in Agronomy from Uttar Banga Krishi Viswavidyalaya, West Bengal, in 2016 and he qualified for ASRB-NET in 2017 and 2019, twice. He completed his B.Sc. (Agri.) Hons. from Palli Siksha Bhavana, Visva Bharati, West Bengal, in 2014. He published 11 research papers, two book chapters, and two magazine articles (ICAR Publication). He reviewed three research articles for the journal "Archives of Agronomy and Soil Science". He is Life Member of the Indian Society of Agronomy, Indian Society of Weed Science, Crop and Weed Science Society, and Society for Advancement of Wheat and Barley Research. He got the best poster presentation award at the International Conference on Sustainable Agricultural Development in Changing Global Scenario organised by Royal Association for Science-led Socio-cultural Advancement (RASSA), New Delhi, and Institute of Environment and Sustainable Development (IESD), BHU. He is currently working as Assistant Professor in the Department of Agronomy, MSSSOA, CUTM.

Iqbal Hossain Moral is currently working as an Academician in the Department of Business Administration, Northern University of Business and Technology Khulna, Bangladesh. His research interests span the topics of Heritage Entrepreneurship, Women Entrepreneurship, AI and Entrepreneurship, Human Resource Management, and Community Psychology.

Archit Kumar Nayak is an agribusiness professional presently working as Research Associate at the Center for Agricultural Market Intelligence, Anand Agricultural University, Anand, Gujarat. He obtained B.Sc. degree in Agriculture from Indira Gandhi Agricultural University, Raipur, Chhattisgarh, in 2013 and MBA degree in Agribusiness Management from the Institute of Agri Business Management, SKRAU, Bikaner, in 2015. He earned his Ph.D. in Agribusiness Management from Sam Higginbottom University of Agriculture, Technology and Sciences, Prayagraj (U.P.). He has also obtained a Post Graduate Diploma in Technology Management in Agriculture from NAARM, Hyderabad, in 2021. He is actively involved in agricultural research with a focus on Value Chain, Supply Chain, and Marketing Analysis of agriculture and allied commodities. He has 10 research publications to his credit published in the form of research papers, popular articles, book chapters, etc.

Subhrajyoti Panda completed his B.Sc. in Agriculture from the College of Agriculture, Orissa University of Agriculture and Technology,

Bhubaneswar, Odisha; M.Sc. in Agriculture (Agricultural Extension) in 2018; and Ph.D. Agricultural Extension from Uttar Banga Krishi Viswavidyalya, West Bengal, in 2021. He qualified for ASRB-NET in Agricultural Extension in the year 2018. Dr. Panda published 10 research papers, 2 book chapters, two books, and four magazine articles. He is Assistant Editor at Agrimeet (Multidisciplinary e-Magazine) and Executive Director at Sabujeema, an international multidisciplinary e-magazine. He is also a Lifetime Member of the "Society for Community mobilization for sustainable Development". He received a University Gold Medal during his M.Sc. in Agriculture in the year 2017. He has also received a Certificate of Appreciation for participating as a reviewer in the International Journal of Agricultural Extension and Rural Development (ISSN 2756-3642). He is currently working as Assistant Professor in the Department of Agriculture Extension, Faculty of Agriculture, Sri Sri University, Cuttack, Odisha.

Shaktiranjan Panigrahy, Assistant Professor and Head of Operations Management at the International Agribusiness Management Institute, Anand Agricultural University, Anand, Gujarat, holds a Master's degree in Agribusiness Management. After completion of his graduation in veterinary science and animal husbandry from Orissa University of Agriculture and Technology, Bhubaneswar, Dr. Panigrahy served as Veterinary Assistant Surgeon in the Fishery and Animal Resource Department, Government of Odisha in 2007. After that, he joined Chaudhury Charan Singh Haryana Agriculture University, Hisar, to pursue a Master's degree programme and was credited with an MBA in agribusiness management in 2012. He joined Anand Agricultural University, Anand, in 2013. He has around 11 years of experience in teaching, research, extension, and livestock treatment. During this period of his academic journey at Anand Agricultural University, Dr. Panigrahy published 26 research papers, 16 articles, five books, and seven book chapters on the subject of agribusiness management. Dr. Panigrahy also handled eight institutional projects and one international project during this period. He is credited with UGC (NET) in management, ICAR (NET), and ICAR SRF (PGS) Fellowship in agribusiness management. His subject areas of specialisation are

Production and Operations Management, Agri-entrepreneurship, Cooperative Management, Agricultural Marketing, and Agribusiness Policies. Dr. Panigrahy has subject knowledge in the livestock sector, fisheries sector, and horticultural sector, specialising in potatoes. He has guided more than 15 students pursuing their Master's degrees in the domain of agribusiness management.

Sunita Pati is an Officer of Odisha Administrative Service working as Assistant Registrar of Cooperative Services in Cuttack city circle, Odisha. She has done her Post Graduation in Agroforestry and Silviculture from Odisha University of Agriculture and Technology and got into OAS, 2015 batch. After joining OAS, she underwent training for a Post Graduate Diploma in Cooperative Business Management from VAMNICOM, Pune. While doing the course, she conducted some surveys and research in the cooperative sector in states like Odisha, Punjab, Himachal Pradesh, and Maharashtra. She has few research publications to her credit in fields of Cooperative and Rural Development.

Vidya Patkar is a Deputy Director at Symbiosis Institute Geoinformatics, Symbiosis International (Deemed University). She has a Ph.D. in Computer Studies from Symbiosis International (Deemed University). Her area of specialisation includes Data Science and Analytics, Software Development, Big Data Handling, Spatial Data Mining, Spatial Decision Support System, and Agro-informatics. She is also associated with different institutes for various educational assignments. She has worked on software development projects at the National Informatics Centre, Pune, and is currently working on different research projects funded by government and private organisations. She has published various research papers in national and international journals and conferences. She is also acting as a Reviewer for national and international journals indexed in Scopus and web of science.

Md. Mizanur Rahman is currently working as an Academician at BRAC Business School, BRAC University, Bangladesh. His research interests include Management, OB, HRM, Entrepreneurship, Artificial Intelligence, Corporate Governance, and Sustainability. Rahman is focusing on quantitative techniques such as PLS-SEM, CB-SEM, and SPSS.

Md. Saidur Rahaman is currently employed as an Academician at the Department of Business Administration, Metropolitan University of Sylhet, Bangladesh. He is interested in many emerging research areas in Management, Human Resource Management, Organisational Behaviour, Artificial Intelligence, Entrepreneurship, and psychology-related fields in many sectors. He has a long list of publications in several journals from various publishers. Mr. Rahaman is currently a Member of the editorial board of several journals of human psychology and serves as a Reviewer for other journals.

K.N. Pavithra is a Ph.D. Scholar, Department of Agricultural Economics University of Agricultural Sciences, GKVK, Bangalore.

Pooja is a Ph.D. Scholar at Department of Agricultural Economics at University of Agricultural Sciences, GKVK, Bangalore.

S.C. Ravi is a Scientist (Agricultural Economics) Division of Post-Harvest Management at ICAR-CISH in Lucknow, India.

P.K. Shajahan is a full-time Faculty at Tata Institute of Social Sciences in Mumbai. His research and publications are mostly in the thematic areas of Social Innovation, People-Centred Development and Social Enterprises, Conflicts and Peace Processes, and Minority Rights. He is currently the Vice-President of the International Council on Social Welfare (ICSW) and represents ICSW at the Task Force on Global Agenda for Social Work and Social Development 2020–2030.

Rahul Waghmare is currently Assistant Professor in the Faculty of Commerce and Management at Vishwakarma University, Pune. Prior to his recent appointment, he completed his Ph.D. from Savitribai Phule Pune University in the field of Organisational Management on the topic of Open Innovation and its relation with SMEs for sustainable development. Dr. Rahul has published a number of papers in referred journals and book chapters in books published by reputed international publishers. Dr. Rahul has also presented papers in a number of international conferences. His major research areas include Innovation Management, SMEs, Social Entrepreneurship, and Sustainability.

Contents

xxi

Chapter 1

A Socio-Economic Scenario of Cooperative Societies Responding to the COVID-19 Crisis

Md. Saidur Rahaman[*,¶], Léo-Paul Dana[†,‖],
Md. Mizanur Rahman[‡,**], and Iqbal Hossain Moral[§,††]

[*]*Metropolitan University, Sylhet, Bangladesh*

[†]*ICD Business School, Paris, France*

[‡]*BRAC Business School, BRAC University, Bangladesh*

[§]*Northern University of Business and Technology, Khulna, Bangladesh*

[¶]*saidurmgt@gmail.com*

[‖]*lp762359@dal.ca*

[**]*mizanur.rahman@bracu.ac.bd*

[††]*iqbalmgt@gmail.com*

Abstract

The motto that motivates people to form cooperatives is *all for one and one for all*. It is primarily dependent on the ownership and control of the cooperative's members, with each person having one vote. A cooperative society is a member-owned business formed for the economic and social growth of any sector in a country. Considering their competency and practical utility, cooperatives are constitutionally recognised as an important economic sector in emerging and developing countries. As a result, every year, on 6 November, Bangladesh commemorates National Cooperative Day. This chapter illustrates that despite the ups and downs in Bangladesh's, India's, and Pakistan's economies, cooperatives are continuously growing and contributing to these nation's socio-economic growth. Through this study, academic scholars, students, cooperative members, administrators, government officials, and other stakeholders can learn about the socio-economic impact of cooperative societies by witnessing those in South Asia's standouts: Bangladesh, India, and Pakistan. The authors acquired all of the data for this study from secondary sources, including government websites, journal publications, newspapers, research community groups, blogs, and social media. After collecting data, the authors narrowed them down and combined them in a usable format to deliver the most relevant data and knowledge for the subject area.

Keywords: Bangladesh, cooperative society, COVID-19, economic, India, Pakistan, social

1. Introduction

Nothing truly valuable can be achieved except by the unselfish cooperation of many individuals.

Albert Einstein

The concept of cooperatives arose to safeguard the interests of society's weaker members. The cooperative society originated due to the industrial revolution, which resulted in the spread of industrial activity around the globe. Therefore, two distinct social classes have emerged: industrialists and labourers. Industrialists exploited labour and mistreated the weaker elements of society (Rajguru, 2019). Cooperatives have been playing an essential role in establishing individual and social life for the labourers in emerging developing countries, such as Bangladesh, India, and Pakistan. They aim to provide a life free of exploitation and discrimination for the most vulnerable members of society (Ferguson, 2012). The key objectives of the cooperatives include socio-economic development, poverty reduction, job creation, women's empowerment, social security guarantees, and most importantly, long-term economic growth (Blair, 1978). Agriculture, fishery and animal husbandry, housing, transportation, milk production, loans and savings, and micro-credit programmes are the major categories of cooperative societies in developing countries (Abul Khair, 2019). Among the 17 specific sustainable development goals announced by the

United Nations for 2015–2030, the goals related to cooperatives include eradicating hunger, achieving food security, promoting nutrition and sustainable agricultural development, and promoting sustainable and participatory economic growth (UNDP, 2016). Creating a conducive working environment, minimising inequities, and preserving production and consumption patterns stability are all priorities for cooperative societies nowadays (Muhammad and Dana, 2015). To attain these objectives, Bangladesh, India, and Pakistan adopt an essential action plan for the cooperative system's implementation, practice, and achievement (Sarker *et al.*, 2016). This study "reflects what practically equates to a controlled experiment in socio-economic development" through cooperatives in Bangladesh, India, and Pakistan, which share a common culture, history, and religion. Furthermore, an effort has been made to perform a complete and comparative examination of the whole scenario pertaining to the evolution of cooperatives in the setting of South Asia. The study aims to create a synthesis of the socio-economic framework adopted by the countries covering a wide range of fields for the expansion of cooperatives while also depicting the countries' significant achievements in the development of cooperatives.

2. Context of the Study

The cooperative movement in the South Asian subcontinent was unable to maintain its original ideals. However, the governments of each country are dedicated to spreading the cooperative movement to assure people's socio-economic and cultural liberty. Recently, most cooperatives are focusing on their socio-economic contribution through the key members of the society: women. The proportion of Bangladeshi women in the labour field has constantly climbed in cooperatives, although it has decreased in India and Pakistan. Pakistan was 70% richer than Bangladesh in 1971, but Bangladesh is now 45% richer than Pakistan. On the other hand, India, which prides itself as a "STAR" of being the only South Asian economy that matters, has contended that it is also weaker in terms of per capita income than Bangladesh. India's per capita income, projected at USD 1947 in 2020–2021, is expected to exceed that of the

Table 1.   Socio-economic statistics.

Socio-Economic Overview			
Dimension	**Bangladesh**	**India**	**Pakistan**
Capital	Dhaka	New Delhi	Islamabad
Population	163,046,161	1,366,417,754	208,570,000
Surface Area	147,630 km^2	3,287,259 km^2	796,100 km^2
Currency	Taka (1 EUR = 100.6212 BDT)	Indian rupees (1 EUR = 86.8440 INR)	Pakistani Rupees (1 EUR = 194.9150 PKR)
Religion	Mostly Islam	Mostly Hindu	Mostly Islam
Belongs to	ACD, BIMSTEC, IMF, UN, SAARC	ACD, BIMSTEC, BRICS, G20, IMF, MGC, UN, SAARC	ACD, ECO, IMF, UN, SAARC
Annual GDP	USD 329,120 M	USD 2,708,770M	USD 262,799M
GDP per capita	USD 2,019	USD 1,982	USD 1,260
Unemployment rate	4.50%		0.044
Standard VAT	15.00%	18.00%	0.17
Top tax rate + SSC	30.00%	42.70%	0.2
Exports % GDP	10.21%	10.45%	0.0836
Imports	USD 52,410.3 M	USD 371,920.0 M	USD 45,847.0 M
Trade balance % GDP	–5.71%	–3.62%	–0.0908
COVID-19 Cases			
COVID-19 — Deaths (as on 12 Sep. 2021)	26,931	442,874	26,787
COVID-19 — Confirmed (as on 12 Sep. 2021)	1,530,413	33,264,175	1,207,508
Fully vaccinated (as on 13 Sep. 2021)	13,632,399	176,940,864	21,962,455
Deaths per million population (as on 12 Sep. 2021)	165.17	324.11	128.43
Doses administered (as on 13 Sep. 2021)	34,288,574	751,496,975	68,227,337

Source: Compiled by authors; countryeconomy.com (2021).

other countries of South Asia. Some of the key statistics of the countries as of 2021 are given in Table 1. According to a Pakistani economist:

> *It is in the realm of possibility that we could be seeking aid from Bangladesh in 2030.*

3. Cooperative Society

A cooperative is a democratic and economic entity that promotes self-help and initiative (Khan, 1979). However, the term "cooperative" implies something more. Since the dawn of civilisation, men have lived in a society in order to work together to attain a common goal. People used to hunt animals together in the pre-civilised culture. Cooperatives are a pragmatic movement in the sense that they are also an effort by a group of people to get out of poverty or improve their economic situation. It gives members the option of forming capital for any initiative that would benefit them (Islam *et al.*, 2014). Cooperatives are now widely acknowledged constitutionally as an essential in many nations as a means of attaining improved efficiency and a more equitable distribution of development gains (Abul Khair, 2019). As a result, it is worthwhile to hold up the cooperatives of Bangladesh, India, and Pakistan as role models.

> *When people get together to achieve their common economic, social, and cultural needs and ambitions, they form a co-operative society. It is a type of social enterprise that is jointly owned and democratically governed. Co-operative Society brings together people from the same socio-economic class to serve one other and work toward common goals.*
>
> Md. Saidur Rahaman

Cooperatives are typically founded by the poorest and most vulnerable members of society, which demonstrates the will of the underprivileged to stand on their two feet (Blair, 1978). A cooperative society is a one-of-a-kind organisation where members work together to develop and improve their economic status through mutual aid. Many firms' principal purpose is to gain money by exploiting their customers, whereas

> *Co-operative is founded on helping each other with available resources and providing commodities to society members without profit or at a*

reduced price, as a means of working together to improve their economic situation at the same time.

Md. Saidur Rahaman

3.1 Cooperative society movements

Since the establishment of the first society in 1844 in Britain, the cooperative society initiated its journey with only 28 weavers in Rochdale, Britain with the capital of GBP 28. Soon, such societies were established in multiple nations at different times with the aim to work for and extend a hand to the economically weaker sections of the society. In 1901, rules and regulations were extensively formed on account of a cooperative society which was started in the subcontinent in 1904 with the approval of the British Government. But considerably for the global economic recession after World War I, the Cooperative Act, 1904 was established in 1912 (NCTB, 2021). The Co-operative Societies Act, 1912 was updated in 1940, which was sanctioned by the Pakistan Government after the partition of India in 1944. With the governing rules and regulations, an increasing number of cooperative societies in East Pakistan stood up to 32,000. Bangladesh in this case barely made progression before independence in 1971, which is presented in Table 2. However, Bangladesh commenced a new cooperative movement with the governance of Cooperative Act, 1940 and Cooperative Rules, 1942. But thereafter, in 1975, unlike Cooperative Rules, 1942, the Cooperative Society's Ordinance, 1974 as Ordinance No. 1 and Cooperative Societies Act, 1987 was ratified. Afterwards, the Cooperative Rules, 1987 was altered in 2004, according to which, Societies Act of 2001, later amended in 2003, led to the establishment of cooperative societies in 2010 (NCTB, 2021).

3.2 Formation and principles governing cooperative society

Cooperative Society Act, 1912, 1925 and 2001 make up the law dealing with cooperative societies in Bangladesh, India, and Pakistan, respectively (Coop Website BD, 2021a; NCUI, 2018a, b; COOP, 2021). Though the acts are different in following but formation procedure is almost similar. A cooperative society must have at least 20 adult members primarily, and

Table 2.   Cooperatives movement.

Issues	Bangladesh	India	Pakistan
Acts	Cooperative Society Act, 2001	Cooperative Societies Act, 1912, India	Cooperative Society Act, 1925
Objectives of forming	Socio-economic development, poverty reduction, job creation, women's empowerment, social security guarantees, and, most crucially, long-term economic growth.	Societies that encourage agriculturists, crafts people, and low-income people to be thrifty and self-sufficient.	Encourage agriculturists and those with similar economic needs to exercise thrift, self-help, and mutual aid to better their living and working situations.
Total numbers of cooperatives	1,95,248	8,54,355	16,146 (All types)
Total members	1,16,03,758	29,00,60,000	53,39,210
Major cooperative categories	Agriculture, Marketing, Industry, Fisheries, Women, Transport, Housing, Milk, and Insurance etc.	Dairy sector, sugarcane, agriculture, real estate, electric power, insurance, health care, and tourism, etc.	Agriculture, Banking, Housing, Industry, and Women Sectors, etc.

Source: Coop Website BD (2021a), NCUI (2018b), COOP (2021).

later at least 10. They could be neighbours, same company employees, members of a similar group, and so forth. The core premise is that everyone who wants to establish a community should have similar goals. The respective concerns of societies receive the appropriate documentation. An administrator scrutinises the documents, and if they meet the requirements, the society's name is entered in the register (Islam *et al.*, 2014). The society is also given a certificate of registration. From the date specified in the certificate, the society becomes a legal entity. The information needed to be included in the application to form a society is shown in Figure 1.

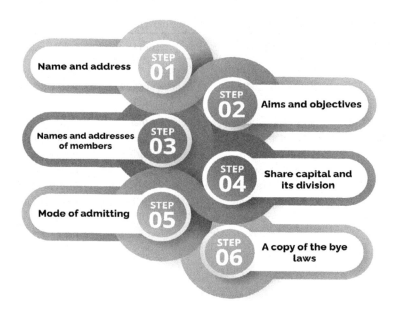

Figure 1.   Information required for forming a cooperative society.

A cooperative is a self-governing group of people who voluntarily pursue a common economic goal. The cooperative forms are based on "self-help, self-responsibility, democracy and equality, equity, and solidarity" (Rahaman *et al.*, 2020).

3.3 Socio-economic scenario of cooperatives in South Asian countries

Co-operatives have a key role to play in the economic, social and environmental pillars of sustainable development.

Juan Somavia, Former ILO Director-General

Cooperatives are usually formed in remote, rural locations, where most poor people live and which are less viable for other enterprises and unattractive to investors due to scattered and low levels of output, high transaction costs, and long distances to market (see Figure 2). Cooperatives help entrepreneurs in developing countries overcome a range of market barriers. Members who engage in agricultural cooperatives to reduce the cost of

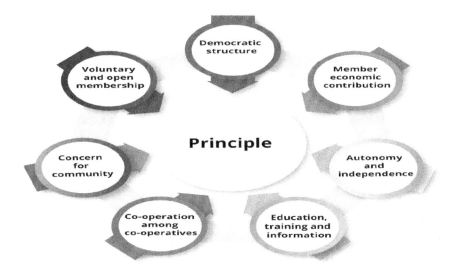

Figure 2.   Principles of forming cooperative society.

growing inputs and increase commercialisation can change areas over time. Credit and savings cooperatives support low-income people who are refused service by commercial banks; insurance cooperatives protect low-income people's assets; and rural electric, health, telecommunications, and housing cooperatives provide community services to the rural poor (Rahman *et al.*, 2021). In the face of adversity and conflict, cooperatives promote trust and solidarity, resulting in societal well-being and stability. Members of the cooperative understand the link between meeting their specific needs and supporting the long-term health of organisations through development efforts. They benefit from leadership, organisational and financial management, member services, and advocacy training. They learn to deliver critical social services while simultaneously fostering social capital and creating trust in their communities. Investing in cooperative development means investing in creating or strengthening sustainable enterprises with the potential for large-scale impact in terms of bringing households out of poverty, delivering services to the undeserved, and protecting the poor's economic assets. The major cooperative societies in South Asia are shown in Figure 3. The following section demonstrates how cooperatives have a sizeable socio-economic impact in Bangladesh, India, and Pakistan.

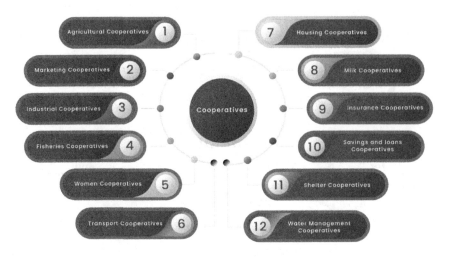

Figure 3.   Major cooperatives functioning in South Asia.

3.3.1. *Bangladesh*

Cooperative societies have served as catalysts for social organisation and togetherness while successfully operating locally owned people's businesses over the years (Ahmed, 2019). There are currently 1,95,248 cooperative societies in Bangladesh, among which 22 are at the national level and 20% are women cooperatives. By embracing this cooperative concept in developing the Golden Bengal, cooperatives play a very influential role in building a middle-income country in 2021 into a developed Bangladesh in 2041. It represents a style of economic activity that prioritises democratic principles and environmental stewardship through their concern for their members and communities. Bangladesh has been motivated by the success of the Millennium Development Goals (MDGs) to summon the courage and passion necessary to attain the objective of sustainable development. Bangladesh's economy is built on the notion of *"development philosophy raised from the country's soil"*, as shown in the spirit of the liberation war. Equal economic opportunity for all citizens, social security, political freedom, performance transparency, and security at all levels are all goals for the country. To promote human development and defend the human rights of individuals from all walks of life, productive investments must be undertaken to boost economic growth and per capita income by creating wide employment, with the benefits reaching all communities. Cooperatives contribute significantly to social integration, job development, and poverty reduction due to their democratic structure and economic orientation. Cooperatives can thus help to stabilise regional economic cycles and create jobs in every region of the country (Khair, 2019). Cooperatives play an important part in the world's economic and social development. Cooperatives, which are based on the ideas of collaboration, help to establish new business and economic ethics and values. They are a great way to build your business, but good politics go hand in hand with strong economics. Cooperatives play an important role in Bangladesh's socio-economic development. Cooperatives play an important role in Bangladesh's socio-economic development, which is presented in Table 3.

3.3.2. *India*

Cooperatives in India have a history that dates back more than a hundred years. The Government of India recognised cooperatives as a third economic sector immediately after independence, recognising the essential role cooperatives may play in the growth of the national economy. They can reach out to the rural people who find it difficult to lead their lives. According to a report, 65% of India's population relies on agriculture and its related businesses, making cooperatives extremely important (Bhattacharya, 2021). Specifically, they were tasked with addressing the needs and ambitions of rural India, with a focus on small and marginal farmers and the poorer sections of society (Dana, 2000). Throughout the years, cooperatives in India have shown to be an efficient means for individuals to take control of their economic futures. More than 8.5 lakh societies with 290 million members are part of the Indian cooperative movement, which is now the world's largest cooperative organisation (NCUI, 2018a). Table 4 presents the overall scenario of India's cooperative movements and socio-economic scenario.

Table 3.   Socio-economic contribution of cooperatives (Bangladesh).

Cooperative Categories	Total Number	Individual Members	Share Capital (Lakh) Tk.	Savings Deposit (Lakh) Tk.	Reserve Fund, (Lakh) Tk.	Net Profit (Lakh) Tk.
Agriculture	72,460					
Marketing	639	27,974	781.79	1,595.56	478.28	167.28
Industrial	3,210	1,29,637	1,366.50	11,700.48		
Fisheries	10,029	3,90,527	2,497.89	5,641.17		1,614.17
Women's	27,388	9,72,349	19,949.56	22,916.40		89.17
Transport	1,346	1,05,227	763.92	6,103.06		
Housing	228	53,899	3,787.03	6,899,74		
Milk	2517	1,17,758	654.06	868.32		185.69
Insurance	(A) 501 (B) 609		(A) 63.77 (B) 8.56		78.88	
Savings and loans	12,381	14,42,513	321.90 crores	1,186.34 crores	29.77 crores	
Water	1,338	4,42,911	903.25	4,243.35	7,053.46	

Source: Annual Report, 2019–2020, pp. 13–17; Bhattacharya (2021).

As the global economy becomes more competitive, it provides a unique tool for accomplishing one or more economic goals. Cooperatives played a key role in India's White Revolution, which has led to the country becoming self-sufficient in dairy products. India has 1,94,195 cooperative organisations in the dairy sector, and 35% of the country's sugar is produced through cooperative mills (Bhattacharya, 2021). Agricultural credit became a secondary function for co-ops in just a few years. Real estate, electric power, insurance, healthcare, and tourism are some of the areas where rural cooperative societies are increasingly expanding. Cooperatives can play a significant role in reducing rural unemployment by training the rural population through cooperatives. There will be a continued growth of the cooperative movement in India. The Indian Government established a separate Ministry of Cooperation on 6 July with

Table 4. Cooperative movement at a glance with contribution in national economy (India).

Indian Cooperative Movement at a Glance	
Total number of cooperatives	8,54,355
Total membership of cooperatives	290.06 million
Share capital (all level & all types)	INR 4,06,886.8 million
Share capital of primary non-credit cooperatives	INR 131,505.2 million
Working capital (credit + non-credit)	INR 125,36,174 million

Percentage Share of Cooperatives in National Economy	
Cooperatives	**%**
Rural network covered by cooperatives	98
Rural network (villages covered by PACS)	90.8
Total agricultural credit disbursed by cooperatives (2016–2017)	13.4
Short term agricultural credit disbursed by cooperatives to small and marginal farmers	19.13
Kisan credit cards issued by cooperative banks + regional rural bank (as on end of March 2017)	67.3
Kisan credit cards issued by cooperatives (as on end of March 2017)	50.2
Fertiliser distributed (2016–2017) estimated	35
Fertiliser production capacity (5.35 million tonnes for the year 2016–2017)	24.92
Fertiliser production (51.62 million tonnes for the year 2016–17)	28.8
Capacity of fertiliser products (10.77 million tonnes for the year 2016–2017)	20.32
Installed capacity of fertiliser manufacturing units (3.638 million tonnes of N Nutrient as on 31 March 2017)	25.6
Installed capacity of fertiliser manufacturing units (1.713 million tonnes of P Nutrient as on 31 March 2017)	23.53
Installed number of sugar factories (284 as on 31 March 2017)	38.63
Sugar produced (5.654 million tonnes as on 31 March 2017)	30.6
Capacity utilisation of sugar mills (as on 31 March 2017)	46.14
Liquid milk marketed out of total milk procured by cooperatives	84.17
Milk procurement to total production (2016–2017)	9.5
Milk procurement to marketable surplus (2016–2017)	17.5
PACS having storage facility (at village level) (2016–2017)	55.5

(Continued)

Table 4. (*Continued*)

Total storage capacity of cooperative sector (2016–2017) 2,277 million tonnes	14.79
Fishermen in cooperatives (active)	20.05
Wheat procurement (4.4 million tonnes during 2017–2018)	13.3
Paddy procurement (7.5 million tonnes during 2016–2017)	20.4
Retail fair price shops (Rural + Urban)	20.3
Spindleadge in cooperatives (3.56 million, as on 31 March 2018)	29.34
Direct employment generated by cooperatives	13.3
Self-employment generated for persons	10.91

Source: Compiled by authors, NCUI (2018b); Annual report, p. 47; Dana (2000).

the stated goal of realising the "Sahkar se Samriddhi" vision ("progress through cooperation"). Officially, the Ministry of Cooperation will offer the country's cooperative movement with a distinctive administrative, legal, and regulatory framework, supporting in the development of cooperatives as a "genuine people-based movement reaching up to the grassroots".

3.3.3. Pakistan

The cooperation began in Europe in the second half of the 19th century as an economic movement. To protect agriculturists against moneylenders, the government founded the cooperative movement in the subcontinent by promulgating the Cooperative Credit Societies Act, 1904 in Pakistan. Their objective was to assist Indian small farmers before the partition of India and Pakistan. Because no other civil group was dedicated to the cause, the subcontinent's government was responsible for encouraging collaboration alone. The Malagan Committee Report on Cooperation, published in 1915, made significant and constructive recommendations for cooperative growth. This study had a significant impact on governmental and civil thought (Coop Website BD, 2021a). The Cooperative Societies Act, 1925 has been slightly modified in the past. However, many conditions and circumstances, such as the cooperative housing sector, remained unaddressed in the stated act. The act also did not sufficiently cover the main component of the cooperative movement. As a result, the Punjab Government revised the act in 2006 to align with the changed realities and tackle the new problems. However, the most recent amendments to the Cooperative Societies Act, 1925 and the Cooperative Societies Rules, 1927 were made in 2020 to make this act consistent with national legislative and regulatory reforms, which were made in response to international standards set by the Financial Action Task Force (FATF) (CoD, Punjab, 2020). Various provinces formed inquiry committees, which eventually boosted the cooperative movement and resulted in the passage of Cooperative Acts in several provinces. Following Pakistan's independence, a succession of legislation were enacted to ensure the safety of public finances and cooperative property, mostly in the form of Governor's Ordinances and later in the form of Regulations of Presidential Ordinances. Cooperatives are a universe unto themselves, with unity in diversity, such as the agricultural, banking, housing, industrial, and women's sectors, all of which operate on cooperative principles and contribute to the success and growth of the province and country, which is represented in Table 5. It is a tremendous effort on the part of the Cooperatives Department to provide residential facilities with fully built infrastructure to their members without demanding financial support from the government. There is no national housing cooperative organisation in Pakistan, and the extent of cooperatives varies widely by region. Housing cooperatives do meet on occasion, and it is worth noting that each province and territory has a cooperative department responsible for encouraging and supervising any type of cooperative development. Some examples are apex societies, housing societies, agricultural societies, and women societies (COOP, 2021).

3.4. Cooperative societies: Success stories

We will not measure the success of the Movement by the number of cooperative societies formed, but by the moral condition of the cooperators.

Mahatma Gandhi

Table 5.   Socio-economic contribution of cooperatives (Pakistan).

The Cooperative Movement

	Pakistan	**Province of Sindh**	**Province of Punjab**	**Province of Baluchistan**	**Province of N.W.F.P**
Cooperatives (all types)	8,073	3,605	2,570	1,236	662
Members	26,69,605	15,46,545	8,26,626	1,47,341	1,49,093
Housing co-ops	2,687	1,275	669	511	232
Members	1,955,190	855,989	647,635	311,250	140,316
Houses/units built	2,274,276	1,050,000	725,000	311, 250	188,026

Cooperative Farming Scheme and Colony Cooperative Farming Union (CCFU)		**Women Societies Rate of Mark-Up**	
No. of cooperatives	132	Total societies	1,484
No. of unions	8	Membership	47,016
Area allocated	147,000 acres	Share capital	PKR 21.232 million
Allotted members	11,117	Working capital	PKR 53.802 million
Members eligible for proprietary rights	10,395	Microfinance advance	PKR 139.497 million
Members obtained conveyance deeds	9,527	Balance outstanding	PKR 38.610 million
Members not granted conveyance deeds	868	Industrial centres	55
Amount deposited	PKR 88.7 million		

Source: Cooperative Department of Punjab (Website) https://www.housinginternational.coop/co-ops/pakistan/.

Growing evidence from cooperatives in Bangladesh, India, and Pakistan suggests that worker cooperatives are more resilient than conventional businesses on average. There are numerous causes for success, including profit not being their primary motivation for flexing in economic adversity. Worker-owners are more dedicated to their workplaces than typical employees, and worker co-ops outperform other enterprises in production (COOP, 2021). The success stories of cooperatives from the three countries are discussed in the following.

3.4.1. *Janata Adarsh Village Development Multipurpose Cooperative Society*

Janata Adarsh Village Development Multipurpose Cooperative Society was established to facilitate the path to social and economic development of every family by utilising all the resources of the village through cooperative societies. Janata Adarsh Gram Unnayan Multipurpose Cooperative Society was established at Thukra village in Khulna in the southern part of Bangladesh. The financial stability and livelihood of the people here are the same as in other villages of the country. Through the efforts of some farmers and youths of this village, Adarsh Gram Unnayan Multipurpose Cooperative Society was established in 1984. At present, the number of members of the association is 183. The association was formed with the aim of socio-economic development of the members of the association and marketing of the products of the farmers as well as overall development of the village. The paid-up capital of the association is BDT 44,862,000. The amount of savings deposit is BDT 525,423,759 and the bank balance of the association is BDT 44,355,063. The present total working capital of the society is BDT 39,450,644. To ensure saving attitude, growth, good relations with each other, mutual cooperation and trust, self-reliance, productive activities, creation of new jobs, profitable investments, and creation of fund for lending among the members and socio-economic status of the members in general, the management committee of Janata Adarsh Gram Unnayan Multipurpose Cooperative Society is working relentlessly and dynamically. The current number of permanent employees in the association is 228. In addition, agriculture, fisheries schools, and garment projects have created employment for about 1,000 people. The total fixed assets of the association are 74.08 acres of land with a current market value of BDT 70 crore (Coop Website BD, 2021b).

3.4.2. *Amul*

The White Revolution in India began in 1970. The Gujarat Cooperative Milk Marketing Federation (GCMMF), an apex marketing organisation for various district cooperatives, was established in 1973 with the goal of pooling resources and expanding the market while lowering advertising costs and eliminating internal competition. The Kaira Union had been utilising the trademark name Amul since 1955, when GCMMF purchased it. It was founded in 1946 by Tribhuvan Das Patel and Verghese Kurean, and Sardar Vallabhai Patel oversaw it. Amul processed 36 million litres of milk per day and various dairy products, such as ice cream, chess, butter, and milk. Amul's revenue in the 2018–2019 fiscal years was INR 9,808 billion; the current market price is INR 50,000 crore. Amul makes a huge difference in the lives of Gujarat is while also contributing to social progress. Amul established India as the world's largest producer of milk. It innovates by producing milk powder for the first time globally and then on a commercial basis. Now, let's discuss strategy and marketing. Amul employs a fluid strategy. People who collect milk are paid instantly by Amul. The Amul approach is referred to as Anand Design. It's a collaborative strategy. It is a three-tiered framework that includes town-level social order, regional dairy associations, and state-level organisation. This technique means that if one person cannot generate capital, another can do so; this is a significant benefit. This type of firm is a bank's first pick for a loan. Amul collaborates with 30 lakh farmers. It's a large family. Amul attained a certain level. This is more than just business success. It is a source of pride for the entire country of India. Amul operates in 222 districts and has 28 marketing federations. Amul is a constant in the lives of the people. Table 6 shows the overview of Amul, the example of cooperative society.

3.4.3. *Pakistan Cycle Industrial Cooperative Society, Lahore*

Pakistan Cycle Industrial Cooperative Society, Lahore, is one of the most renowned industrial cooperatives in Punjab. It was founded in 1953 and manufactures bicycles under the brand names "RUSTAM" and "SOHRAB", as well as several kinds of motorcycles under the brand name "SOHRAB".

Table 6.   Overview of Amul at a glance.

Brand	Amul
Founded	14 December 1946
Headquarters	Anand, Gujarat
Amul Full-Form	Anand Milk Union Ltd.
Revenue	INR 38,550 crores (USD 5.4 billion) in 2020
Managed by	Gujarat Co-operative Milk Marketing Federation Ltd.

Source: Varad Kitey (2021); Rahman *et al.* (2021).

This society exemplifies a well-managed and successful industrial cooperative. In addition, the society exports bicycles, motorcycles, and replacement parts. Initially, just a few bicycle spare components were manufactured locally, with the remainder imported from elsewhere. Over time, the situation began to improve, and today, about 98% of bicycle spare parts are manufactured in-house or by vendors.

It now has 228 members, compared to 22 earlier. The factory's daily output has doubled from 5 to 2,000 bicycles (approximately). It is a source of pride for the society as it is the only company in the country that produces bicycles (for men and women), heavy-duty cyclovans, wheelchairs, pushchairs (both fold and fixed varieties), exercise cycles, and tricycles. The last two gadgets listed above, as well as heavy-duty cyclovans delivered to Yemen were created with disabled people in mind and are provided at no cost.

The society has an essential role in the cycle manufacturing industry as a leader. It is progressing because of the precision, planning, and dedication of its staff, including managers, administrators, and engineers, who are always eager to put in the effort and take on any challenge bravely. The Rustam & Sohrab cycle plant is now owned by Pakistan Cycle Industrial Co-operative Society. Finally, this society has expanded to encompass as follows: (1) computerised electroplating factories; (2) plants for electrostaticspray painting; (3) brasing plant that is fully automated; (4) the shell plant Bottom Bracket (B.B.); (5) a heat treatment facility; (6) the axel on the bottom bracket; (7) B.B. cup; (8) axles for the pedals; (9) let your imagination run wild; (10) manufacturing factory for cranks and 11. Motorcycle Project (Citysearch, 2021).

3.5. Cooperatives response to the COVID-19 crisis

With the spread of COVID-19, the economic and social consequences of the globe are entering an unprecedented period of instability. It is a period when previously inconceivable things have become a reality (Rahaman *et al.*, 2020; Salamzadeh & Dana, 2021; Rahman *et al.*, 2021). Closure of non-essential companies and confinement of billions of people to their homes are reshaping communities and the economy. The impact is unevenly spread across households, workers, and companies, aggravating already existing inequalities. Cooperatives and their employees and communities are similarly impacted, albeit asymmetrically, depending on the sectors and stage of the virus's spread in their region or country (ILO, 2020). Some countries' economic recovery from the COVID-19 pandemic has resulted in positive GDP growth, but the outlook for many others remains shaky and uncertain Vorobeva and Dana (2021). The "uneven recovery", notably in South Asia, is an ongoing concern that impedes efforts to improve global prospects. In the post-COVID-19 era, a new social contract is essential to rebuild better and accomplish the 2030 Agenda and SDGs. Historically, during times of crisis, the principles of cooperation, solidarity, and mutualism gain appeal. Cooperatives worldwide are rallying to give help to their workers, members, and communities in the aftermath of the COVID-19 outbreak. Cooperatives play an essential role in the social contract because they prioritise people over profit in their operations. They are founded to provide equal opportunities and access to employment/decent labour for everybody and high-quality education and primary healthcare (UN, 2021). Table 7 lists some examples of how cooperatives have responded during the COVID-19 crisis.

3.6. Problems and prospects of cooperatives

At present, many cooperative initiatives in Bangladesh are currently unable to function; they are no longer active projects (Ahmed, 2019). Cooperative problems in South Asia include poor management, ineffective cooperative structures, corruption and embezzlement, a lack of working capital, a lack of cooperative democracy and education, weakness of supporting institutions, and, in general, an inability to compete in a

Table 7. Cooperative responses to COVID-19.

Country	Initiatives	Cooperatives	Example
Pakistan	Social assistance	Karachi Cooperative Housing Societies	Assist the community social work
India	Distribution of medical supplies and food	SEWA Cooperative Federation	Provides food and health kits, offers food-related direct cash transfers
	Production and donation of medical supplies and other initiatives	SEWA Lok Swasthya health cooperative	Produces low-cost hand sanitisers and masks, gives food to children and the elderly Provides educational materials on social distancing and other preventative measures, medical supplies are provided
	Provision of medical supplies	IFFCO	Farmers and labourers are given masks, soaps, and other protective gear. A USD 3.6 million donation to the PM Cares Fund will go towards relief operations in India.
Bangladesh	**A case study on how Bangladeshi cooperatives responded to the COVID-19 crisis is provided at the end of the chapter.**		

Source: https://europa.eu/capacity4dev/file/103591/download?token=3cVyzZG7.

liberalised market economy Rajguru (2019). The major challenges for the cooperative societies in Bangladesh, India, and Pakistan are discussed in a summary as follows in Figure 4.

First, many people in South Asian countries have no idea how to register as a cooperative organisation with the appropriate authority. On the other hand, obtaining registration from the relevant sources is difficult due to the registration process's numerous bureaucratic issues (Abul Khair, 2019). Second, female participation in cooperatives is lower than male membership, which creates an obstacle in ensuring accurate and rapid socio-economic benefit for any country (McCarthy & Feldman, 1983).

Third, internal conflict among cooperative members acts as a tailback also. It happens due to the cooperatives' preponderance of the vested interests of a specific person or class. Because members are unaware of running a cooperative properly, there is a shortage of professional management. Fourth, political influence can sometimes pose a serious threat to the sector's success. Finally, members' limited capital supply causes financial challenges, preventing them from taking advantage of new chances.

Cooperative societies can play a significant role in social and economic development if the government promptly addresses the aforementioned issues. As a result, a periodic campaign programme on

Figure 4.   Photographs showing cooperative activities. *Photo credit*: Md. Saidur Rahaman.

this subject will encourage the general public to form appropriate type of cooperatives in urban areas also. To boost the sector, adequate education and training to develop management and business skills can help members increase their ability to sustain the society and contribute to the economy by creating new jobs and generating a substantial profit (Sharma, 2018). Relevant consulting services and assistance in structuring money, on the other hand, will aid cooperatives in avoiding financial difficulties (Milovanovic & Smutka, 2018). Again, the concerned authority's promotional measures will promote cooperative confidence (Sultana, Ahmed, & Shiratake, 2020). Finally, higher-level stakeholders are under-motivated to promote the benefits of forming cooperatives and advise how to obtain appropriate help from the relevant government.

4. Conclusion and Way Forward

In the three South Asian countries considered, there are many cooperatives functioning, such as consumer, producer, credit, marketing, diary, and housing. Though these cooperative have had huge impact towards the individual, social, and national level, the Asian subcontinent's cooperative movement could not maintain its original ideology. However, the governments of each country are dedicated to spreading the cooperative movement in order to assure people's socio-economic and cultural liberty (Palalic *et al.*, 2021). Finally, it can be stated that Bangladesh, India, and Pakistan have all had ups and downs, but cooperatives are steadily growing and contributing to each country's socio-economic development as a result of collaborative and unwavering efforts built within the nations. The government should create a wave of cooperative organisations to achieve SDGs in order to influence their own destiny as well as the progress of their country.

5. Case Study: "Al-Amin Sarbik Gram Unnoyon Shombay Somiti"

In the last part of the 2019–2020 financial year, the COVID-19 pandemic spread to Bangladesh along with the rest of the world. This has a serious impact on the normal life and livelihood of the people and the production and marketing system of the country. But the officials and employees of the cooperative department and the cooperative societies are taking risks and the government has continued to work in compliance with the declared health rules. In the first four months of this pandemic, 98 cooperative societies, with their own funding and management, distributed relief items worth BDT 9.44 crore to 1,96,434 affected members. They have carried out publicity and propaganda among the members and the general public about the observance of hygiene rules.

As a result of the global pandemic, people have become disoriented, but in this situation, enlivened by the cooperative ideal "Al-Amin Sarbik Gram Unnoyon Shombay Somiti" along with some local public representatives and socially prominent personnel donated to 150 poor helpless people with 10 kg rice, 2 kg pulse, 1 kg oil, 1 piece of Lux soap, 2 kg onion, and 2 kg potato. From the society, they have also donated 300 masks during the pandemic. Moreover, employees working in the cooperative divisions, administrative personnel from district and upazila were also assisting in their donations and promotions. The pandemic has also proved that cooperatives are the welcome mantra for overcoming any kind of misery.

Due to the COVID-19 pandemic, it was not possible to achieve the target of 100% performance of some activities of the Cooperative Department in the financial year 2019–2020, such as audit, selection, training, and inspection. But in the midst of the pandemic, as much as possible, efforts have been made to do all that work. Our colleagues have done their best.

In the financial year 2019–2020, in the midst of the pandemic, the development projects of the Cooperative Department were being implemented and success has been achieved. At the same time, we have been working on new development project proposals and the success is significant. On the other hand, the officers and employees of the Cooperative Department have been participating in the relief and promotion work under the leadership of the local administration at the divisional, district, and upazila levels. The pandemic has also proved that cooperatives are the infallible mantra for overcoming any kind of misery (Annual Report, 2019–2020).

References

Ahmed, F. U. (10 September, 2019). Socio-economic importance of co operatives: Bangladesh context, mismanagement, mistrust, irregularities, are harming the cooperative societies. https://m.theindependentbd.com/post/214894.

Annual Report. (2019–2020). Local Government Department, Rural Development and Cooperatives, People's Republic of Bangladesh, http://www.coop.gov. bd/site/view/annual_ reports/-.

Annual Report. (2019–2020b). Department of Cooperatives, Government of the People's Republic of Bangladesh, pp. 13–17. http://www.coop.gov.bd/site/ view/annual_reports/-.

Blair, H. W. (1978). Rural development, class structure and bureaucracy in Bangladesh. *World Development, 6*(1), 65–82.

Citysearch. (2021). https://cooperatives.punjab.gov.pk/industrial_societies.

CoD, Punjab. (2020). History. https://cooperatives.punjab.gov.pk/history.

Coop Website BD. (2021a). Cooperative at a glance. http://www.coop.gov.bd/ site/page/e2a17178-811f-4143-a759-c7ada72b205e/-.

Coop Website BD. (2021b). Success stories of cooperative society, pp. 16–20. shorturl.at/fkrMW.

COOP. (2021). About Pakistan. https://www.housinginternational.coop/co-ops/ pakistan/.

Countryeconomy.com. (2021). Country comparison Bangladesh, India and Pakistan. https://countryeconomy.com/countries/compare/bangladesh/pakistan and https://countryeconomy.com/countries/compare/bangladesh/india.

Dana, L. P. (2000). Creating entrepreneurs in India. *Journal of Small Business Management, 38*(1), 86–91.

Ferguson, J. A. (2012). Generating sustainable livelihoods; the role of cooperatives. Canadian cooperative association, Paper presented at the Harnessing the Cooperative Advantage to Build a Better World, Ottawa, 4–6 September, 2012.

ILO (2020). Cooperatives and wider SSE enterprises respond to COVID-19 disruptions, and government measures are being put in place. https://www.ilo. org/global/topics/cooperatives/news/WCMS_740254/lang--en/index.htm.

Islam, M. J., Azim, M., Karim, M. M., & Begum, M. A. (2014). An overview on co-operative societies in Bangladesh. *European Journal of Business and Management, 6*, 33–40.

Khan, A. R. (1979). The Comilla model and the integrated rural development programme of Bangladesh: An experiment in "cooperative capitalism". *World Development, 7*(4–5), 397–422.

Khair, M. A. (2019). The role of cooperatives in the economy, Daily Jugantor.
Retrieved on 24 September 2022 from https://www.jugantor.com/todays-
paper/window/239174/%E0%A6%85%E0%A6%B0%E0%A7%8
D%E0%A6%A5%E0%A6%A8%E0%A7%80%E0%A6%A4%E0%A6%B
F%E0%A6%A4%E0%A7%87-%E0%A6%B8%E0%A6%AE%E0%A6%A
C%E0%A6%BE%E0%A7%9F%E0%A7%87%E0%A6%B0-%E0%A6%A
D%E0%A7%82%E0%A6%AE%E0%A6%BF%E0%A6%95%E0%A6
%BE.

McCarthy, F. & Feldman, S. (1983). Rural women discovered: New sources of
capital and labor in Bangladesh. *Development and Change, 14*(2), 211–236.

Milovanovic, V. & Smutka, L. (2018). Cooperative rice farming within rural
Bangladesh. *Journal of Co-operative Organization and Management, 6*(1),
11–19.

Muhammad, N. & Dana, L. P. (2015). Barriers to the development and progress
of entrepreneurship in Rural Pakistan. *International Journal of Entrepreneurial Behavior and Research, 23*(2), 279–295.

NCTB. (2021). Unit 6: Cooperative Society, p. 106. http://www.ebookbou.edu.
bd/Books/Text/OS/HSC/hsc_1885/Unit-06.pdf.

NCUI. (2018a). Annual report. p. 47. https://ncui.coop/hindi/main-images/
Statistical_Profile_2018.pdf.

NCUI. (2018b). Indian cooperative movement. https://ncui.coop/hindi/main-
images/Statistical_Profile_2018.pdf.

Palalic, R., Ramadani, V., Mariam Gilani, S., Gërguri-Rashiti, S., & Dana, L.
(2021). Social media and consumer buying behavior decision: What entrepreneurs should know? *Management Decision, 59*(6), 1249–1270.

Pallab Bhattacharya. (2021). India's new cooperatives ministry will it lead to
cooperation or confrontation? https://www.thedailystar.net/views/opinion/
news/indias-new-cooperatives-ministry-2128376.

Rahaman, M. S., Rahman, M. M., & Moral, I. H. (2020). Informative knowledge
and challenges of home quarantine during COVID-19 in Bangladesh.
International Journal of Technology Transfer and Commercialisation, 17(4),
354–367.

Rahman, M.M. (2021, Access Year). Social protection and economic development through co-operative. http://bea-bd.org/site/images/pdf/088.pdf.

Rahman, M. M., Uddin, M. B., Chowdhury, M. S., & Rahaman, M. S. (2021).
Psychological status of private commercial bank employees in Bangladesh
during COVID-19. *Journal of Business Strategy Finance and Management,
2*(2), 66–73.

Rajguru. (2019). Features of cooperative society, economic discussions. https://www.economicsdiscussion.net/cooperative-society/features-of-cooperative-society/31770.

Salamzadeh, A. & Dana, L. P. (2021). The coronavirus (COVID-19) pandemic: Challenges among Iranian startups. *Journal of Small Business & Entrepreneurship*, *33*(5), 489–512.

Sarker, A. R., Sultana, M., & Mahumud, R. A. (2016). Cooperative societies: A sustainable platform for promoting universal health coverage in Bangladesh. *BMJ Global Health*, *1*(3), e000052.

Sharma, N. (2018). Contribution of social learning in counterproductive work behaviors. In A. Sandu and A. Frunza (eds.), *Ethical Issues in Social Work Practice*, pp. 260–281. IGI Global.

Sultana, M., Ahmed, J. U., & Shiratake, Y. (2020). Sustainable conditions of agriculture cooperative with a case study of dairy cooperative of Sirajgonj District in Bangladesh. *Journal of Co-operative Organization and Management*, *8*(1), 100105.

UN. (2021). Expert group meeting on "The Role of Cooperatives in Economic and Social Development". https://www.un.org/development/desa/dspd/2021-meetings/coops.html.

UNDP. (2016). United Nations. Sustainable development solutions network. Transforming our world: The 2030 agenda for sustainable development. Retrieved 5 March 2016 from http://bit.ly/1P1zfHH.

Varad Kitey. (2021). Amul case study — History & present of the taste of India. https://startuptalky.com/amul-case-study/.

Vorobeva, E. & Dana, L. P. (2021). The COVID-19 pandemic and migrant entrepreneurship: Responses to the market shock. *Migration Letters*, *18*(4), 477–485.

https://doi.org/10.1142/9789811253799_0002

Chapter 2

Cooperatives and the United Nations' Sustainable Development Goals

Satarupa Modak[*,‡], Triptesh Mondal[*,§], and Subhrajyoti Panda[†,¶]

M.S.S.S.O.A., Centurion University of Technology and Management, Odisha, India

†*Sri Sri University, Odisha, India*

‡*satarupa.modak@cutm.ac.in*

§*triptesh.mondal@cutm.ac.in*

¶*subhrajyotip1992@gmail.com*

Abstract

Sustainable development goals aim to address various global challenges by 2030. This chapter aims to explore the role of cooperatives in reaching the sustainable development goals. This chapter discusses the history of cooperatives, their classification, formation, and role in reaching the sustainable development goals. Adopting and incorporating sustainable development goals into the core objectives of the cooperatives will lead to sustainability.

Keywords: cooperative, credit, livelihood, organisation, sustainable

1. Introduction

A cooperative, often also known as co-op or coop, is "an autonomous association of persons united voluntarily to meet their common economic, social and cultural needs and aspirations through a jointly-owned enterprise" as per International Cooperative Alliance. Cooperatives play a very crucial in the achievement of sustainable development goal (ILO, 2002). Industrial revolution prompted the genesis of this special form of organisation called cooperative or cooperative society to safeguard the weaker section of the community involved in various activities including business activities (FAO, 2012). This intention to help protect the interests of the weaker sections of the society — the concept of cooperation — gave rise to the mottos, "each for all and all for each" and "self-help through mutual aid" (ICA, 2013).

2. Features of Cooperatives

Cooperatives are voluntary associations democratically owned by their members with equal voting rights to elect the board of directors. Cooperative societies are often registered as separate legal entities with a service motive for the distribution of surplus under state control, especially to eliminate middlemen from agricultural commodity markets, provide facilities of cash trading, audit, and also offer democratic management, perpetual existence, open membership, one-man–one-vote, raising capital, management of affairs of co-operative, dividend distribution from the surplus, disposal of surplus, and fixed return on capital. Cooperatives work under the principle of self and mutual help, promotes the spirit of cooperation, common interest to equality of vote, distributive justice, limited capital, morality, and ethics.

3. Most Common Forms of Cooperatives in India

There are various types of cooperatives (Schwettmann, 2012; Brichall, 2004). There are six types of cooperatives in India, described as follows.

3.1 Consumer cooperative society

These types of cooperatives offer household goods at reasonable price for the member and non-member consumers since they procure bulk goods at wholesale rate directly from the producer. Capital is raised by issuing low-denominational shares to the members who also get dividends on the shares and mostly use word-of-mouth publicity. Examples for this type of cooperatives are Kendriya Bhandar, Apna Bazar, Sahkari Bhandar and Samabayika in West Bengal, and Aitorma in Tripura.

3.2 Producer cooperative society

In this type, mostly small-scale producers pool resources together to increase marketing volume in order to minimise risk from competitive capitalistic markets. This type of cooperatives produce and manufacture goods at producer level and distribute them to consumers without an intermediate link. Handloom societies such as APPCO, Bayanika in Odhisa, Haryana Handloom, and Tantumita in Tripura are examples of this type.

3.3 Cooperative credit society

Cooperative credit societies serve as a financial society to provide loans to members at low rate of interest for various purposes and also provide almost all banking services. These societies are regularly aided by state and national government subsidies and funding. Some examples are village service cooperative societies and urban cooperative banks.

3.4 Marketing cooperative society

These cooperatives help producers to sell their produce at the best market price and also educate them about marketing components, credit facilities, input availability, and pooling together to stabilise supply against demand to ensure facilitates such as grading, processing, storage, and transport. They act as a safeguard measure for producers from market exploitations and profits distributed among producers on the basis of quality of produce. Examples for this type of cooperatives are milk cooperatives in Gujarat, Maha Grape in Maharashtra, Sugarcane Co-operative Marketing Society, Cotton Co-operative Marketing Society, Oilseed Growers Co-operative Marketing Society, and KASAM in Odisha.

3.5 Housing cooperative society

To help their members to own a decent housing facility, these cooperative societies have been developed, which provide affordable housing to the middle- and low-income groups. One can purchase shares to become member of these housing cooperative society and payments collected in instalments. These societies are mostly found in the semi-urban and urban areas.

3.6 Cooperative farming society

Resource-poor farmers can opt for one of the following types of cooperative farming society services: farming cooperatives, cooperative better farming, cooperative joint farming, co-op tenant farming, and collective farming co-ops.

4. Why Form a Cooperative Society?

Among the various types of business organisations, cooperatives are more preferred by agrarian communities because they are easy to form, open for membership, and provide democratic management with equal rights to vote, limited liability, stability and durability, economical operation, government support, low management cost, mutual cooperation, no speculation, economic advantages, service motive, internal financing, income tax exemption, cheaper goods based on collective bargaining principle, elimination of middleman, equality, perpetual existence, and scope for self-government.

5. Role of Cooperatives in Sustainable Development Goals

Sustainable development goals are mainly focused on economic, social, cultural, and environmental aspects; these are three-dimensional aspects of marginalised and weaker section of the community. It has been proven that grassroot organisations play a vital role in any developmental activity. Cooperatives are profoundly appropriate and important in the realisation of the proposed sustainable development goals. Some of the highlights of sustainable development goals, as proposed by eminent persons in the post-2015 Development Agenda (HLP, 2013; Wanyama, 2014), are as follows.

5.1 Poverty reduction

Cooperatives are operating with self-help and mutual-help mechanisms create opportunities, extend protection, and facilitate empowerment for wholesome benefit of the community. This provides a platform to identify economic opportunities for their members, empowers the disadvantaged to defend their interests, provides security to the poor by allowing them to convert individual risks into collective risks, and mediates member access to assets that they utilise to earn a living. Cooperatives give employment for millions of people around the world in conjunction with small- and medium-sized endeavours; they are the most noteworthy source of modern business (ILC, 2007). Additionally, cooperatives have contributed to food security by supporting individuals to diversify the production and marketing of food (Sizya, 2001; Wanyama *et al.*, 2008; Khurana, 2010; IFAD, 2012).

5.2 Gender equality

Cooperatives are contributing towards gender equality by developing women's participation in social and economic sectors. Cooperatives are supporting vulnerable sections of community by mainstreaming them in cooperative societies. Gender balance can be improved by empowering women and adolescence girls to reach their full potential by providing equal access to resources and economic opportunities and building women's capacity to impact decision-making by dispensing with discrimination against women in administration and open life (HLP, 2013; Puri, 2013).

5.3 Quality education and lifelong learning

Cooperatives can help directly or indirectly to accelerate facilities to attain quality education and lifelong learning. Cooperatives improve standard of living as well as economic and purchasing power of individual members, which indirectly facilitates and increases the scope of spending on children education as organisation participation has proven its impact on improving quality of life. Here, cooperative members work as a cohesive groups exchanging knowledge and understanding on various aspects of life; through knowledge sharing, one can open up the technological advantages related focused group target areas. Lifelong learning is provided to the members through skill training and knowledge development by many cooperatives, as well as literacy and numeracy for members who did not attend school.

5.4 Health

Cooperatives work not only for economic empowerment but also include social activities, such as providing healthcare service to the people. The cooperatives are mainly helpful for giving the service through this fourth sustainable development goal. The areas of health service include reduced maternal mortality rates, reduced burden of disease from HIV/AIDS, tuberculosis, malaria, neglected tropical diseases, and priority non-communicable diseases.

5.5 Food security and good nutrition

In cooperative joint-farming models, member farmers can collectively purchase agricultural inputs and jointly perform various agricultural operations to reduce labour cost. Also, collective marketing facilitates bargaining power for better price realisation. Cooperatives also promote nutrition gardens with access of quality seeds, nutritious crop varieties, and seed banks with local crop cultivars (FAO, 2013). Thus, resource-poor farmers not only get food security but are also ensured access to good nutrition.

5.6 Access to water and sanitation

Food security and good nutrition alone can defend various malnutrition issues, but access to clean water and proper sanitation facilities are equally important. Water cooperatives are mainly dedicated for accessing and providing clean water to the people (McIntyre, 2012). In Ghana, Ethiopia, and South Africa, water cooperatives work with the community to drill boreholes and establish local groups for maintenance. In the United States, water cooperatives provide safe, reliable, and sustainable water service at reasonable cost in small suburban and rural communities (International Labour Organization and International Co-operative Alliance, 2015). Sanitation is another major issue dealt with the help of cooperatives. Access to safe drinking water, sanitation, and hygiene is important for nutrient assimilation.

5.7 Sustainable energy

In developing countries, cooperatives are helping farming communities with not only basic amenities but providing sustainable and clean energy like biomass, solar power, windmill, etc. Cooperatives can be formed to access areas where there is less public outreach and too costly for the private sector to afford. Such success stories include a biomass-based power cooperative in Karnataka, India; Dhundi Saur Urja Utpadak Sahakari Mandali is India's first solar cooperative of Dhundi Village in Gujarat's Kheda District, which launched a solar energy-based irrigation pump system.

5.8 Create jobs, sustainable livelihoods, and equitable growth

Cooperatives have created many jobs directly or indirectly over the decades especially for the weaker section of the society, giving them economic empowerment by improving their collective bargaining power, building social capital, and equitable distribution of economic resources (Das & Mazumdar, 2019). At present, there are approximately 6 lakh cooperatives in India, and these cooperatives have made remarkable improvements in employment, fertiliser delivery, sugar production, handloom sectors, fishery sectors, and gender cooperatives (Anonymous, 2016). In India, dairy cooperatives help not only provide livelihood security but bring white revolution and increase per capita consumption of milk up to 225 g/day (Biswas, 2021).

5.9 Manage natural resource assets sustainably

Among grassroot-level organisations, cooperatives are considered a better model for conservation and maintain long-term sustainability of natural resources. This is because the cooperative model is able to meet these goals better than other models, especially in terms of efficiency, sustainability, equity, and resource user's satisfaction (Singh & Ballabh, 1993). If necessary prerequisites are fulfilled, then cooperative organisations can lead successfully towards sustainable social construction for natural resources (Hagedorn, 2013), such as Sustainable Agricultural Cooperatives in Netherlands, Social Cooperatives in Italy, and Social Forestry in India.

5.10 Ensure good governance and effective institutions

Good governance is deeply rooted in the mechanism of cooperatives. The most important characteristics of transparency in operation, boosting responsibility among members, accountability for operation and functions, encouraging participation, responsiveness for community, meet people's need and interest, and respect for rules and laws (Puri, 2018) are the blood and vein of any successful cooperative.

5.11 Ensure stable and peaceful societies

As cooperatives work with the principle of mutual help, peaceful business operations and effective conflict management among members or customers can be established. For instance, in Israel, cooperative movements can help in bringing together Israeli Jews and Palestinian-Israeli Arabs to live and work together peacefully. Cooperatives are comparatively successful in bringing peaceful environment between member and non-member communities with effective conflict management strategies, fostering community development activities, and enabling sustainable livelihood opportunities, market access, risk mitigation measures, promote integration and interaction with local communities, and access to health care facilities helps to create a stable and peaceful society (www.thenews. coop).

5.12 Create a global enabling environment and catalyse long-term finance

By joining cooperatives, members can attain fair marketing also enable to get entry into the global market. Cooperatives help members with financial assistance and many long-term benefits. Thus, they enable small and marginal producers to enjoy the essence of global trade.

6. Conclusion

As a grassroot organisation, cooperative plays a vital role in the economic development of the members and can foster holistic development of the society as a whole. From the above discussion, it is clearly understood that to attain sustainable development goals, cooperatives will be effective and helpful.

References

Anonymous (2016). Cooperatives can play a very important role in creating job opportunities in rural areas: Radha Mohan Singh, cooperatives largest movement in India: Agriculture & Farmers Welfare Minister Ministry of Agriculture & Farmers Welfare, Press Information Bureau, Government of India. Retrieved 24 September 2021 from https://pib.gov.in/newsite/PrintRelease.aspx?relid=153711.

Biswas, B. (2021). Cooperative best business model to ensure job creation, says Amul's RS Sodhi, featured article under Business segment. Retrieved 24 September 2021 from www.cnbctv18.com.

Birchall, J. (2004). *Cooperatives and the Millennium Development Goals.* Geneva: International Labour Organization.

Das, A. & Mazumdar, M. D. (2019). Contribution of Cooperatives on Employment Generation Evidence from West Bengal Milk Cooperative in Burdwan District, Implementing the Sustainable Development Goals: What Role for

Social and Solidarity Economy? UN Inter-Agency Task force on Social and Solidarity Economy, Draft paper of UNTFSSE (2018), 1–11.

FAO (2012). Agricultural cooperatives: Key to feeding the world. http://www.fao. org/fileadmin/templates/getinvolved/images/WFD2012_ leaflet_en_low.pdf.

FAO (2013). The state of food insecurity in the world. (Rome, FAO). http://www. fao.org/publications/sofi/en/.

Hagedorn, K. (2013). Natural resource management: The role of cooperative institutions and governance. *Journal of Entrepreneurial and Organizational Diversity, European Research Institute on Cooperative and Social Enterprises,* 2(1), 101–121.

HLP (2013). A new global partnership: Eradicate poverty and transform economies through sustainable development. New York: United Nations. http:// www.post2015hlp.org/wp-content/uploads/2013/05/UN-Report.pdf.

ICA (2013). Cooperative identity, values and principles. Retrieved 15 November 2013 from http://ica.coop/en/whats-co-op/co-operative-identity-values-principles.

IFAD (2012). Agricultural cooperatives: Paving the way for food security and rural development. Retrieved 27 September 2013 from http://www.ifad.org/ english/institutions/yic_flyer.pdf.

ILO (2002). Recommendation 193 concerning the promotion of cooperatives. Geneva: ILO. http://www.ilo.org/images/empent/static/coop/pdf/english.pdf.

ILO & ICA (2015). Cooperatives and the sustainable development goals. A Contribution to the Post-2015 Development Debate, Policy Brief. Retrieved 2 September 2021 from www.ilo.org.

Khurana, M. L. (2010). Cooperatives for improving living conditions in slums. Retrieved 26 August 2013 from http://www.naredco.in/Article. asp?prYear=2010&mon= Jan&foo=bar&page=2.

McIntyre, N. (2012). How will climate change impact on fresh water security? In *The Guardian,* retrieved 21 December from http://www.theguardian.com/ environment/2012/nov/30/climate-change-water.

Puri, D. L. (2018). Impact of good governance on performance of cooperatives in Nepal. *Management & Marketing, XVI*(2), 208–224.

Rajguru, K. Features of cooperative society. Retrieved 20 September 2021 from www.economicsdiscussion.net.

Schwettmann, J. (2012). Cooperatives — A global vision. Paper presented at a Symposium on "Perspectives for Cooperatives in Southern Africa", Friedrich Ebert Stiftung, Lusaka, Zambia, 20–21 August.

Singh, K. & Ballabh, V. (1993). Cooperatives in natural resource management, Workshop Report 10, Institute of Rural Management, pp. 1–59.

Sizya, M. J. (2001). The role cooperatives play in poverty reduction in Tanzania. Paper presented at the United Nations in observance of the International Day for the Eradication of Poverty, Retrieved 17 October, from http://www.un. org/esa/socdev/poverty/papers/poverty_panel_sizya.pdf.

Wanyama, F. O. (2014). Cooperatives and the Sustainable Development Goals: A Contribution to the Post-2015 Development Agenda, ILO.

Wanyama, F. O., Develtere, P. & Pollet, I. (2008). Encountering the evidence: Cooperatives and poverty reduction in Africa. *Journal of Cooperative Studies*, *41*(3), 16–27.

https://doi.org/10.1142/9789811253799_0003

Chapter 3

Strengthening Resilience and Solidarity in Cooperatives: Pathways for a New Ministry of Cooperation in the Post-COVID-19 Era

Neha Christie[*,§], Darshnaben Mahida[†,||], and P.K. Shajahan[‡,¶]

School of Social Work, Tata Institute of Social Sciences, Mumbai, India

†*Dairy Economics, Statistics & Management Division, ICAR-National Dairy Research Institute, Karnal, India*

‡*Centre for Community Organisation and Development Practice, School of Social Work, Tata Institute of Social Sciences (TISS), Mumbai, India*

§*nehachristie@gmail.com, neha.christie@tiss.edu*

||*darshnapmahida93@gmail.com*

¶*shajahan@tiss.edu*

Abstract

Cooperatives have been given much-needed attention now by the Indian government through forming a separate Ministry of Cooperation. However, a lot has to be done before taking pride in the same. This chapter emphasises on the cooperative model to promote local institution-building in the post-COVID-19 era. Influenced by the institutional theory, the chapter discusses the gaps at the ground level and also provides suggestions to strengthen the cooperative sector in the country. A case is discussed from the successful dairy cooperatives in India that played a significant role in times of the COVID-19 crisis. The findings of the case discuss the interventions of the cooperatives in generating awareness towards safety, solidarity, accountability, providing stability, maintaining the value chain, securing finances, and supporting community welfare even during the time of the pandemic. Through this, the chapter highlights the cooperatives' abilities in generating inclusive development in the country even during the time of crisis. This chapter is based on the primary information collected through a qualitative research method that includes in-depth interviews with the cooperative members.

Keywords: sustainability, dairy cooperatives, crisis, livelihoods, economy

1. Introduction

The concept of resilience emerged while there were debates concerning sustainable development. Later, new understandings grew towards social resilience that included the aspects of socio-economic, governance, and human–nature systems. In this chapter, social resilience is considered as a product of solidarity and collective action through the cooperative model. In today's time of the global pandemic, resilience and solidarity are the priority needs of the community survival. The world has been witnessing the diverse effects of the COVID-19 pandemic due to the spread of the coronavirus. Every nation is taking necessary precautions to deal with this global crisis and the situation of uncertainty. The sudden step of lockdown has not only affected the national economies but also caused traumatic physical and mental conditions, loss of family, home, work, and an increase in crime and inequality. In India, a huge population resides under the label of marginalised; however, among all, the condition of small farmers and migrant labourers was the most vulnerable. Studies have shown that most of the farmers reported negative impacts on production, sales, prices, and incomes. Among all, 80% of farms reported a decrease in sales ratio and 20% of farms reported devastating failures by selling almost nothing. Over 80% of farmers said that the prices of commodities decreased, and 50% of farmers reported a decrease in price by 50%. The income from the farm was reduced by more than half for 60% of farms (Harris *et al.*, 2020). On the one hand, the global crisis has its negative impacts, while on the other, it has generated new possibilities, learnings, and ideas for the way forward. In the case of India, the role played by the local interventionist institutions and non-government organisations has created an environment of hope, empathy, and solidarity across the nation. According to Dutta and Fischer (2020), It has also given new lessons and evidence to prove the present need for decentralisation of power in the country. At present, developing sustainable solutions to save the rural economy is one of the biggest challenges for the country.

Cooperatives are local organisations that are grown through collectivity and human relations. They are known for their double nature that ensures both social and economic empowerment of the communities. Such local organisations are based on networks and social capital with high interpersonal relations between the members (Górriz-Mifsud *et al.*, 2016). Cooperatives are member-owned organisations and therefore hold collective efforts, quality, longevity, and sustainability in their nature. This chapter discusses the cooperative model for its role in ensuring communities' social resilience and abilities in promoting community participation, integration, distributing resources, and gaining sustainability (Tailor-Gooby, 2004). It focuses on the micro, mezzo, and macro levels of the cooperative system responsible for resilience and development in the community. The chapter refers to the institutional theory that explains the role of the institutions and the necessity to deal with the change effectively. It rationalises that it is the need of the hour that the country should invest in developing local institutions that involve strong people's participation. To support the argument, this research studies the case of dairy cooperatives of Gujarat State in India that are known for their collective action and success and highlights their significant role during the global crisis due to COVID-19.

2. Cooperative Identity and a New Ministry of Cooperation in India

Collective action, voluntary membership, shared goals, and member benefits are the first and known characteristics that generally form an identity of the cooperatives. A deeper understanding of cooperative identity can be achieved through relating the cooperative laws, principles, and values with different circumstances. These circumstances can be the role of the state, market strategies, situation of the cooperative members that directly and indirectly affect the cooperative sector (Bandyopadhyay, 2004). In terms of extending our understating, we have to be aware of not only these external circumstances but also the internal components that form the cooperative identity. These components can be the network of members, structure, and norms that build the governance system, the reciprocity among the members, and the resources produced by the members. A cooperative is an interventionist organisation that highly depends on its members. The cooperative members form a network that generates social capital which is the base of the organisation. It is important to moderate the network with a robust governance system to generate positive outcomes that are beyond financial profit (Jankauskas & Šeputienė, 2007). In terms of claiming the cooperative identity, one requires to develop a holistic perspective towards the members' benefits. There are essential dimensions of the cooperative that foster sustainable solutions and community empowerment.

Recently, the Indian Government formed a new ministry of cooperation to strengthen the cooperative movement in the country, the cooperatives were established a long time ago. The interventions to establish cooperatives were initiated during the colonial period, looking at the success of the cooperative movement in Europe. In the year 1904, the Cooperative Credit Society's Act was established to boost cooperative movements in the country and observe the output. The act was modified in the year 1950 based on the observations (Ilbert, 1914). Later, the cooperatives grew with varying structure and output as per the geographical locations. At present, there are various types of cooperatives in the country, the reasons behind their growth are the diverse culture, social capital, and the interventions of the state (Birthal & Joshi, 2009). A report by the National Cooperative Union of India in 2018 recorded 854,355 cooperatives societies in the whole country. Today, social scientists have mixed views towards the cooperative structure and their performance in the country. The cooperative is of interest to the states; therefore, the structure of the cooperative varies as per the state rules in India. The state government implements its programmes through cooperatives and the cooperatives are given various subsidies by the state. Most of the time, with the change of the political leadership in a state government, the cooperative political environment also changes. This situation directly or indirectly affects the cooperative members (MoSPI, 2013).

3. Case Study

This study was conducted on dairy cooperatives of Anand District of Gujarat State that has one of the oldest dairy cooperatives in the state. The cooperatives are known for their robust governing system, milk collection capacity, and running the business with high turnover (Rajendran & Mohanty, 2004). The reason to select the cooperatives of Anand District was to study the cooperatives' ability in generating resilience and solidarity during times of crisis. It can be enlightening for the rest of the country to rethink the local institution-building through the cooperative sector. The study narrates the farmer milk producers' experiences during the COVID-19 crisis and the way dairy cooperatives of Gujarat dealt with their day-to-day challenges.

3.1 Research methodology

The research follows a qualitative research methodology to develop a case study through in-depth interviews (Creswell, 2009). There were 38 in-depth interviews were conducted in eight dairy cooperative societies (DCSs) in the Anand District of Gujarat State. The samples included 38 active milk producer members from the eight DCSs. The selection criteria for DCS included the registration period, homogeneous or heterogeneous governing board composition, milk procurement capacity, and geographical distance. The sample selection of the members included chairpersons, secretaries, and active members. The identified participants were informed about the study objectives and informed consent was taken. The secondary data were collected through annual reports, news articles, and other literature available in the public domain.

3.2 Limitations of the study

The findings of the study are limited to the dairy cooperative sector in Anand District in Gujarat State in India. However, the learnings can be applied to the general cooperative sector in the country as the research promotes local development through the cooperative model. This research also tries to develop linkages between micro, mezzo, and macro levels of the cooperative sector.

3.3 Findings

3.3.1 *Generating solidarity and accountability*

The cooperatives were able to function with cooperation and necessary precautions. The members were provided masks, sanitisers, and COVID-19–related information and guidelines regularly. The members followed social distancing and other important rules effectively. The consumers in urban areas were regularly guided to reduce panic purchases.

3.3.2 *Ensuring stability against unorganised sector*

The dairy cooperatives were able to procure even more milk during the lockdown phase as the unorganised sector stakeholders were not able to procure milk due to the shutdown of hotels and restaurants. The milk cooperative handled the situation with great collaboration and moderated the supply chain.

3.3.3 *Micro to macro supply chain management*

Throughout the lockdown period, the dairy cooperatives were able to procure a regular amount of milk every day from the village DCSs to district milk unions and supply to the urban regions of the state. The consumers were informed of the new timings of the milk collection centre.

3.3.4 *Economic security*

Most of the farmer milk producers claimed that they didn't face many difficulties as they didn't face much difficulties as they could pour their milk to the DCSs and earned income regularly. In one case, the cooperatives faced issue as there was no bank in the village. However, later, an ATM was fixed in the village for the convenience of the cooperative members.

3.3.5 *Community welfare*

The dairy cooperatives of Anand District had set up an oxygen plant at the local welfare hospital in the district that is run through a welfare society. The hospital provides subsidised medical treatment and is known in the entire Gujarat State. The oxygen plant generates 20,000 litres per hour of oxygen (*Times of India*, 2021).

A few common quotes from the interviews with milk producer members are mentioned in Table 1 as supporting statements to the findings discussed above.

Table 1.   Common quotes from the respondents (milk prouder members).

No.	Themes	Common Quotes From the Respondents (Milk Prouder Members)
3.3.1	Generating solidarity and accountability	*Our cooperative societies followed the guidelines given by the government and took necessary safety measures while milk collection process.* (active members)
		The cooperative society gave us the masks and strictly informed us to wear them while pouring the milk.
		In case of any member was tested COVID positive then that member was told to stay at home and not to visit the society. (active members)
		The cooperative societies have made circles in ques where we have to stand and maintain social distance. (active members)
		We have been informing the consumers that there is enough milk collection and they do not have to purchase in bulk. (director of the state cooperative federation)
3.3.2	Ensuring stability against unorganised sector	*We are able to collect more milk from the milk producers as those who used to sell some milk to the restaurants have also started pouring milk to cooperatives now.* (managing director of the state federation)

(Continued)

Table 1.   (*Continued*)

No.	Themes	Common Quotes From the Respondents (Milk Prouder Members)
3.3.3	Micro to macro supply chain management	*So far the supply chain has been maintained well and we have not heard of any issue. We are regularly supplying milk to the district union through tankers.* (secretaries of the eight Village Dairy Cooperative Societies (VDCS)) *We received regular income and haven't faced any difficulty in supplying the milk.* (active members)
3.3.4	Economic security	*We did not face any issue during the pandemic as we could regularly pour milk at the society and collect money.* (secretaries of the eight VDCS) *We do not have a bank in our village, so every time one person used to go to the city and withdraw money for all of us. Now we have ATM in our village so this issue is solved.* (auditor of a society)

3.4 Discussion

The dairy cooperatives effectively dealt with workforce management, consumer demands, transportation, surplus milk, decreased demand for milk and milk products, and protection of farmers and livestock (Parmar & Misra, 2020). As discussed earlier, the cooperative has also set up an oxygen plant at a well-known charitable hospital in the state. This facility can treat up to 60 patients in a day. The cooperative is also in the process of initiating more oxygen plants in other districts of the state (*Times of India*, 2021). The networks, reciprocity, and internal communication system are the reasons that the cooperatives have done well even during the global pandemic. However, unfortunately, there are milk producers in other parts of the country that are connected with passive cooperatives and unorganised sector, including private companies and small vendors. These milk producers have been facing great difficulties due to the non-functionality of the unorganised sector during the lockdown (*India Today*, 31 March 2020). The market is one of the biggest external challenges for cooperatives in India. A report claims that the scale of milk demand will be higher than the scale of supply by 2040 (Reincke *et al.*, 2018). In such a situation, the country may be under greater pressure to produce more milk and develop new pathways to procure more milk from the farmer milk producers. This market pressure can create conflict situations between the state and the milk producers. The collective organisations like cooperatives will also suffer as the big farmer milk producers may move towards private business rather than staying with cooperatives. Such a market can manipulate cooperative values. In this situation, the state's take on market principles is very important as it affects the relationship between the state and the interventionist organisations like cooperatives.

In its recent budget, the government of India has allocated INR 3,289 crore for animal husbandry and dairying. There are different central government schemes, such as the Dairy Entrepreneurship Development Scheme (DEDS), National Programme for Dairy Development (NPDD), and DIDF (Dairy Processing and Infrastructure Development Fund) (Parida & Yadav, 2020). These funds and schemes can be utilised to establish and strengthen the process of institution-building, collective action, and individual participation to empower the marginalised population through cooperatives.

4. Lessons Learnt Towards Strengthening Resilience and Solidarity in Cooperatives

The dairy cooperatives of Anand District in Gujarat State have been able to achieve a standard that is quite recognised at the international level. This section, rather than classifying threats, opportunities, strengths, and weaknesses in two-by-two quadrants, discusses the way the cooperative sector in India can use its strengths and weaknesses in the given internal and external environment (Minsky & Aron, 2021).

4.1 Requirement of charismatic leadership

The success of the dairy cooperative movement in the Anand District of Gujarat depended highly on the dedicated, visionary, and collaborative local leaders. These leaders possessed charismatic leadership characteristics that were farmer sensitive. Most of the cooperative members acknowledged the contribution of the former charismatic leaders. In the present condition, the accountability and dedication of the board members have comparatively decreased. Land ownership, political affiliation, and belongingness to a particular community carry a lot of weightage to be a cooperative leader. These conditions inhibit the opportunity for genuine leadership in cooperatives. Effective norms for the election process and a farmer-sensitive system can help in such cases.

4.2 Moderating networks of members

At present, there are states in India with a high number of marginalised populations and passive cooperatives. This raises a question about the state's role as an agent to uplift the small and marginal farmers of the country. In a developing country like India, the growth of small farmers is critical. The ability of cooperatives to preserve their resources and equal share of member benefits is threatened by many internal and external factors. The dense networks of cooperative members at the village level need moderation for better choices and perspectives. The network of social capital is required to measure the trust, drivers of trust, and its consequences to save the institution. In terms of making cooperatives active, the country needs to invest in micro-level networking, strengthening systems, members' capacity building, etc.

4.3 Inclusion of small farmers and marginalised population

India has a long history of establishing rural institutions that have been serving the rural economy by generating collective action. A report by the Ministry of Agriculture and Farmers' Welfare in India recommended developing a system that can rework farmers' welfare goals, representation in decision making, more grassroot-level participation, social security, and more access to knowledge (Government of India, 2020). Today, the pandemic has invited new challenges for the lower-middle class and marginalised population. Many vulnerable groups including manual workers, small-scale farmers, and landless labourers have lost their sources of livelihood and faced the worst situations among all (Workie *et al.*, 2020). In such a scenario, creating a separate ministry of cooperation can be considered as a step towards local institutional development in India. This ministry will require to pay special attention to the present requirement of these marginalised populations. The country requires a strong system and new strategies to support and secure the livelihood of these groups majorly including labourers and farmers. This can be done faster by establishing networks and collective efforts that bring not only economic stability but also uplift the socio-psycho situation of the poor. In recent times, the lockdown, lack of income, and search for security made many labourers heading back to their hometowns. The role of the states has become more crucial especially where the migrants have returned and farmers are suffering from multiple challenges. The states should ensure plans that can channelise and utilise the skills of the labourers.

4.4 Dealing with social capital

The cooperative model has the ability to utilise dense social capital with a robust structure. This has been the reason that earlier the dairy cooperatives in Anand District in Gujarat State could achieve their common goals through voluntary member participation. There is a lot of scope for the development of cooperatives through collective action and networking in other parts of India. Dairy cooperatives in Anand have given many lessons to realise the present requirements of decentralisation and institution-building that can strengthen the role of local institutions in the country. The three-tier cooperative model in Anand District involves active partici-pation and cooperation between farmers and professionals at each level. It generates a system that fosters integration and effective resource utilisation.

4.5 Promoting cooperative model

Cooperatives consist of networks, norms, reciprocity, and trust. The structure of cooperatives is built on the principles of open and voluntary membership, democratic member control, members' economic participa-tion, autonomy, independence, education, training, and information, coop-eration, and concern for the community (Bandyopadhyay, 2004).

The cooperative model has the ability to provide a good lift to India's rural economy and possesses a lot of calibre in taking care of small farmers. However, it is essential to reinvest and regenerate the attention in strengthening the governing system of the cooperatives and preparing the farmers for future challenges. Regions including Kerala, West Bengal, Telangana, Odisha, and Tamil Nadu are the budding milk-producing states and can rise in milk production as the ratio of marginalised farmers are high (National Cooperative Union of India, 2018). The northeast region should also be motivated to establish cooperatives. The supply chain also requires a strong networking system that can monitor micro- and macro-level processes (Francesconi *et al.*, 2010). The states should develop a strong network-based system that can generate collective action and democratic individual participation can boost growth and preserve the rural economy at this moment in India.

4.6 Forming effective policies for passive cooperatives

Cooperatives can stay firm as they are focused on their members. The cooperative interventions are developed towards its member benefits. It has the ability to equally distribute the power among its members through one-member–one-vote system. The reciprocity and trust among the members develop mutual understanding and prevents opportunistic behaviour in the group (Billiet *et al.*, 2021). Cooperatives play an effective role in community development as they involve local participation from various communities. Decentralisation of power and a strong and democratic governance system can produce fruitful, effective, and sustainable interpersonal relations among members. Such a system automatically gains strength to deal with the challenges. It can also be a great tool to help the farmers to fight against market domination. An effective cooperative network can provide a stage for effective communication and learning (Tailor-Gooby, 2004). The present situation is quite tough for the country and therefore the considered and supportive role of the state becomes very important.

For solving some major issues of the cooperatives, such as restrictive rules and lack of professional management and leadership, producer companies which are also being called as new-generation cooperatives present an alternative, the concept of milk producer company (MPC) in the villages has been promoted that were either uncovered by the cooperative network or the non-functional cooperatives. This situation has gained traction among district-level cooperative unions as well (Sood, 2014). Instead of forming new groups of companies, it is easier to strengthen the passive cooperatives and utilise the social capital with a strong structure and implementation system.

4.7 Handling global competitiveness

There was a perception in the Indian economy that the cooperatives will not be able to thrive and deliver in light of the increasing global competition. However, with increasing liberalisation, the cooperative sector, especially the marketing cooperatives, now faces global competition and they have to compete in the open market. There is a lot of pressure to improve the standard of cooperative performance to sustain in the market. For instance, although India opted out of the Regional Comprehensive Economic Partnership (RCEP), but owing to the World Trade Organization (WTO) commitments, it has permitted the import of 10,000 million tonnes (MT) of milk and milk products with a 15% concession on import duty during the year 2020 (Bhandari & Lal, 2020).

Given the situation of global competition, cooperatives will have to work towards uplifting their quality standard that can be more sustainable, inclusive, and people-centred by promoting solidarity among people, greater accountability, and fair rules and standard, which offer equal opportunities to all. Cooperatives have a special identity owing to their social and economic objectives, the basis of values and community, people-oriented and network of linkages gained through cooperative movement. Thus, by being authentic to their basic principles, cooperatives can also be in line with the United Nations Sustainable Development Goals (UNSGDs) and be the vital agent for dealing with the challenges of globalisation (MoSPI, 2013). Indian cooperatives, such as AMUL and IFFCO, are slowly taking their place among the topmost global processors and marketers; however, they also have to contribute effectively towards the sustainable development of the country's marginalised population. While most of the country's cooperatives need to strengthen their system, these topmost cooperatives can be good learning lessons. India needs to focus on quality improvement as per the international standards, diversification of processed product profile, upgrading manpower skills, infrastructure development, and global marketing for making the cooperatives globally competitive (Singh, 2016).

4.8 Improving the infrastructure

One of the major hurdles that India faces in expanding cooperatives is lack of infrastructure: inadequate transportation, lack of processing or manufacturing facilities, storage in required facilities, etc. These situations lead to an increase in the wastage of perishable commodities. It also affects the cost calculation. On the other hand, increasing the marketable surplus of produce through cooperatives requires the creation of effective additional processing, products manufacturing, and storage infrastructure. Further, lack of quality testing facilities and standards fail to pay a remunerative and appropriate price to the producers, thereby reducing the trust of producers in the cooperatives (Punjabi, 2009). Thus, cooperative societies need to have basic overall infrastructural facilities to ensure effective and efficient conduct of the business. Cooperatives have contributed significantly to the generation of institutional infrastructure and private capital formation in rural areas and have great potential in the future (Soni *et al.*, 2013). Besides, it is highly required to be globally competitive and facilitate real innovation in cooperatives through information technology upgrades. The government has started initiatives in this area such as digitally connecting the village-level societies to district level and further the national-level cooperatives through NABARD (Roychaudhary, 2021); however, the efforts need to be implemented faster and with effective follow-up.

4.9 Relaxation in restrictions and government control

A few of the cooperative laws should be modified to let the cooperative practice as autonomous business entities. (ALC India, 2019). Political and bureaucratic interference is another hindrance. The inability of these institutes to keep social and political affiliation away at various levels (village, union, and state levels) results in working inefficiency, corruption and hence remain ineffective in improving the livelihood of its members (Rajendran & Mohanty, 2004). The imprudent external intrusion in the dealing of cooperatives worsens their performance which ultimately renders them unfit for the competition (Amul, 2020). The institutional arrangement based and operative on the democratic principle is inherently more fair, feasible, and sustainable and hence should be encouraged and strengthened (Sudan, 2019). Cooperatives could bring optimistic conditions in the forthcoming era of globalisation if they are restructured into independent organisation administered by the elected officials of their members, professionally managed and free from needless restraints (Singh, 2016).

4.10 Governance and performance of cooperatives

Literature suggests that the implementation of any community-based institution rests upon the five pillars of good governance that are transparency, accountability, participation, predictability, and rule of law (Gupta, 2004). The lack of members' awareness about governance and ineffective participation in business operations, inadequate transparency and accountability, corruption, lack of willingness and commitment among committee members, and lack of training of members as well as the committee members are the factors that led to poor performance of cooperatives (Dhyananand, 2013). Small cooperatives are unable to afford the services of a professional manager; moreover, they fail to encourage the employees due to low incentives and salaries. Superfluous manpower and poor technical skill of workers are worrisome areas for cooperatives (Amul, 2020). Such cooperatives need to optimise the number of their employees along with upgrading their skills through proper education, adequate training, and apt advisory and support services. At village-level societies, inactiveness and unawareness of the executive (secretary) and managerial committee in transferring benefits of various schemes/services to the members hinder the development and welfare of the member producers. Hence, such a lack of accountability of employees also renders the cooperatives ineffective in the area. The planning commission (2003) also suggested to strengthen the accountability and management skills of the employees in cooperatives.

4.11 Ensuring commitment

In many cases, cooperatives are headed by bureaucrats who hold the position for just 1–2 years and fail to deliver desired results due to their short tenure (Business Today, 2021). Experience reveals that capable and dedicated professionals working for a reasonably long period in cooperatives, mostly, are vital for the success of cooperatives (Amul, 2020). Thus, for better performance, cooperatives should be headed by dedicated professionals instead of government officers who are posted on deputation. It can also help in increasing the pace of decision-making. Quick two-way communication mechanisms from ground to top level can help in making timely decisions and help the cooperatives in grabbing new opportunities.

4.12 Increasing the members' effective participation

Increase in membership is one of the indicators of an increase in farmers' collective action and participation. To attract new members and also retain the old ones, cooperatives should essentially be active to identify and fulfil their needs. Besides, effective member participation ensures vigilance which is important for enhancing the sense of responsibility among the executives/board members (Dhyananand, 2013). The cooperatives have to chalk out the appropriate strategies to adequately meet the obligations of the farmers up to their satisfaction. This involves the supply of required support services, such as inputs, veterinary care infrastructure, and extension services at reasonable rates to their members. For dairy farmers in dairy cooperatives, we need more attention in the form of scientific management, value addition for the products, customer services, managing the financial sustainability, maintaining the welfare of the farmers, etc. The irregular and insufficient cattle feed supply, rare visits by veterinary staff, non-accessibility to the veterinary staff on an urgent basis, and irregular meetings by the cooperatives condense members' interest in the cooperatives (Chaudhary & Pawar, 2004). Rigorous efforts to improve awareness about services offered by cooperatives are essential to reach out to more of the beneficiaries, which will eventually improve the economic outcomes (Sudan, 2019). Non-functional dairy cooperatives can also be revitalised by optimising the input delivery, payments to producers on committed dates, training the new entrant staff, and keeping party politics away. The active participation of member producers in business affairs is essential for their goods as well as for the cooperatives to be effective and efficient. Hence, the passive participation of members just as a silk supplier will not serve the motive of the cooperation. The provisions of holding free, fair, and timely elections are toned to be ensured legally by the Government (Amul, 2020). The cooperative's supervision by the representative of the member farmers could minimise the likelihood of underperformance and guaranteed milk procured can be maintained. If the cooperative societies are supervised by the dairy farmers' elected representatives, the chances of underperformance will be minimised and guaranteed procurement will be possible during the year (Subbhuraj *et al.*, 2015).

4.13 Regularise the payment methods

Studies have shown that amount and time of payment to the farmers strongly affects the quantity of production and growth of cooperatives (Rajendran & Mohanty, 2004). For example, states like Haryana and Uttar Pradesh have witnessed low performance even after having higher milk production capacity, while the relatively lower milk producer states like Bihar and Odisha have higher procurement levels. Milk unions in Haryana and Uttar Pradesh offer very low prices for both cow and buffalo milk leading to lower procurement compared to the unions in Gujarat. Along with paying competitive prices, the timing of payment is also important. Instantaneous and marginally high payment attracts producers rather than large payments per litre, but at the end of the year in form of an annual bonus to the farmers by dairy cooperatives, especially in the economically backward areas. The government announced an interest subvention of up to 4% on working capital loans to the dairy sector in order to help the cooperatives and producer organisations in making timely payments to the farmers when revenue of most of the dairy processing units shrank significantly during the COVID-19 lockdown and they were running short of working capital (Ministry of Fisheries, Animal Husbandry and Dairying, 2020). Along similar lines, cooperatives need to develop their mechanism for ensuring timely payments during normal times.

4.14 Handling large unorganised sectors

For example, in the dairying business, major disposal of milk through unorganised sectors is an ongoing issue. At present, the organised sector in India handles only 35% of the total milk production (Shashidhar, 2019). In this situation, there is an immediate need to bring reforms in the laws and regulation that could help cooperatives to increase their market share and contribute towards the welfare of the community on which it is based. Resolving the issues on pricing and marketing and establishing the much-needed infrastructure, starting from milk collection to processing and the packaging and distribution through cooperatives, can alter the minds of producers.

4.15 Promoting product diversification and effective marketing strategies

Being competitive in today's marketing environment essentially involves an enhanced role of advertising and making the packaging attractive. Unsuccessful cooperatives generally fare poorly on both fronts making it imperative to re-orient their marketing strategy. The cooperatives can consult marketing experts who will not only suggest better resource utilisation by diverting more resources towards the products yielding better returns but will also enhance the sales of those traditional products whose sales have declined by building the brand value (Shashidhar, 2019). Moreover, products are available only at their booths reducing their reach to more customers. Along with procurement, the distribution network should also be strengthened for growth and profitability. The use of modern marketing channels, such as online ordering facilities and kiosks, can further prove helpful in this regard.

4.16 Dealing with overdependence on the government

The cooperatives face financial resource constraints as their funds barely have a share in the portfolio of operational capital. With a weak stance on owned financial resources, their borrowings from the central funding agency are significantly conditioned. Historically, this has challenged to meet the adequate credit needs of the current as well as to be members (Franco & Nagrale, 2020). To avoid these conditions, effective interventions are required to generate the financial resources of cooperatives.

4.17 Setting out the way forward

Despite their overwhelming immense importance to India's rural economy, numerous factors have implicated the financial viability of most of the cooperatives. This is due to a variety of reasons including inner and peripheral internal and external constraints. There comes the role of strategic management which involves analysing, decision-making, implementing, and evaluating the actions to generate and sustain competitive advantage. The internal and external analysis of the institution serves as a roadmap to decide the appropriate strategy. External analysis helps an institution to identify the serious threats and opportunities in the existing competitive environment. On the other hand, the internal analysis helps the institution to identify its strengths and weaknesses. In other words, it helps to segregate the resources and capabilities of an institution that are more prospective. Furthermore, it helps the cooperatives to be more productive through guiding the resource allocation and achieve the desired goals (Gurel & Tat, 2017).

5. Conclusion

Dairy cooperatives of Gujarat State have presented the institutional strength of the cooperatives during the current global pandemic. The cooperatives have given many lessons to realise the present requirements of networking, decentralisation, and institution-building at micro level. The networking ability of the dairy cooperatives has united the rural population for their survival and to fight against the challenges. It has demonstrated that decentralisation of power and strong governance system can produce effective and sustainable interpersonal relations among the community members.

Local institution-building strategies can guard the farmers of India and their rights. The cooperative model can function as a saviour if it can be governed through a robust monitoring system. The cooperatives' networks create subsystems that promote social inclusion. It provides a great opportunity for negotiation against the market monopoly. A strong network provides effective bargaining power and economic and social security. The model enables various sustainable options for survival through community spirit. It enables easy information exchange and trust-building.

The recent step by the Indian Government has brought the cooperative model into the limelight and gained a lot of thought processes across the country. Many consider it as a political step and not an immediate necessity as there is a special cooperative department. With the combination of compliments and criticism, the new Ministry of Cooperation will have to act tactically to promote local institution-building through cooperatives. The new ministry should ensure the upliftment of marginal populations, equal gender representation, and involvement of youth by ensuring an intergenerational environment. It will have to be more attentive towards micro-level issues in the cooperative system and develop a healthy democratic institutional environment.

Declaration of interest statement

The author has no conflict of interest to be disclosed.

Funding

The authors have not received any funding for this research.

References

ALC India (2019). Autonomy and independence of cooperatives in India. A report prepared by ALC India (Hyderabad) for International Cooperative Alliance: Asia and Pacific. Retrieved from https://www.ica.coop/en/node/14835.

Amul (2020). A note on the achievement of dairy cooperatives. Retrieved from https://www.amul.com/m/a-note-on-the-achievements-of-the-dairy-cooperatives.

Bandyopadhyay, A. (2004). Hundred years of co-operative movement–vision and mission 2020. *Indian Cooperative Review*, *42*(1), 1–25.

Banerjee, A. (1994). Dairying systems in India. *Indian Dairyman, 46*, 592–593.

Bhadari, G. & Lal, P. (2020). Is Indian dairy sector buoyant enough to sail through COVID-19 crisis? *AgriculturePost.com*. Retrieved from https://www.researchgate.net/publication/343336242_Is_Indian_dairy_sector_buoyant_enough_to_sail_through_COVID-19_crisis_-_Agriculture_Post-pages-1–4.

Billiet, A., Dufays, F., Friedel, S., & Staessens, M. (2021). The resilience of the cooperative model: How do cooperatives deal with the COVID-19 crisis? *Strategic Change, 30*(2), 99–108.

Birthal, P. S. & Joshi, P. K. (2009). Efficiency and equity in contract farming: Evidence from a case study of dairying in India. *Quarterly Journal of International Agriculture, 48*(4), 363.

Chaudhary, H. & Pawar, J. S. (2004). Dairy cooperative societies-perceptions of milk producer members. *Social Change, 34*(3), 53–63.

David Creswell, J. D. & Creswell, J. W. (2009). *Research Design: Qualitative, Quantitative, and Mixed Methods Approaches* (Vol. 20). SAGE Publications, Inc. 2455 Teller Road Thousand Oaks, California 91320.

Dayanandan, R. (2013). Good governance practice for better performance of community organizations — Myths and Realities!! *Journal of Power, Politics & Governance, 1*(1), 10–26.

Dutta, A. & Fischer, H. (2020). The local governance of COVID-19: Disease prevention and social security in rural India. *World Development, 138*, 105234.

Francesconi, G., Heerink, N., & D'Haese, M. (2010). Evolution and challenges of dairy supply chains: Evidence from supermarkets, industries and consumers in Ethiopia. *Food Policy, 35*(1), 60–68.

Franco, D. & Nagrale, B. G. (2020). *Dairy industry: Hurdles ahead in economic perspective*. In J. Minj, A. Sudhakaran V and A. Kumari (eds.), *Dairy Processing: Advanced Research to Applications*, pp. 263–281. Springer Science and Business Media LLC.

Górriz-Mifsud, E., Secco, L., & Pisani, E. (2016). Exploring the interlinkages between governance and social capital: A dynamic model for forestry. *Forest Policy and Economics, 65*, 25–36.

Government of India. (2018). Vision (2022): National action plan for dairy development. New Delhi: Ministry of Agriculture and Farmers' Welfare.

Government of India. (2020). "Doubling farmers' income", comprehensive policy recommendation, volume XIV, the Ministry of Agriculture and Farmers' Welfare, New Delhi.

Gupta, A. (2004). Governance issues in cooperative: Need for role clarity and new institutional arrangements. Background paper prepared for IRMA Silver

Jubilee Symposium workshop on Governance Issues in Cooperatives, IRMA, Anand, 17–18 December 2004.

Gurel, E. & Tat, M. (2017). SWOT analysis: A theoretical review. *Journal of International Social Research*, *10*(51), 994–1006.

Harris, J., Depenbusch, L., Pal, A., Nair, R. M., & Ramasamy, S. (2020). Food system disruption: Initial livelihood and dietary effects of COVID-19 on vegetable producers in India. *Food Security*, *12*(4), 841–844.

Ilbert, C. (1914). British India. *Journal of the Society of Comparative Legislation*, *14*(1), 70–76.

India Today. (2020). Amul MD talks to India Today on Looming National Milk Crisis. Retrieved 30 March from https://www.youtube.com/watch?v=27dkIXdzRF8.

Jankauskas, V. & Šeputienė, J. (2007). The relation between social capital, governance and economic performance in Europe. *Verslas: Teorija ir praktika*, *8*(3), 131–138.

Ministry of Agriculture & Farmers' Welfare statistical profile. (2018). Indian cooperative movement (15th ed.). New Delhi, India: Cooperative Union of India. Retrieved from https://ncui.coop/wp-content/uploads/2019/04/Statistical_Profile_2018.pdf.

Ministry of Fisheries, Animal Husbandry and Dairying (2020). Interest subvention on Working Capital Loans for Dairy sector due to lockdown. Retrieved from https://pib.gov.in/PressReleasePage.aspx?PRID=1623843.

Minsky, L. & Aron, D. (2021). Are you doing the SWOT analysis backward? *Harvard Business Review*, *21*, 1–8.

MOSPI (2013). Chapter-44 Cooperative Societies from Statistical year book of India-2013. Retrieved from http://mospi.nic.in/sites/default/files/Statistical_year_book_india_chapters/CO-OPERATIVE%20SOCIETIES-WRITEUP.pdf.

Parida, Y. & Yadav, D. (2020). India's dairy sector has helped lift the rural economy and improve livelihoods. *The Hindu Business Line*. Retrieved 1 June from https://www.thehindubusinessline.com/opinion/indias-dairy-sector-has-helped-lift-the-rural-economy-and-improve-livelihoods/article31722467.ece.

Parmar, P. & Misra, H. (2020). Dairy sector handled the lockdown well. Retrieved 28 September from https://www.thehindubusinessline.com/opinion/dairy-sector-handled-the-lockdown-well/article32717902.ece.

Planning Commission Report (2003), Evaluation Study on Integrated Dairy Development Project. Programme evaluation organisation. Government of India, New Delhi, India.

Prathap Reddy, K., Srinivasan, R., Sriram, M. S., & Raju, K. V. (2004). Democratic governance and member capital stakes in cooperatives. Background Paper Prepared for IRMA Silver Jubilee Symposium workshop on Governance Issues in Cooperatives, IRMA, Anand, 17–18 December 2004.

Punjabi, M. (2009). India: Increasing demand challenges the dairy sector. Retrieved from http://www.fao.org/3/i0588e/I0588E05.htm.

Rajendran, K. & Mohanty, S. (2004). Dairy co-operatives and milk marketing in India: Constraints and opportunities. *Journal of Food Distribution*, *35*(2), 34–41.

Reincke, K., Saha, A., & Wyrzykowski, Ł. (2018). The Global Dairy World 2017/18 Results of the IFCN Dairy Report 2018.

Rouchaudhary, A. (2021). Cooperatives to play key role in making India a $5-trillion economy, says Amit Shah. Moneycontrol. Retrieved from Cooperatives to Play Key Role in Making India a $5-trillion Economy, Says Amit Shah (moneycontrol.com).

Shashidhar (2019). Losing flavor: Dairy cooperatives need to shed their political tone and focus on business to stay afloat. Retrieved from https://www.businesstoday.in/magazine/the-hub/story/losing-flavour-219868-2019-08-05.

Singh, S. K. (2016). Problems and prospects of the cooperative movement in India under the globalization regime. *The International Journal of Indian Psychology*, *3*(59), 154–165.

Soni, A. K, Kapre, A. K., & Saluja, H. P. S. (2013). Study on socioeconomic development of Kabirdham: Role of cooperatives. *Special issue in International Monthly Refereed Journal of Research in Management & Technology*. Retrieved from https://www.researchgate.net/publication/267476677_STUDY_ON_SOCIOECONOMIC_DEVELOPMENT_OF_KABIRDHAM_ROLE_OF_COOPERATIVES.

Sood, J. (2014). New milky ways. Down to Earth. Retrieved from https://www.downtoearth.org.in/coverage/new-milky-way-43368.

Subbhuraj, M., Ramesh Bab, T., & Subramonian, B. S. (2015). A Study on strengthening the operational efficiency of dairy supply chain in Tamilnadu, India. *Procedia — Social and Behavioral Sciences, 189*(2015), 285–291.

Sudan, F. K. (2019). Role of dairy cooperatives in achieving the economic dimension of SDGs: Experience and lessons learnt from India. A report of UN Agency Taskforce on Social and Solidarity Economy. Retrieved from https://knowledgehub.unsse.org/wp-content/uploads/2019/06/135_Sudan_Role-of-Dairy-Cooperatives-in-India_En-1.pdf.

Taylor-Gooby, P. (2004). Open markets and welfare values. Welfare values, inequality and social change in the silver age of the welfare state. *European Societies, 6*(1), 29–48.

Times of India. (2021). Amul Dairy sets up oxygen plant in Anand. 12 May. Retrieved from https://timesofindia.indiatimes.com/city/vadodara/amul-dairy-sets-up-oxygen-plant-in-anand/articleshow/82557831.cms.

Vaidyanathan, A. (2013). Future of cooperatives in India. *Economic and Political Weekly, 48*(18), 30–34.

Workie, E., Mackolil, J., Nyika, J., & Ramadas, S. (2020). Deciphering the impact of COVID-19 pandemic on food security, agriculture, and livelihoods: A review of the evidence from developing countries. *Current Research in Environmental Sustainability, 2*, 100014.

Yadav, D. & Misra, H. (2019). Stepping on the gas: Now, a women's cooperative for processing animal dung in Gujarat. *The Indian Express*, Retrieved 26 December from https://indianexpress.com/article/india/stepping-on-the-gas-6185008/.

Chapter 4

Understanding the Business Model of Uralungal Labour Contract Cooperative Society: India's Oldest Workers' Cooperative

Rahul Waghmare[*,‡], Naman Sharma[†,§], and Yogesh Desale[*,¶]

Vishwakarma University, Pune, India

†*Indian Institute of Foreign Trade (IIFT), Kolkata, India*

‡*rahul.waghmare@vupune.ac.in*

§*namanshandilya@gmail.com*

¶*yogesh.desale@vupuen.ac.in*

Abstract

The world has accepted cooperatives as alternative business models for socio-economic development. Asian and especially Indian cooperatives have seen significant success in cooperative sector. Uralungal Labour Contract Cooperative Society (ULCCS) is one of the oldest workers' cooperative sustained profitably for 90 years through its participative and direct democracy process and approach in decision-making and day-to-day activities. Despite challenges such as poor infrastructure, skilled personnel, administrative concerns of being a democratic organisation which other cooperatives are trying to address, the success of ULCCS is inspiring and enlightening for other cooperatives. This chapter presents the history of ULCCS, its organisational structure, and functioning.

Keywords: cooperatives, workers' cooperatives, democracy, business sustainability

1. Introduction

Cooperatives are known for their distinctive business models, which has more focus on the specific community. The cooperative firms have been found to be an effective way to build a network and upsurge the social capital for greater good. Uralungal Labour Contract Cooperative Society (ULCCS) is the worker's cooperative emerged and sustained in India to provide benefits to workers, especially construction workers.

ULCSS is known for their democratic and participative way to conducting business activities. The business practice of ULCSS is inspirational and a model for many existing and future cooperatives for sustainable organisation. ULCSS is the appropriate example for adaptation and reflection of the definition of cooperatives given by the International Cooperative Alliance. A cooperative society that began as an association of lower-caste manual labourers in the Malabar region of Kerala, India, nine decades ago has grown into a multi-billion-dollar business conglomerate that includes an information technology (IT) park, the first of its kind in the world, and is worth hundreds of crores of rupees.

International Cooperative Alliance (ICA) defines cooperative as "an autonomous association of persons united voluntarily to meet their common economic, social, and cultural needs and aspirations through a jointly-owned and democratically-controlled enterprise" (International Cooperative Alliance, 1995).

The cooperative operates under the principles of self-help, democracy, equity, and solidarity. They hold universal human principles such as ethics, social responsibility, honesty, and holistic development in high regard. International Cooperative Alliance also provides the guidelines for cooperatives bring values into the practices as follows (International Cooperative Alliance, 1995):

 i. voluntary and open membership;
 ii. democratic member control;
 iii. member economic participation;
 iv. education, training, and information;
 v. cooperation among cooperatives;
 vi. concern for community.

The outline of this chapter is as follows: introduction to worker's cooperatives and ULCCS, organisational structure of ULCCS, functioning of ULCCS through the various practices, and takeaways for the other cooperatives and social enterprises to improve upon their sustainability.

The chapter has used secondary data such as published reports, journal articles, news articles, and websites to understand the functioning of ULCCS.

2. What is Workers' Cooperatives?

Workers' cooperatives emerged as alternative business models for addressing contemporary issues or changes in the world of work. Many definitions are available for it, but in brief, it can be referred as the cooperatives or firms owned and controlled by its workers.

The workers are entitled to the right of ownership of the firm. The workers' cooperatives are a kind of organisation that forms a group of workers to work together. The revenue from the business activities are shared among the members, i.e. workers. Cooperative can be involved in business activities such as production of goods or services, distribution, generating and managing of funds, and providing the necessary skills and training to the members to increase the bargaining power of workers.

The workers' cooperatives functioning and governance has more varied characteristics than other for-profit business organisations. Indeed, cooperatives also adopt business functions and management functions like other businesses but have the following distinguishing features (Sapovadia & Patel, 2013):

- Registered under the Cooperative Act applicable in the region, which allows them to conduct the business.
- Members of cooperatives elect the board of directors (BOD). The BOD prepares and sets the policy for governance and day-to-day activities.
- Fundamentally addressed or represented by workers, for the most part, offers an inclination to their individuals in employment.
- Decision-making and ownership remain with the workers. Revenue and benefits are disseminated among members as per the works and labour contribution.

- Members put in their effort voluntarily, adopting and following cooperative principles.
- Workers' cooperative comes under the category of employee-owned and run by democratic approach.
- Adopts and practises self-development.
- Usually, members of cooperatives have multiple roles, such as employee, director, investor, and owner.

According to Sapovadia and Patel (2013), the critical success factors for the cooperatives are member participation and member control. The functioning of a cooperative has an influence of ownership by workers, but cooperative performance depends on the level of association and interactions. A remarkable aspect of cooperatives is that the structure of a cooperative allows each member to be involved in the day-to-day business affairs, unlike people cooperatives.

The members are considered as active catalysts for the performance and success of the cooperative. Though the active participation of workers is encouraged in decision-making, it may lead to chaos and differences that need to be controlled and managed by the leadership, i.e. the BOD.

"In summary, worker co-operatives are a radical break from the conventional business model. The worker co-operatives primary goal in operating an enterprise is for service to its employees and its community rather than service to the owners of capital. The goal is to provide the best possible employment conditions for the members and to provide the customers and community with a service or product at a fair price that meets their needs and leads to a sustainable community" (Canadian Workers Co-op foundation, 2019).

3. Workers' Cooperatives in India

The cooperative movement in India holds an important place in the socio-economic development of the Indian economy. Agricultural Credit Cooperative Society is the first cooperative society formed under the Cooperative Credit Societies Act, 1904.

"Although in pre-independence India, co-operative movement was spontaneous, various princely states did support the movement as engine for social and economic development. Predominant among these are the states of Mysore and Baroda. British India also followed suit. In post-independence India, cooperative sector was considered as essentially to be faster for all-round economic growth, especially in rural and agrarian sectors" (Karnataka State Souharda Federal Cooperative Ltd., 2021).

The years 2012–2015 have seen exponential rise in registrations of cooperative societies in India, especially credit societies and agricultural societies, under the Multi-State Co-operative Societies (MSCS) Act, 2002. In total, Maharashtra State has the maximum number, i.e. 621 cooperatives registered under MSCS Act, 2002.

As per the information available on the website of MSCS, Ministry of Cooperation, Govt. of India, a total of 1,050 cooperatives are registered under the MSCS Act, 2021. Figure 1 depicts the number of registered cooperative societies registered from 1986 onward.

More than 20% of the cooperatives registered are under the liquidation process, which is not a favourable sign for the cooperative movement

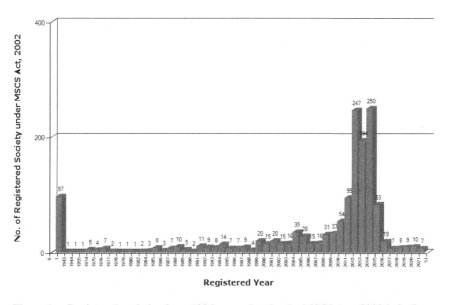

Figure 1.   Registered societies from 1986 onward under the MSCS Act, 2002 in India.
Source: https://mscs.dac.gov.in/ChartYear.aspx.

in India. Singh (2016) has identified the following challenges or causes for the slow progress and failure of cooperatives in India:

- government's over interference;
- mismanagement and manipulation in the organisation;
- lack of awareness about objectives of cooperatives;
- restricted scope and coverage in terms of purpose and number of members;
- functional weakness: inadequacy of trained personnel.

The functioning of cooperatives suffers from several weaknesses such as inadequate infrastructure, lack of disciplined management processes, overreliance on the government, inactive membership, irregularity in the conduction of elections, inadequate human resource policy, organisation communication structure, and public relations initiatives.

ULCCS is considered as India's and Asia's oldest workers' cooperative. The following are significant workers' cooperatives in India:

1. ULCCS
2. Amul: Gujarat Co-operative Milk Marketing Federation Ltd.
3. Indian Coffee Houses: affiliated to All India Coffee Workers' Co-operative Societies Federation
4. Lijjat: women's worker cooperative
5. Milma: Kerala Co-operative Milk Marketing Federation
6. Co-optex: Tamil Nadu Handloom Weavers' Cooperative Society
7. Nilenso: The first software workers' cooperative

4. Uralungal Labour Contract Cooperative Society

ULCCS is a classic case of how labourer becoming the owners. The journey of ULCCS, the INR 6,600-crore cooperative, started with 14 people and a capital of 6 annas (37 paise) for catering to the needs of the lower strata in Northern Kerala. The upper castes denied them jobs in retaliation to their attempts to reform the society challenging the caste discrimination prevalent then. Initially, the society took up small road works and slowly gained a name for itself for completing projects with utmost quality.

ULCCS was formed in 1925 by 14 labourers, inspired by the teachings of Vagbhatanandan, one of the most outstanding socio-religious leaders of the Kerala Renaissance from Malabar. His philosophy of "Atmavidya" gained an organisational form in Atmavidya Sangham in 1917.

ULCCS is renowned in Kerala for delivery of projects on time with quality that can match international standards. There are occasions when ULCCS delivered projects in less than the estimated amount and gained the confidence of both the public and government authorities in Kerala. Quality and predictable delivery helped ULCCS receive major projects from government and non-government agencies. Till now, ULCCS has completed more than 7,500 major projects, and more than 500 projects are in various stages of execution.

Today, it is one of the largest workers' cooperatives in Asia. The ULCCS Group, while adhering to its formation agenda, has branched out to new realms and is growing stronger, addressing the career concerns of upcoming generations. Table 1 illustrates the timeline of the ULCCS history.

Table 1. Timeline of ULCCS history.

Year	Brief description
1917	A few young men from Uralungal went to Mahe to listen the speech of Vagbhatanandan, in whom they found a leader for the long-awaited social reformation.
1917	After returning from the Mahe speech, these youngsters invited Vagbhatanandan to their hamlet. Responding to the humble invitation, Vagbhatanandan visited Karakkad, which led to the formation of Kerala Atmavidya Sangham.
1922	Inspired by the teachings of Vagbhatanandan, Kerala Atmavidya Sangham determined to find their means of life and labour with dignity and stability, which were denied by the influential upper castes. They first formed "United Credit Cooperative".
1924	They initiated a labour contract cooperative society to provide labour and income to the natives by contracting local constructions.
1925	Strenuous labour of these youngsters was turned to a registered entity as a venture on 13 February 1925, "Uralungal Labourers' Mutual Aid and Co-operative Society", which was renamed later as the Uralungal Labour Contract Cooperative Society.

(Continued)

Table 1.   (*Continued*)

Year	Brief description
1925	The first "project" they undertook was resilience to rebuild bunds of farmlands that collapsed in the 1924 flood. The stock yards of fishermen that collapsed in the 1924 floods were rebuilt by youngsters of ULCCS as their "Resilience Project".
1925	Pathways were built by ULCCS which connected villages of North Malabar regions of Madras Providence.
1944	ULCCS was awarded the contract for the widening of Canoli Canal, Kozhikode.
1949	With a zest for learning and thirst for skill development, these youngsters explored methodology incorporating essentials of "Road Engineering" by hiring skilled resources.
1952	Paleri Kanaran Master became President of ULCCS (he served as president for 32 years continuously).
1954	ULCCS opened its headquarters near Nadapuram Railway Station in Madappally.
1963	ULCCS was awarded a significant work of constructing a bridge in Vengara in the neighbouring Malappuram District.
1982	A highly acclaimed work of Helipad and Road to Madappally College Ground was awarded to ULCCS.
1995	Remeshan Paleri was chosen as President of ULCCS and he continues at the helm of the Society.
1995	For its own construction purposes, ULCCS started a crusher unit in Neettikotta, Pasukkadavu, Kuttiyadi.
1997	As another path to self-sufficiency, ULCCS started its own hollow bricks unit in Iringal Kozhikode.
1999	Major contribution to the Seminar on Functioning of Labour Contract Societies in Kerala held at Onchiyam.
2001	ULCCS took up the construction of ROB at Chorode and its approaches and construction of realignment.
2001	ULCCS set a model for civic responsibility by expressing willingness to decimate the functional headquarters when the highway is supposed to be expanded and erected a new headquarters building.
2003	ULCCS started the construction of Kozhikode Bypass Phase III.
2005	ULCCS was honoured with the membership in National Labour Co-operative Federation.

Table 1. (*Continued*)

Year	Brief description
2005	UL Technology Solutions, the IT subsidiary of ULCCS was inaugurated.
2006	As part of expanding its operations in Kerala, ULCCS started a new office in the capital, Thiruvananthapuram.
2009	ULCCS IT Infrastructure was registered for UL Cyber Park.
2011	ULCCS ventures into art and tourism and launches Sargaalaya Kerala Arts and Crafts Village.
2011	As a philanthropic arm, ULCCS Charitable & Welfare Foundation was registered.
2013	Design and construction of aesthetically appealing Thusharagiri Bridge to connect Wayanad with Kozhikode.
2013	The United Nations decides to document the success story of ULCCS by producing a documentary film on it.
2015	Started UL Care Nayanar Sadanam Institute of Vocational Training & Placement for adults with intellectual challenges.
2016	ULCCS takes up District Flagship Infrastructure Projects (DFIP).
2016	A bypass construction with a deadline of 36 months was accomplished by ULCCS in 16 months.
2017	Finance Minister Dr. T.M. Thomas Isaac and Academician Michelle Williams co-authored *Building Alternatives: The Story of India's Oldest Construction Workers' Cooperative* which describes the empirics and ethics of ULCCS.
2018	ULCCS inaugurated another institution under UL Care: Madithattu Centre in Vadakara for senior citizens.
2018	Diversifying into education, ULCCS launches Indian Institute of Infrastructure and Construction in Chavara, Kollam.
2018	As a major step in education sector, DDU-GKY UL Skill Academy was inaugurated.
2019	Resilience initiative by Drone & Field Survey indexing Flood Devastation (2018), which distributed resources and compensated material loss in Ponnani Municipality initiated by the MLA of the constituency, P Sreeramakrishnan, Speaker, Kerala Legislative Assembly.
2019	ULCCS becomes a member of International Co-operative Alliance (ICA)
2019	UL Housing initiated its first apartment project named UL Apartments.
2020	Kerala Arts and Crafts Village was opened at Kovalam, a tourism hot spot, to provide a better livelihood to the craftspersons, exploring the potential of the global market.

Source: https://ulccsltd.com/timeline.

ULCCS was formed with following values and purpose (ULCCS Ltd., 2021):

> ULCCS was formed as part of a social movement to fight against social injustice, marginalization and other social anarchies prevalent during the pre-independent era. The prime objective of this society is to provide employment opportunities and livelihood support to the people in need with a vision to grow as a whole ecosystem. Today, it is looked up to for zero corruption, fair trade practices and credibility.

ULCCS is a cooperative registered under the Cooperative Societies Act. Presently, the cooperative has more than 2000 workers as members. ULCCS acquires the contacts for the projects through bidding process conducted by the government and other reputed organisations. The cooperative works with the mission of accomplishing the acquired project in decided the time. The important aspect considered while doing this is to provide the workers job opportunities and in turn uplifting the society. The processes and responsibilities are well defined, and because of this, ULCSS has received ISO 9001:2008.

ULCCS also provides education and training of necessary and contemporary skills, which helps make the members employable. ULCCS has established its own manufacturing facilities and laboratories. Till date, ULCSS has accomplished more than 3,800 tasks successfully, and many good initiatives are still going on.

ULCCS conducts monthly meetings to review work progress and workers are motivated to join the review meeting. The meetings and the overall work environment discipline maintenance is observed and expected from the members. The BOD had the authority to punish or, if required, suspend default members. However, the board of directors don't have the right to remove the members.

ULCCS emphasises having a professional governance structure to draft and formulate the policies and overall execution of business activities. Whenever required, they also approach professional bodies, such as IIM Kozhikode, for policy decisions.

"Our model is simple. You treat the workers well and pay them well, and they will work well with commitment. And you can produce quality work, able to finish it much before the time and make a profit out of the time and cost savings," Rameshan Paleri shares the secret of the society's success.

4.1 Organisational structure of ULCCS

The organisational structure of ULCCS is well articulated to implement and execute the decisions of the BOD and make policy-related decisions. ULCCS puts emphasis on setting up the professional governance structure in the drafting of the policy and execution.

> The ULCCS has defined the objective of society to promote the economic interests of the labourers of the society and to find suitable and profitable employment for them (Thomas Isaac & Williams, 2017, p. 81).

Membership of ULCSS comprises five classes as listed in Table 2.

Members working for the organisation holds the A-, C-, and D-class memberships. All the members are entitled to employee benefits, such as an employee provident fund, insurance, gratuity, shares, welfare fund, mediclaim scheme, and interest-free loans (SetuMadhavan, 2020).

ULCCS has no restriction of age for retirement. Workers can work as long as they can. But they are entitled for employee provident fund benefits till 60 years of age.

Table 2. ULCCS membership categories.

Member Category	Description and rights
A-class	Members are permanent with voting rights
B-class	Related to governmental shares which forms 90.59% of the share capital, has no vote
C-class	These members are not entitled for voting rights. After few years, they become A-class members.
D-class	Those who joined the organisation recently, has no vote
E-class	Shareholders and are entitled to receive incentives but not having voting rights

Source: Setumadhavan (2020, p. 330).

The elected governing body serves for the duration of five years. A-class members democratically select the directors for the board. The BOD meets on a daily basis to review the work progress. Meetings are headed under the leadership of the chairman.

Governing body of ULCCS includes 13 directors, including three women members, elected democratically by the members of the cooperative. One director post on the governing body is reserved for a representative from SC/ST caste. The chairman and vice chairman leads the governing body. The members can be elected as directors for more than one term continuously according to their performance. The current chairman has been leading the organisation for more than three decades.

The Cooperative Act mandates that annual general body meetings be held. While the organisation employs a member, the cooperative holds his or her shares until the member leaves. The governance of ULCCS enables its employees to work with sincerity, devotion, and efficiency.

Workers at ULCCS thrive in leadership and teamwork, which contributes to greater job efficiency and productivity. In the workplace, there are established communication and leadership channels. They can work with the utmost sincerity and commitment because of this work culture. Each project is overseen by a director who is assisted by team leaders.

Employee benefits, including free lunch, are provided to all employees. In addition, workers get all kinds of leave of absence, such as casual leave, annual leave, and medical leave, according to the company's policies. This ensures that workers' involvement in increasing productivity is vital, displaying the characteristics of a high-performance workplace.

4.2 Understanding the business model of ULCCS

The major explanation behind the success of ULCCS is its commitment to participative and direct democracy in the functioning of cooperative.

4.2.1 *Decision-making and worker democracy*

How do cooperatives guarantee meticulous coordination and proficient creation without the commonplace industrialist procedures of discipline

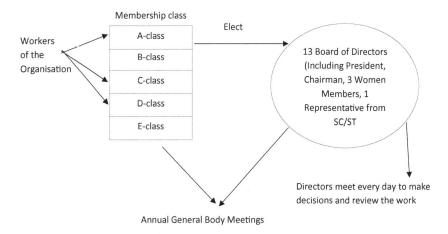

Figure 2.   Organisational structure of ULCCS.
Source: Altman *et al.* (2020, p. 330).

and motivators? How would they guarantee that labourer proprietorship doesn't sabotage the forces of administrators or lead to labourers evading their obligations? More explicitly, how did ULCCS prevail with regard to making a prudent mix of chain of importance and investment? To respond to these inquiries, we should take a gander at ULCCS's encounters in fostering a work cycle that is both productive and participatory.

ULCCS conducts the annual general meetings (AGMs) as per the guidelines of the Cooperative Act. The BOD is elected in the AGM and reviews the performance during the previous year. Unlike capitalist companies, at ULCCS, the directors work as managers of cooperatives and take decisions in line with organisation culture, innovation, work structure, and policies (Figure 2).

Site pioneers drive the building destinations browsed among the labourers in an interaction through which just specialists with demonstrated administrative capacity and who appreciate broad regard and trust are chosen. Labourers and site pioneers ceaselessly examine the division of work and methodology at worksites, for instance, over an aggregate lunch (ready by the helpful). While there is a lot of comprehensive consultation, once a choice is made, everyone is obligated to adhere to it. Defying site pioneers' directions, neglect of obligation, monetary abnormalities, or intentional breaches in execution can prompt discipli-nary activity — albeit such activity is seldom required.

Majority rule measures are kept up with through ordinary correspond-ence inside the agreeable. Site pioneers go to everyday gatherings with the directorate. All site chiefs, board individuals, and specialised staff go to weekly gatherings, while all labourer individuals take an interest in the monthly gatherings, where new improvements are accounted for and where individuals can raise reactions. Full budget summaries are talked about at yearly comprehensive gatherings. While countless such gather-ings include time and energy, it additionally creates a feeling of aggregate possession, fortitude, and normal mission, improving efficiency.

4.2.2 *Participation and market competitiveness*

The major challenge for ULCCS is to get the work contracts which is mostly tender based, where low-cost manufacturing or low budget needs to be submitted as against the private contractors. Being a workers' coop-erative, it is a difficult challenge to address as they cannot compromise on the workers' benefit and quality of materials used to complete projects.

The competitive advantage ULCCS has is work efficiency coming through the innovation practices and expertise, persistent labours which are very advantageous in the construction industry. The most critical aspects of skills and commitment are core to the labours persistence for ULCCS. ULCCS has also encouraged the involvement of the labour in the decision-making and a similar practice is followed while deciding salaries and working environment.

4.2.3 *Strategy of diversification*

One of the prominent factor for the success of ULCCS is the way they have adopted and executed the diversification in their business activities. They have started with construction and infrastructure development and then gradually entered into IT, IT infrastructure, tourism, skills training, handicrafts, housing, agriculture, and social welfare. Table 3 depicts the highlights of ULCCS diversification.

Table 3. Highlights of ULCCS diversification.

Sectors	Name of the organisations/subsidiary	Year
Construction and Infrastructure Development	ULCCS	1925
IT	UL Technology Solutions	2005
IT Infrastructure	ULCCS IT Infrastructure Pvt	2009
Tourism	Sargaalaya Kerala Arts and Crafts Village	2011
Handicrafts	Sargaalaya Kerala Arts and Crafts Village	2011
Housing	UL housing	2019
Skills training	UL Care Nayanar Sadanam Institute of Vocational Training & Placement, DDU-GKY UL Skill Academy	2018
Social Welfare	ULCCS Charitable & Welfare Foundation	2011

4.2.4 *Management and discipline*

ULCCS has a military-type discipline among the board members, including the president, member/non-member workers, and employees. Irrespective of project site location, the workers are expected to maintain utmost discipline with the local community.

Violations are very rare in the cooperative since the punishments are severe, ranging from ordering of such delinquents to undertake hard manual work alone to termination of membership. Indiscipline in financial matters by any cooperative member is subject to the termination of his/her position regardless of the amount involved.

4.2.5 *Assurance of quality*

ULCCS is an ISO 9001:2008 organisation and has refined development hardware to finish the tasks viably. Even though the labourers of the society hail from rustic regions, they utilise modern, cutting-edge innovation in their exercises.

One might say that ULCCS is a fruitful model for how innovation reception at grassroot levels can roll out wonderful improvements in the standard of life of a community.

4.2.6 *Concern for community*

The cooperative members have concern for the community and are continuously engaged in building better relationships with society at large. They showed marvellous generosity in constructing houses for tribal people of Muthukadu Tribal Colony, Wayanad District. The proactive approach can be seen in their cooperative's preparedness to solve the problems of natural calamities, such as tsunamis and landslides. The president reported that the cooperative has undertaken a massive effort to rehabilitate tsunami victims. He further said that they provided them with transport facilities for evacuating the people, food, and financial assistance.

5. Conclusion

ULCCS has survived and grown in line with the demands of the 21st century. While it is embedded in a socialist culture, it has not deviated from its core values.

ULCCS was established in 1925 to uplift the living standards of the country's working class. Its goal was to build a favourable environment for the growth and development of industries, individuals, and communities. Through the years, the organisation has evolved into a multi-sectoral body that addresses the needs of different sectors. ULCCS is a leading organisation in the field of infrastructure development. It has a track record of continuous improvement and is regarded as one of the most reputable organisations in the industry.

Sargaalaya, Cyber Park, and the Indian Institute of Infrastructure and Construction are three examples of how ULCCS has successfully planned, created, and operated big institutions that the government would have otherwise operated on its own behalf.

UL Cyber Park is the first of its kind in the Malabar region. Designed by Nikken Sekkel, a Japanese architect, it has a built-up area of about 2.7 million square feet.

The performance of ULCCS is recognised and awarded by national and international agencies. Its efforts in social welfare and community development is well recognised by ULCCS's association with the United Nations, UNDP, and ILO.

Cooperatives are an improvement over the capitalist system of production. They offer key lessons in self-management and democracy, but the competitive pressures of the market bind them. This chapter offers important lessons in formulating a democratic and participatory work process as an alternative to for-profit and market-oriented activities and shows that a satisfied workforce contributes to higher productivity and thus ensures higher productivity and competitiveness in the market.

References

Altman, M., Jensen, A., Kurimoto, A., & Tulus, R. (2020). *Waking the Asian Pacific Co-operative Potential*, 7th edn. Academic Press, USA, p. 330.

Canadian Workers Co-op foundation. (December 2019). Retrieved from https://canadianworker.coop/about/what-is-a-worker-co-op/.

Karnataka State Souharda Federal Cooperative Ltd. (2021). Retrieved from http://www.souharda.coop/index.html.

ULCCS Ltd. (2021). Retrieved from www.ulccsltd.com, https://ulccsltd.com/aboutus.

International Cooperative Alliance. (1995). Retrieved from https://www.ica.coop/en/cooperatives/cooperative-identity.

Sapovadia & Patel. (2013). What works for workers' Cooperatives? An Empirical Research on Success & Failure of Indian Workers' Cooperatives. 15 January 2013. doi: 10.2139/ssrn.2214563.

Setumadhavan T. (2020). Successful cooperatives across Asia: ULCCS — the icon of successful cooperatives in India. In M. Altman and A. Jensen (eds.), *Waking the Asian Pacific Cooperative Potential*, 1st ed. Academic Press, pp. 365–367.

Singh, S. (2016). Problems and prospects of the cooperative movement in India under the globalization regime. *International Journal of Indian Psychology*, *3*(4), 59.

Thomas Isaac, T. & Williams, M. (2017). *Building Alternatives*. 1st ed. LeftWord Books, p. 81, New Delhi.

Williams, M. (2016). Uralungal: India's oldest worker cooperative. *The WIRE*, Retrieved from https://thewire.in/labour/uralungal-indias-oldest-worker-cooperative.

https://doi.org/10.1142/9789811253799_0005

Chapter 5

Cooperative Societies: Classification and Subclassification

Pooja[*,‡], K.N. Pavithra[*,§], and S.C. Ravi[†,¶]

Research Scholar, Department of Agricultural Economics, University of Agricultural Sciences, GKVK, Bengaluru 560065, Karnataka, India

†*Scientist (Agricultural Economics), ICAR-CISH, Lucknow, India*

‡*poojabkori77@gmail.com*

§*pavithraharsha6@gmail.com*

¶*ravisc3@gmail.com*

Abstract

The concept of a cooperative society is not new. It is almost a global concept that exists in all countries. In a country like India, cooperatives play a very important role. Cooperative societies operate in every country on the planet and are represented in every industry, including agriculture, food, finance, and healthcare. The cooperative society is founded to protect the interests of the weaker sections of the population. It is a non-profit organisation whose primary goal is the well-being of its members. The cooperative society is based on the idea of mutual aid and welfare. As a result, the principle of service dominates its operations. If there is a surplus, it is dispersed to the members as a dividend in accordance with the society's bye-laws. Cooperatives have been around in India for over a century. Their presence is substantial, with over a lakh grassroots cooperatives. Despite considerable increases in rural outreach and coverage of small and marginal farmers made by cooperatives, their financial health has been a source of worry. This research aims to learn more about the elements that influence cooperatives' financial health as measured by their recovery performance. Knowing about classification of cooperatives gives a clear knowledge about the cooperative societies, and in this chapter, a very clear understanding of the types of cooperative societies in India is recorded.

Keywords: cooperatives, principles of cooperatives, classification of cooperatives, agricultural credit cooperatives, producers' societies

1. Introduction

A cooperative is defined as an autonomous association of persons united voluntarily to meet their common economic, social and cultural needs and aspirations through a jointly owned and democratically controlled enterprise. The cooperative principles are a unique charter that crosses cultures, politics, languages and religion. Cooperatives serve a variety of purposes and provide loans, technical help, farm inputs, storage and handling, marketing, and processing to their members (Frederick, 2016). Agricultural cooperatives are important institutions in agricultural development (Frederick, 2016). In India, the cooperative movement is extremely important in the agricultural, banking, and housing sectors. Many cooperative organisations, especially in rural regions, boost political engagement and are used by prospective politicians as a stepping stone. Cooperatives have been around in India for over a century. Their presence is substantial, with over a lakh grassroots cooperatives. Despite the significant progress cooperatives have made in terms of rural outreach and coverage of small and marginal farmers, their financial health has been a source of concern (Misra, 2006). Credit cooperatives in India make up one of the largest rural financial systems in the world (Misra, 2010). Following the 2012 International Year of Co-operatives, the blueprint for a cooperative decade provides a great opportunity to examine how the cooperative movement has progressed in recent years and to draw some future trends from it (Vezina & Girard, 2014). Cooperative firms are configured as an optimal business alternative to meet these challenges. They are business organisations whose management is designed to benefit all stakeholders. In recent years, various studies have highlighted the value of these companies as a vehicle for improving the business sector in local areas, boosting economic development in these areas (Kindling Trust, 2012). It has also been found that the very nature of cooperative firms implies socially responsible behaviour. Their objectives (meeting the needs of their partners), democratic governance (one partner one vote), and ownership and control (mostly belonging to the partners–workers–users) result in cooperative firms being a model of sustainable economic development.

2. Importance of Cooperative Societies in India

Every Indian citizen should recognise the value and relevance of cooperative organisations as they contribute significantly to economic equality and welfare. A thriving network of cooperative societies, as agents of change and reformation, enhances the standard of living of the weaker and middle-income sections of a society, despite the fact that they are not the dominant public or private financial institutions. They provide an economic model with a higher level of entrepreneurial or social sustainability, and they frequently act as lobbying groups to represent their members' interests in a larger market. As a producer and a consumer, belonging to a co-op increases your creditworthiness. The cooperative movement has made a substantial contribution to rural development. The members of these societies have developed a sense of brotherhood and a desire to work together. Furthermore, the people are instilled with a genuine feeling of democracy. Many people have benefited from cooperative marketing institutions, which have helped them escape the clutches of money lenders and protected them from exploitation by middlemen. Farmers receive assistance in saving money from moneylenders through these committees, and as a result, they develop the habit of saving. As a result, they are better able to deal with their problems on their own.

3. Principles of Cooperatives

There are seven principles of cooperatives which are stated as follows:

  i. voluntary and open membership;
 ii. democratic member control;
iii. member economic participation;
 iv. autonomy and independence;
  v. education, training, and information;

vi. cooperation among cooperatives;
vii. concern for community.

A report by Dale *et al.* (2013) concludes that cooperatives are involved in the social, economic, and environmental dimensions of sustainability, and that the cooperative principles are more closely aligned with the social dimensions of sustainability.

The definition of a sustainable cooperative by Dale, A. *et al.* (2013) is that a cooperative is sustainable when it fully implements all seven co-op principles and maintains or restores the ecosystem as a viable business.

4. Classification of Cooperatives in India

i. Consumer cooperatives
   a. National Cooperative Consumer Federation
   b. Primary societies
   c. Cooperative federations
   d. Central/Wholesale societies
ii. Producers' co-op
   a. Manufacturing cooperatives
   b. Industrial service cooperatives
iii. Cooperative marketing societies
iv. Cooperative farming societies
   a. Collective farming
   b. Tenant farming
   c. Cooperative joint farming societies
   d. Cooperative better farming societies
v. Cooperative credit societies
   a. Non-agricultural credit cooperatives
   b. Agricultural credit cooperatives
vi. Cooperative housing societies
vii. Multi-stakeholder cooperatives
   a. Social cooperatives
   b. Multi-stake holding in retailing
   c. New generation cooperatives

viii. Worker cooperatives
    a. Business and employment cooperatives
  ix. Other cooperatives
    a. Labour and construction cooperatives
    b. Processing cooperatives
    c. Platform cooperatives
    d. Volunteer cooperatives

5. Consumers' Cooperative Societies

Consumer cooperatives operate along the same lines as a business. They are founded to handle distribution of basic consumer items. In most cases, only shareholders and subscribing members are able to purchase their needs from such cooperatives. Anyone can become a shareholder or a member of such a society by purchasing a share or paying a small fee. Consumers create a consumer cooperative association in order to receive good-quality products at cheap prices. By acquiring things in bulk directly from manufacturers or wholesalers and selling them to members, the organisation hopes to cut out the middlemen. If there are any profits or surpluses, they are split among the members in proportion to their capital contributions or purchases. These cooperative societies safeguard the interests of consumers who want to buy high-quality goods at low prices. This organisation buys items in bulk from wholesalers and sells them at the lowest possible retail price to its members, who are consumers. Their goal is to cut out the middlemen and distribute profits to all members.

The shareholders and members have control over the company. Regardless of a shareholder's or member's investment or capital contribution, the principle of "one man, one vote" is carefully upheld. Consumer cooperatives have been useful in mitigating the negative impacts of monopoly. They have also contributed to a more equitable distribution of wealth in their own way. Even a person with minimal resources can join a cooperative and benefit from all of the benefits that come with it. Consumer cooperatives have also aided in the creation of socially beneficial goods. Consumer cooperative organisations were formed to assure a consistent supply of vital consumer goods of a high quality at reasonable rates. The goal of such societies is to cut out the middlemen by connecting directly with the producers or their agents. This strategy results in buying of lower-cost products. A consumers' cooperative society's earnings is put to good use according to its bye-laws, which may include paying dividends and awarding bonus shares to its members.

The National Cooperative Consumers' Federation of India (NCCF), based in New Delhi, is a national consumer cooperative organisation that serves the entire country. It was founded in October of 1965 and is governed by the Multi-State Cooperative Societies Act of 2002. NCCF has 148 members as of 31 March 2017, including the Government of India, three national cooperative organisations (National Cooperative Union of India (NCUI), National Cooperative Development Corporation (NCDC), and National Agriculture Cooperative Marketing Federation of India (NAFED)), and the NCDC.

5.1 National Cooperative Consumer Federation

On 16 October 1965, the National Cooperative Consumer Federation (NCCF) was founded. It is the country's functional body for consumer cooperatives. NCCF operates a network of 29 branch offices all over the country. The Multi-State Co-operative Societies Act of 2002 is the act through which NCCF is registered. The Indian National Cooperative Consumers Federation has begun to create trade relationships with manufacturers, including government entities. It aids in the acquisition, sale, and distribution of various consumer goods. NCCF has also worked on infrastructure development and other construction projects. The major goal of NCCF is to assist consumer cooperatives in supplying consumer goods to other distributing organisations. The distribution of consumer items happens at a fair pace. Technical guidance is given to consumer cooperatives

5.2 Central/Wholesale cooperatives

A cooperative wholesale society (CWS) is a type of federation in which the members are often consumer cooperatives. A cooperative wholesale society's goal is to coordinate "bulk purchasing" and, if possible, production. Such a society is a type of federal cooperative through which consumers can buy items at wholesale prices and, in some situations, operate factories or farms collectively.

Cooperative federalism, a school of thinking in cooperative economics that favours consumer cooperative societies, has argued for cooperative wholesale societies. Consumer cooperatives should form cooperative wholesale societies, according to the cooperative federalists, and these societies should purchase farms or factories through such partnerships. They maintained that profits (or surpluses) from these CWSs should be distributed to member cooperatives as dividends rather than to workers.

6. Producers' Cooperative Societies

Producers' cooperatives, also known as industrial cooperatives, are businesses that work together to produce goods. As a result, small producers may form cooperatives in order to compete with large producers. This can be accomplished in two ways. To begin with, producer members may manufacture items on their own (not as members of the society) but with the assistance of the society's raw materials, tools, and other equipment. Producer-members' goods can be sold to the society for resale or distribution among the society's members or to outsiders. Rather than working on their own, the producer-members may join the cooperative as employees or labour for a wage. The society also maintains its members supplied with raw materials, tools, and other equipment in this type of organisation. The items created as a result of this process may be sold to outsiders and/ or dispersed among the society's members. Small producers create a producers' cooperative association in order to obtain inputs for products production to meet consumer demands. They've been developed to compete with large-scale producers. They are also called industrial cooperative societies. These societies are created by local small producers to combat the competitiveness of major producers by assisting its members who require capital, equipment, materials, and other resources to apply their abilities in the production of goods. These organisations also engage in marketing operations in order to promote the items created by its members.

These safeguard the interests of small producers seeking a good return on their investment. These companies provide raw materials and other inputs to producers as well as purchasing their goods. They allow small businesses to compete with large corporations. Profits are dispersed based on the amount of capital invested by members. The society wishes to strengthen small producers' negotiating power in order to combat huge capitalists. The society does this by providing raw materials, equipment, and other inputs to the members, as well as purchasing their output for resale. Profits are dispersed among the members based on their contributions to the society's overall pool of products produced or sold.

i. **Manufacturing Cooperatives:** These organisations treat their members as employees and pay them for their services. These societies provide the members with enormous quantities of raw materials and tools for production, which they use to produce under one roof or at their homes. The societies sell the products in the market and distribute the proceeds to the members after collecting the production from the members.

ii. **Industrial Service Cooperative:** The producer members of these organisations operate independently and sell their industrial output to the cooperative. The members of these cooperative societies receive raw materials and other tools from these cooperative groups. The society is in charge of marketing the members' final products. Producers' cooperatives include handloom societies such as Haryana Handloom and Boyanika.

7. Cooperative Marketing Societies

Producers band together to promote their wares in cooperative marketing groups. The products of various members are pooled, and the society agrees to sell them at a reduced price by cutting out the intermediaries. A marketing cooperative is a group of producers who work together to sell their products. When the market is favourable, goods are sold. Because of their limited resources, individual producers may not be able to wait for longer periods of time. A marketing cooperative society is a non-profit organisation made up of small independent producers who want to sell their products through a single centralised agency. Producers who want to get fair rates for their goods are among the group's members.

The products of various members are pooled, and the society takes on the task of selling them without the need of middlemen. These organisations also execute marketing activities, such as transportation, warehousing, and packaging, to ensure that the output is sold at the greatest potential price. Profits are divided among the members according to their contributions to the common pool of output. Small producers form these societies to manage the marketing of their products. These societies pool the products of small-scale producers and market them on a big scale, relieving members of the burden of selling their products in fragmented markets. The revenues created by the societies are dispersed among its members in proportion to their contributions. These organisations were formed to assist small manufacturers in selling their goods at a profit. They pool the members' output and make arrangements for shipping, warehousing, and packaging in order to sell their products at a profit. They assist in the elimination of intermediaries, allowing them to enhance their profit margin. Profit is divided among members in proportion to their initial investment.

The three-tier structure's pattern is described as follows:

i. **Primary Cooperative**: Primary cooperative marketing societies exist at the grassroots level. These organisations promote the products of the area's producer members. Depending on the production of rural products in the area, they may be single-commodity or multi-commodity societies.

ii. **District-level Cooperative Societies**: There are cooperative marketing societies that span a bigger area or a district after the core cooperative societies that operate at the block level. These cooperative societies at the district level are known as federations or marketing unions. These are in charge of purchasing, selling, and granting loans to basic cooperative organisations. Their major responsibility is to market the produce brought to market by the area's leading cooperative marketing groups. These are found at secondary wholesale markets and usually give a better deal on produce.

iii. **State Cooperative Marketing Societies**: State Cooperative Marketing Societies, which serve the entire state, are the apex entity at the state level. Their members include both primary cooperative societies and the State's Central Cooperative Union. They have progressed above the level of central cooperative marketing societies to become a provincial society. They are in charge of extending credit to cooperatives that are in need and deserving.

Need of cooperative marketing:

a. Elimination of malpractices: Different types of malpractices that exist in the rural marketing system, such as arbitrary deductions from weights and measures, price manipulation, and collusion between brokers and company purchasers, deserve special attention. The Royal Commission deemed these misdeeds to be nothing less than scientific theft.

b. To reduce the price spread: Cooperative marketing can reduce the "price spread" between the producer and the consumers, thereby giving fair return to the producers, without affecting the interests of the consumers. If efficiently and honestly organised, co-op marketing will be able to reduce prices paid by producers and consumers.

c. Need for integrated programme: Cooperative marketing has developed as a concomitant of large-scale expansion of cooperative credit. Marketing societies will be acting as the agents to collect or to recover the loans advanced by cooperative credit societies. The successful working of credit cooperatives depends largely on the development of marketing societies.

d. For stabilisation of agricultural prices: Price stabilisation, which is a necessary component of a balanced economic development, is unlikely if the market mechanism is left to the free will and caprice of private intermediaries. So long as the private sector prevails, the "profit incentive" will have the upper hand, even if typical market conditions stray from healthy practices to risky speculation.

8. Cooperative Housing Societies

In most cases, housing or building societies are created in urban areas where housing is a serious issue. All those who wish to own a home or who want to rent a home at a reasonable price can join such cooperatives. However, because a large portion of such cooperatives' assets are in the form of immovable property and because there is always a need for ready cash to lend to needy members, membership is also open to people who do not meet either of the two criteria above but have sufficient funds to invest in such societies. Members deposit money with the cooperatives and the cooperatives pay them interest. They lend the money to needy members in exchange for a mortgage on property or other assets. Housing cooperatives sometimes supply building materials to their members in addition to financial help. Roads, street lights, parks, a post office, water, power, sanitation, and other civic services are also provided by these societies. People who want to get residential homes at a lesser cost form a cooperative housing association. Such organisations assist low-income persons in building dwellings at an affordable cost. The society's goal is to help members with their housing troubles by offering the option of paying in instalments. The group either builds the flats or offers members with sites on which they can build their own homes. There are two methods in which housing associations work as follows:

(i) They seize land and sell the plot to their members so that they can build their own home.
(ii) They build houses or apartments for their members and allow them to pay in instalments.

Members can get loans and financing from banks and other financial organisations through the housing societies. Housing societies are divided into two categories: primary housing societies at the individual level and Apex Co-operative Housing Finance (ACHFS) at the state level. According to a Shodhganga housing cooperative profile dissertation, these ACHFS have roughly 92,000 housing cooperatives across the country, with about 31,000 of them associated with state-level ACHFS for financial assistance. The remaining cooperatives are those that receive funding from other sources and have fully repaid their loans.

Types of housing cooperatives based on type of ownership:

(1) **Ownership Housing Societies:** Members own the houses and the society holds the land on a lease or freehold basis.

(2) **Co-Partnership Housing Society:** These housing societies own both land and buildings, and allot flats to its members on a leasehold or freehold basis.

(3) **House Mortgage Societies:** These organisations lend money to their members to help them build homes. The members must construct their own home.

(4) **House Construction or House Building Societies:** Members of the society are given money to build and live in houses. The money spent is repaid in the form of a loan.

9. Cooperative Credit Societies

The Co-operative Credit Organizations Act of 1912 was the first to establish cooperative credit societies in India. These are setup to provide members with short-term financial support and to encourage them to be thrifty. Credit cooperative society is established to provide members with short-term financial help in the form of loans. The society's goal is to safeguard members from predatory lenders who demand exorbitant interest rates on loans. The society lends money to its members using the money it has accumulated as capital and deposits, with low interest rates. Credit cooperatives come in a variety of shapes and sizes. Credit cooperatives are classified as follows:

(i) Agricultural credit cooperatives: Agriculture and cooperatives are mutually beneficial. They can't exist in a vacuum. India's agricultural credit cooperatives are one of the world's largest rural banking systems. These credit cooperatives are critical in the distribution of loans, particularly in rural areas. They are well-equipped to deal with issues that arise in rural areas.

(ii) Non-agricultural credit cooperatives, depending on the field they serve.

10. Cooperative Farming Societies

The major impediments to the implementation of planned agricultural production in India include factors such as increasing population pressure on land, uneconomic size of holdings, primitive and unscientific methods of cultivation, inequitable land distribution, and poverty and ignorance of the peasantry. Cooperative farming, on the other hand, which entails the pooling of disparate and unprofitable land holdings and their cooperative management, will go a long way towards advancing agriculture. Small farmers create these societies to pool their resources in order to cooperatively cultivate their properties. They want to organise agriculture on a big scale in order to boost agricultural productivity and enhance farmers' economic conditions. Cooperative farming enables mechanisation of farming as well as the provision of improved seeds and other agricultural inputs, irrigation infrastructure, and other agricultural-productivity-enhancing measures. These organisations offer low-cost inputs such as seeds, fertilisers, and manures, as well as novel approaches. They assist small-scale farmers in forming cooperatives and collaborating on farming tasks. Farmers gain from large-scale farming in this way.

The farming cooperation may be of the following types:

(i) **Cooperative Better Farming Societies:** The cooperative farming programme might be said to be built on the foundation of the better-farming society. Its main goal is to educate and prepare farmers to adopt the new agricultural system. They do this by holding demonstrations of improved agricultural technologies. The most prevalent activity conducted by these societies is the use of improved seeds, manures, and equipment. Besides, a variety of other activities are carried out, such as the sale of farm goods at reasonable costs and the procurement of vocational requisites. Individuals retain ownership and management of land in this sort of cooperative farming.

(ii) **Cooperative Joint Farming Societies:** Joint-farming societies are well-suited to address land fragmentation and the cultivation of unprofitable properties. The land of small landowners is pooled together, resulting in a larger unit of cultivation. Members of the society collaborate on the pooled land in accordance with the society's programme. Cultivators on the farm are compensated for their efforts. In contrast to land ownership, owner cultivators receive a dividend or rent based on the worth of the land. The development of crop programmes, shared purchasing of farm requisites, joint cultivation, mobilisation of finances for land improvement, and joint selling of farm produce are all common functions of these types of societies. Small landowners are encouraged to pool their property and establish a larger farming unit. Land for farming can also be purchased or leased by the society.

(iii) **Tenant Farming Societies:** The cooperative tenant farming society provides financial aid, tools, and seed services to its members. The society owns or leases land, but it does not engage in farming. The land is divided into blocks, and each block is rented to a planter who follows the society's plan for cultivation.

(iv) **Collective Farming Societies:** The society either owns or leases land, which its members collectively farm. The majority of these societies are setup on government-owned wastelands. Members are compensated for their effort, and if profits are made, a bonus is paid in proportion to their earnings. On the share capital, no dividend is paid. The land does not belong to the members of the collective agricultural cooperative, and they do not have any ownership or property rights in it. The movement is gradual since cooperative farming societies rely mostly on government properties that are leased out on a short-term basis and are often on hilly slopes that need a lot of labour and money to cultivate. Only one cooperative farming organisation in the Miraj taluka, Salagare, had a permanent plot of land.

11. Multi-stakeholder Cooperatives

Traditionally, cooperatives have taken their membership from a single group of stakeholders: producers own producer cooperatives, workers own worker cooperatives, and consumers own consumer cooperatives, for example. Multi-stakeholder cooperatives are co-ops in which more than one type of membership class, such as customers, producers, workers, volunteers, or community supporters, owns and controls the cooperative. Individuals or organisations such as non-profits, enterprises, government agencies, or even other cooperatives might be considered stakeholders. A multi-stakeholder cooperative (MSC) is a co-op governed by two or more stakeholder groups, as the name implies. Workers, producers, consumers, business owners, volunteers, and community supporters are examples of these groupings. In their study, Kindling Trust (2012) opines that cooperatives allow and bring together different types of membership, often consumers and providers of services and goods, but sometimes also workers and buyers. The genius of MSCs, also known as solidarity cooperatives, is that they have a shared vision that stresses equality, sustainability, and social justice among multiple stakeholder groups throughout a company.

Shareable reached out to Bauwens to learn more about MSCs, their potential for social and environmental transformation, and why, as the extractive economy reaches its nadir, rethinking how cooperatives operate is vital. MSCs are a relatively new form of cooperative (Lund, 2012).

12. Worker Cooperative

A worker cooperative is one in which the workers own and run the business. This control can refer to a company in which each worker-owner has one vote and participates in democratic decision-making. It can also refer to a company in which management is elected by each worker-owner who has one vote. Workers' cooperatives might be thought of as firms that manufacture a product or provide a service for profit and have members or worker-owners, despite the fact that there is no commonly agreed definition. Worker-owners are those who work in the company, rule it, and administer it. Unlike traditional businesses, a worker cooperative's ownership and decision-making power should be placed completely in the workers, and ultimate authority should remain with the workers as a whole. Worker-owners have control over the cooperative's resources and the labour process, such as wages and working hours.

13. Other Cooperatives

There may be many different cooperatives that deliver the benefits of cooperative effort to its members in addition to the types of cooperatives already mentioned.

Cooperatives can be formed to bring together people who work in occupations such as dairy and poultry farming, fisheries, cold storage, and the processing of agricultural products, e.g. sugarcane, cotton, and oilseeds.

(i) **Processing Cooperatives:** Processing agricultural produce is critical in India because it is an agrarian economy. It not only aids in value addition but also in the creation of jobs and the export of agricultural products. NCDC has been promoting cooperatives that process food grains, plantation crops, and oilseeds by giving financial aid to these cooperatives through state governments as well as directly to the processing societies. These organisations are typically established in rural regions with the goal of processing agricultural raw materials for delivery to industries. This category includes cooperatives that process sugar cane, cotton, jute, paddy, oilseeds, and other crops.

(ii) **Labour and Construction Cooperatives:** These organisations are typically established in rural regions with the goal of processing and supplying raw materials to industries generated by farmers. Sugarcane, cotton, jute, paddy, oilseeds, and other crops processing cooperatives fall into this group.

14. Conclusion

Cooperatives are founded to meet the requirements of their members, according to cooperative ideals. They are self-help democratic organisations that are owned and governed by their members. Cooperative membership is open and voluntary. Any person who can use the services and accepts the responsibilities of membership is eligible to join without discrimination. The entire system is democratically governed. The members elect their representatives to run their cooperatives' operations. A very good example of successful cooperative society in India is Anand model, and it clearly shows us the importance of potential of a cooperative society in India. The clear-cut classification and subclassification of the cooperative societies gives a greater understanding about the cooperatives.

References

Dale, A., Duguid, F., Lamarca, G., Hough, P., Tyson, P., Foon, R., Newell, R. and Herbert, Y. (2013). Co-operatives and Sustainability: An investigation into the relationship. International Co-operative Alliance. Co-operatives and Sustainability Report. Sustainability Solutions Group Community Research Connections.

Boadu F. O. (2016). *Cooperatives in Sub-Saharan Africa.* In *Agricultural Law and Economics in Sub-Saharan Africa: Cases and Comments.* Academic Press. pp. 263–281.

Misra, B. S. (2006). Performance of primary cooperatives in India: An empirical analysis. *Indian Economic Journal*, *53*(4), 95–113.

Misra, B.S. (2010). *Credit Cooperatives in India: Past, Present and Future* (1st ed.). London: Routledge, pp. 1–192. https://doi.org/10.4324/9780203854938.

Vézina, M. & Girard, J. P. (2014). Multi-stakeholder co-operative model as a flexible sustainable framework for collective entrepreneurship: An international perspective. In Gijselinckx C., Zhao L., & Novkovic S. (eds.), *Co-operative Innovations in China and the West*. London: Palgrave Macmillan. doi: 10.1057/9781137277282_5.

Lund, M. (2012). Multi-stakeholder co-operatives: Engines of innovation for building a healthier local food system and a healthier economy. *Journal of Co-operative Studies*, *45*(1), 32–45.

Kindling Trust. (2012). Growing Manchester(S) Veg People — A Guide to Setting up a Growers' and Buyers' Co-operative. Retrieved from http://www.sustainweb.org/publications/?id=214.

Chapter 6

Sustaining Cooperative Banks in South Asia: Lessons with Special Reference to Sustainable Models of Cooperative Banks from Kerala, India

B.P. Pillai[*,¶], R. Jayalakshmi[†,‖], and Sneha Kumari[‡,§]

*Agricultural Co-operative Staff Training Institute (ACSTI),
Thiruvananthapuram, Kerala, India*

†*Vaikunth Mehta National Institute of Cooperative Management, Pune, India*

‡*Symbiosis School of Economics,
Symbiosis International (Deemed University), Pune, India*

¶*bppillai7@gmail.com*

‖*jayalakshmi17@hotmail.com*

§*snehakumari1201@gmail.com*

Abstract

The Kerala model of cooperatives has won international attention for its achievement in building sustainable models. Collective actions have been facilitated by the people to build up a socially, economically, and environmentally feasible society. The credit sector has built up considerable financial assistance and support for the people to sustain their livelihood. Driven by the need for detailed examination, this study highlights the cases of three cooperative banks, namely Kodiyathoor Service Co-operative Bank, Kizhathadiyoor Service Co-operative

Bank, and Peringandur Service Co-operative Bank, which have built a sustainable model in the cooperative sector. This study is based on primary and secondary data collected to understand the process and practices in cooperatives. This study is also a contribution towards a cooperative model for sustainable growth in banks.

Keywords: cooperative, collective, credit, bank, sustainability, growth, financial performance

1. Introduction

The Kerala model for cooperatives has set up an example for Asian cooperatives on sustaining credit and financial performance (Viren, 2001). The principal objective of credit cooperatives is to accumulate savings and create a source of credit for the members and the poor sections. Credit cooperatives have always been looking for sustainability. The sustainability of credit cooperatives can be assessed from the ability to facilitate the smooth operation of financial institutions by overcoming all challenges and attaining profitability (Filene, 2011). Sustainability is often measured in terms of operational efficiency and financial self-sustainability (Meyer, 2002). There has been a number of cooperative banks that claim to work for the poor, but they are not able to sustain themselves. There is a need to work on the credit cooperatives since they work to serve the financial needs of the rural sector. There has been a scarcity of research on sustainable cooperatives. This has led to the research question of what could be a sustainable cooperative model for financing the poor. This study aims to examine the sustainability and outreach performance of the Kodiyathoor Service Co-operative Bank, Kizhathadiyoor Service Co-operative Bank, and Peringandur Service Co-operative Bank in Kerala, India. This research employs a case-study approach, exploring the financial performance of credit cooperative banks.

This chapter is organised as follows. Section 2 describes the research methodology adopted. Section 3 elaborates the cases of Kodiyathoor Service Co-operative Bank, Kizhathadiyoor Service Co-operative Bank, and Peringandur Service Co-operative Bank. Section 4 focuses on concluding remarks on documenting the cases and a way forward for the cooperatives in Asia to sustain the credit sector.

2. Research Methodology

This research is based on a case-study approach. Kodiyathoor Service Co-operative bank, Kizhathadiyoor Service Co-operative Bank, and Peringandur Service Co-operative Bank have been selected as samples for the case study as these cooperative banks are among the best models for sustainable credit cooperatives. The study has highlighted the sustainable indicators for the credit cooperatives. The diversified strategies, organisation structure, and bank activities have been explored through the case. The authors have collected secondary data from the cooperative banks and primary data from the members of the credit cooperatives. Once the data have been collected, they have been analysed and presented in the form of cases.

3. Results and Discussion

This section explores the cases of the credit cooperatives selected in detail. Kodiyathoor Service Co-operative Bank, Kizhathadiyoor Service Co-operative Bank, and Peringandur Service Co-operative Bank are among the leading cooperative banks in the Indian state of Kerala. The following sections explain each case study in detail.

3.1 Case study of Kodiyathoor Service Co-operative Bank

Its outlook and approach are towards the progress and prosperity of society. The bank is classified as Class I Super grade Bank on account of its performance and has been awarded the best co-operative bank in the Kozhikode district. The bank had a humble beginning in September 1988 with a share capital of INR 29,500 held by members and is registered under the Co-operative Societies Act 1987 under the leadership of visionaries in the area. Today, the bank has become one of the best cooperative banks in the state, having five branches operating at various localities of the Kodiyathoor panchayat and a corporate office at Eranjimavu town in its building. Agri Marketing Center located at Eranjimavu was built under the DMI scheme of the Government of India. Now, the bank has

25,000 members. The bank has reported an increase in deposits and advances. The bank has maintained steady growth since its inception. The bank has launched different loan schemes tailor-made to suit the needs of various types of customers. The procedure for sanctioning loans under various schemes has been simplified and relaxed to attract new customers and facilitate speedy loan sanctions. The bank is providing investment opportunities to all sections of people in the form of attractive deposit schemes and interest rates. All the five branches and the corporate office have been computerised to provide quality services to customers. The bank is committed to spreading a network of branches throughout the Kodiyathoor panchayat and providing the much-needed banking services to the people, who have been deprived of banking facilities. The bank has always endeavoured to provide satisfactory customer service with the help of the latest technologies, such as RTGS/NEFT, mobile banking, ATM facility, with utmost care for its customers. In a nutshell, it can be said that this bank is acting as a lifeline for the socio-economic growth of the area as a whole. The bank has got five branches in Kodiyathoor panchayat, with three branches working in the building. The main branch started functioning on 19 August 1988 at Pannikode in its building. The main branch functions from 8 a.m. to 8 p.m., and all other branches function from 9 a.m. to 6 p.m. The fertiliser unit is functioning under the main branch. The other branches of the bank are given in Table 1.

Table 1.   Bank branches and their features.

Bank Branch	Feature
Thottumukkom branch	Thottumukkom branch started functioning on 2 February 2001 and has also got a fertiliser depot which is functioning well.
Chullikkaparambha branch	Chullikkaparambha branch started on 6 June 2004 and in April 2017 moved to its building complex which consists of a supermarket, Janaushadi Kendra, and medical shops.
Kodiyathoor branch	Kodiyathoor branch started its operation from 15 December 2007.
Gothamba Road branch	Gothamba Road branch started functioning on 19 February 2011, and a supermarket is functioning under the bank.
Pannikode branch	Started on 22 October 2017; a Neethi store, Milma booth, photostat and fertiliser depot are working under the branch.

The board members include Shri. V. Vaseef (President), Shri. Santhosh Sebastian (Vice President) and the directors are Shri. E. Ramesh Babu (Director, Kerala Bank), Shri. P. Shino, Shri. P. P. Abdul Nazr, Shri. Ahammedkutty Parakkal, Shri. V. K. Aboobakker, Smt. Asmabi Parappil, Shri. Nisar Babu. A. C., Smt. Reena Boban, Smt. Sindhu Rajan, and Shri. K. Baburaj (Secretary).

Apart from the banking business, the Kodiyathoor Service Co-operative Bank has proved to be successful in all its areas of business such as coconut oil factory, gas agency, petrol bunk, medical laboratory and polyclinic, Neethi Medicals, agro centre, fertiliser depot, consumer store, Neethi store, milk product stall, frozen meat store, bakery, and cool bar, photostat centres, Jenasevana Kendra, coconut and copra procurement, steel and cement depots, and library. The details of the businesses are shown in Table 2.

There is an account for every home in Kodiyathoor Service Co-operative Bank and the bank has thus successfully implemented the project of one account in each home. The bank's board of directors and staff have approached 5,710 homes in 16 wards of Kodiyathoor panchayat as a team and accounts have been successfully opened for every home.

3.1.1 *Contribution towards the agricultural sector*

Suvarnam Organic Vegetable Market with a vision of "Pesticide-free Vegetable for Onam" and to motivate organic cultivation, farmer groups along with the bank and Karshaka Sevana Kendram cultivated organic vegetables in the land owned by the bank. This was inaugurated by honourable District Collector Shri. N. Prashant, Indian Administration Service, in the presence of Shri. Kunjahammad Kutty, President, Organic Producers Group, Kozhikode. The vegetable harvesting has been inaugurated by Shri. Vatsaraj (Joint Registrar, Co-operative Department) in the presence of Shri. E. Ramesh Babu, (President, Kodiyathoor Service Co-operative Bank). As part of the government scheme Suvarnam, to sell organic vegetables to the people, an organic vegetable market has been organised under the bank and Karshaka Sevana Kendram. All vegetables are made available in the market along with a variety of rice, different home-made products, spices, etc. The official inauguration of the organic

Table 2.　Diversified businesses of Kodiyathoor Service Co-operative Bank.

S. No.	Business	Features
1	Natural Coconut oil	The bank has a coconut oil factory equipped with all-new technology-enabled machinery at Pannikode, which started its production in 2011, and the coconut oil is marketed under the brand name "Natural Coconut Oil" which has a huge demand in the market.
2	Natural Gas Agency (Bharat Gas)	Kodiyathoor Service Cooperative bank is an authorised LPG distributor of Bharat Gas. Natural gas has been successfully able to capture the market at the time of inception, with around 6,000 connections within a few months. Natural Gas has got a go-down at Pannikode and an exclusive showroom at Mukkom.
3	Unity Diagnostics & Research Center	Unity Diagnostics & Research Center is a unit of Kodiyathoor Service Co-operative Bank in the medical diagnostic field to serve the public in the medical area at an affordable price. The unit is located at its head office (HO) building at Eranjimavu. The diagnostic centre is dedicated to providing the most accurate analysis and seamless patient care. A team of qualified and experienced diagnostic professionals, aided with the latest technological developments and modern diagnostic equipment, helps them deliver analytical reports with utmost precision. Infrastructure has been designed following the most modern facilities for doctors as well as for the patients.
4	Neethi Medicals	To ensure the availability of all medicines to the public at an affordable rate, the bank has started Neethi Medicals at HO Eranjimavu, where the public has access to all the facilities, including consultation with doctors, medical diagnostics, and medicines at an affordable rate.
5	Fertiliser Sales Depot	The bank has two fertiliser sales depots for the distribution of fertilisers for the locality, yielding a high profit with a sale of INR 63 lakh during this year.
6	Neethi Consumer Store & Milk Product Stall	Neethi Consumer Store has been functioning from the HO building to provide all household commodities at a reasonable rate.
7	Karshaka Sevana Kendram	The bank has been selected by the government as a Karshaka Sevana Kendra for acting as a nodal agency for coordinating and improving agriculture practices. The farmers will be given inputs and training on farming practices through the Karshaka Sevana Kendra and most modern agricultural machinery are leased to the farmers at reasonable rates. Karshaka Sena, a trained group of people formed under Karshaka Sevana Kendra for agricultural labour is available at the centre to overcome the shortage of trained agriculture labour.

8	Agro Center	Through the Agro Center, all agri-related machinery, fertilisers, and all other equipment are made available for the farmers.
9	Natural Bakes & Cool Bar	The bank has initiated a bakery and cool bar at its HO in Eranjimavu.
10	Jenasevana Kendra	To facilitate all the online services, including personal account number (PAN) card registration, online ticket booking, internet café, PSC registration, government certificate applications, and DTP, for the public.
11	Library	The bank's library has been equipped with all kinds of books, including references for competitive exams, which is very useful for the younger generation. The bank has been thinking of a digital library concept with online books.
12	Auditorium	The bank has constructed an auditorium with a capacity of 200 persons and a mini training centre which is rented out.
13	Steel & Cement Depot	To make available civil construction materials (cement, steel, and allied materials) for the public at an affordable rate, a depot has been started adjacent to the HO building in Eranjimavu. The bank has started the initiation for setting up of a hardware, electrical, and plumbing outlet in the same building.
14	Cattle feed Distribution	The bank has taken up Amul cattle feed distribution in Kozhikode, Kannur, and Kasargode districts.
15	Kosco Ventures Pvt. Ltd.	Kosco Ventures Pvt. Ltd. is a company formed under the bank with the aim of diversification into different sectors with the participation of the shareholders. Shares are distributed to the public, and the majority share is owned by the Kodiyathoor Service Co-operative Bank.
16	Career Arcade	To step into the educational sector, the bank has started a competitive exam training centre for government job aspirants. Career Arcade has made a tie-up with TIME as an academic partner and has been conducting coaching for many exams. Apart from language training, computer training is also being offered.
17	Center For Employability Enhancement & Training (CEET)	CEET has been established to provide all types of training to the workforce especially for cooperative staff for enhancing their productivity. Training for business people and students are also planned.
18	Petrol pump	The bank is running a Hindustan Petroleum dealership at Valillapuzha, and another pump dealership with Indian Oil is in process.

vegetable market was marked by the honourable Minister of Legislative Assembly (MLA) Shri. George M. Thomas selling vegetables to Shri. Rameshan Panikkar. The then bank president, Shri. E. Ramesh Babu presided over the function. Sales amounting to INR 59,802.50 have been reported through the vegetable market. Natural Bharat Gas Agency stall has also been inaugurated.

Under the leadership of the bank with assistance from the National Bank for Agriculture and Rural Development (NABARD) and Krishibhavan, seven farmers' clubs have been formed, namely Kairali, Kathir, Kissan, Haritha, Gramashree, Yuva, and Pratheekasha. All these farmers' clubs are functioning well.

3.1.2 *Cattle farm loans (DEDS, NABARD)*

To promote cattle farming, with the assistance from Dairy Department and Dairy Training Center, Kodiyathoor Bank has invited applications for loan with subsidy. In cooperation with women and self-help groups (SHGs), such as Kudumbhasree, majority of the applicants who are of the same category have been given continuous training from department heads at Kodiyathoor Service Co-operative Bank. As a part of this, INR 8,680,000 has been sanctioned for 39 farmers for dairy farming and INR 2,246,700 has been availed as a subsidy.

3.1.3 *Interest-free poultry loan with cage*

To help the weaker section and make them self-sufficient by enabling them to earn regularly, interest-free loans have been provided to individuals along with a poultry cage set and training from the poultry department has been given to all those who have availed the loan. A consultation service has also been provided to them on a regular basis. The poultry cage set includes 24 chicks of two weeks old, two months of food, and other medical aids. Being a part of the Surakshitha 2030 project, the eggs have been collected back from the farmers at a decent rate. Loans amounting to INR 924,000 have been given during the first phase, with 25 farmers benefiting, and in the second phase, 15 farmers have benefited through this scheme. The inauguration of the first phase was done by the Municipal Chairman, Shri Kunjan Master, and the second was inaugurated by Smt. Swapna Ariyangothchalil, Vice President, Kodiyathoor Grama Panchayat.

3.1.4 *Milking machine*

Loans for milking machines have been given to those farmers who are eligible for subsidy. Fifteen farmers have benefited through this scheme with a subsidy of INR 25,000 per machine.

3.1.5 *Seminar for coconut farmers*

To help the coconut farmers in this area, a meeting for forming a consortium for coconut farmers has been called at the bank's head office (HO) on 8 June 2017 to discuss future projects related to coconut. Coconut farming tips have been given to the farmers through the seminar conducted by scientists from Krishi Vigyan Kendra, Peruvannamuzi, Calicut. Bank President Shri. E. Ramesh Babu inaugurated the seminar. These seminars were really helpful for the farmers regarding fertilisation and marketing of their products.

3.1.6 *Coconut procurement centre*

To promote coconut farming, a collection depot has been started at Thottumukkom which is used to collect coconuts from farmers at a rate higher than the market rate. Bank President Shri. E. Ramesh Babu, along with Shri. V. M. Sunny, Grama panchayat Standing Committee Chairman, inaugurated the collection centre.

3.1.7 *Paddy cultivation seminar*

To utilise barren wetlands, a meeting for interested farmers was conducted at the bank's auditorium. The meeting was organised to make plans regarding paddy cultivation. Kodiyathoor Panchayat and agriculture department along with Kodiyathoor Service Co-operative Bank have initiated the project.

3.1.8 *Haritham Sahakaranam*

As a part of the Kerala government's Haritham Sahakaranam project, organic vegetables have been cultivated in a one-acre land along with financial assistance from the agriculture department under Haritham Sahakaranam project. A subsidy of INR 93,000 has been assigned through this scheme; a Green Army team under Karshaka Sevana Kendra has made all the arrangements for the production.

3.1.9 *Vegetable cultivation district-level award*

The bank has secured the first position in organic vegetable cultivation at the district level for the combined effort put forward by the bank in the agriculture sector. Green Army under Karshaka Sevana Kendram has done all the arrangements for the cultivation; modern equipment has been used for the cultivation in a one-acre land owned by the bank. Smt. M. M. Sabeena, Agriculture Officer, Kodiyathoor Service Co-operative Bank has been awarded the best agriculture officer related to this.

3.1.10 *Haritham Sahakaranam: Plantation of trees*

In connection with a project by the Kerala government along with the cooperative department to plant one crore trees all over Kerala, the bank has taken up a huge role in this project and has distributed various varieties of plant seedlings to the Kudumbhasree ADS in Kodiyathoor Panchayat.

3.1.11 *Onam–Bakrid fair*

With assistance from the consumer federation, an Onam–Bakrid fair has been conducted at Pannikode and this has been continuing every year. The bank honours those who contribute to society every year, with a cash award and memento presented to them as a token of appreciation.

Shri P. S. Prashant Master, National Teacher award winner has been honoured and a memento was awarded as a token of appreciation.

3.1.12 *Free water supply*

The bank has been continuing the free water supply to drought areas in Kodiyathoor Panchayat every year. The water supply was carried out from April to May in the affected areas every year.

3.1.13 *Old-age pension distribution*

The bank has been recognised as the best bank in the district for the speedy distribution of old-age pension from the government to the members who come under the bank working area. This year, pensions amounting to INR 34,360,500 have been reportedly distributed to 2530 pensioners on time.

3.1.14 *Recreation club*

The contributions by the bank's recreation club towards social activities are appreciable. The recreation club has been directly involved in various activities concerning the society; as a part of this, cleaning activities have been carried out in the entire panchayat in every season. Health awareness seminars have been conducted in all schools before the monsoon every year.

3.1.15 *SURAKSHITHA 2030*

Kodiyathoor Service Co-operative Bank has initiated a new concept of integrated farming project called "SURAKSHITHA 2030" — a 22-crore project in the agriculture sector — with the assistance of Animal Husbandry Department, Agricultural Department, Fisheries Department, Dairy Development Department, District and Industries Center. This project comprises a cattle farm, poultry, organic vegetables, farm tourism, etc. with a mission to spread agriculture practices to every corner of the society and to eradicate harmful pesticide-dipped vegetables from other states (Table 3).

Table 3.   New proposals for sustaining the cooperative.

A convention centre with all facilities at Pannikode for which land extending about
115 cents by the side of Airport Road has been purchased by the bank recently, and
the registration process of this purchase would be completed within a few weeks.

A godown-cum-sales-outlet for cement, steel, and other construction materials in the
land owned by the bank in front of the HO of the bank by the side of the main road,
extending to about 37 cents.

The bank has initiated a new concept of integrated farming Project, "SURAKSHITHA
2030", comprising cattle farms, poultry, organic vegetables, farm tourism, etc., and the
service of Karshaka Sena is also utilised through this concept. The farms are intended
to be an enterprise that will generate employment in the locality and provide
knowledge inputs to the communities around without dilution of the focus on
profitability and sustainable agricultural practices. For this purpose, land measuring
five acres has been purchased by the bank. This project, by providing all inputs for
farming and good value for the cultivated products, motivates people to turn to
agriculture. These products will be marketed under the brand name, Natural.

Recent studies pointed out that 90% of the vegetables coming from other
states use high levels of pesticides and chemicals, which are more dangerous to the new generation.

For this project, the bank has acquired agricultural land in Kozhikode
Village, in Chatamangalam Panchayat measuring five acres, where the
agro-industry unit has been planned. In these five acres of land, a mini
agro-industrial unit, model farms (cattle, poultry), agro-tourism centre,
health tourism, etc. have been planned. In this agro-industry unit, the
farmers can bring their cultivated products (potato, banana, tapioca, etc.,
which can be processed into value-added products); apart from this, various inputs, including fruits collected from the farmers, can be processed
and marketed under the brand name of Natural. This project also gives
importance to agro-tourism: packaged tours can be arranged for corpo-
rates and foreigners, through which the tourists have the opportunity to
stay in the heritage centre at the farm and can directly participate in the
agricultural activities.

All inputs for vegetables, poultry, cattle farms will be provided by the
bank along with all the financial assistance, including regular visits and
training, and the final products will be taken back from the farmers at a
good price and will be marketed using delivery vehicles. For this, the bank

has already purchased two vehicles, and for more vehicles, the bank has discussed with the employment centre and agreed to provide subsidy and other assistance for the project. The project has been planned to be implemented in three stages. The first stage aims to cultivate the vegetables and make arrangements for the farm, and the remaining — processing plant and centralised marketing including the agro-industries centre — has been planned for the next stage. The tentative balance sheet of the bank is shown in Table 4.

3.2 Case study of Peringandur Service Co-operative Bank

Peringandur Service Co-operative Bank was registered on 12 August 1932 and started functioning from 1 January 1933. Peringandur, Minaloor, Parlikkad, and a part of Mundathicode Village come under its area of operation. The bank is now functioning in a five-storied building under a centralised air-conditioned environment (Tables 7–11). The bank has three branches. Besides banking operations, the bank has also undertaken non-credit activities, such as Neethi Medical Store, supermarket, textile shop, and manure depot. The bank is situated at Athani near Thrissur Medical College.

3.2.1 *Save old-age people programme*

The bank had envisaged a programme three years ago by surveying the area of operation. Under this programme, the bank has intended to help adults aged above 70 years by providing financial assistance and physical care. This project came into force during 2017–2018. As a first step, the bank identified 618 persons for assistance. A yearly pension of INR 1,200 is given to meet the day-to-day expenses. As a part of this programme, a portion of expenses incurred on dialysis for kidney patients, cancer patients, etc. is absorbed by the bank.

3.2.2 *Rural Haat*

This is a programme co-sponsored by National Bank for Agriculture and Rural Development (NABARD). The bank provided an 8,000-square-feet

Table 4. Tentative balance sheet as on 31 March 2021.

Liabilities		Assets	
Particulars	**Amount (Rs.)**	**Particulars**	**Amount (Rs.)**
Share Capital	72,279,999.00	Cash Balance	
Deposits	3,476,504,218.50	Cash on hand	47,859,123.80
Borrowings		Cash at Bank	452,876,616.90
District Bank	465,657,450.00	Shares of Other Institutions	28,255,414.00
Government	544,195,704.64	Other Investments	0.00
Others	50,000,000.00	Reserve Fund Invested	7,550,130.00
Reserves & Funds (Distribution of Net Profit)	0.00	Employees PF Invested	29,399.00
Reserve Fund	8,332,180.47	Employees Security Deposit Invested	174,057.00
Agrl. Credit Stabilisation Fund	4,421,443.96	Loans & Advances to Members	3,367,097,736.75
Other Funds	16,559,523.88	Interest Receivable	582,59B,735.00
Funds & Provisions (Charging P & L account)	0.00	Miscellaneous Assets (Interest on Investments)	15,345,427.00
Depreciation Fund	33,826,555.40	Group Deposit Scheme	229,687,574.05
Other Funds & Provisions	68,123,376.60	Movables	51,463,405.98
Reserve for Overdue Interest	40,769,157.00	Immovables	148,996,119. 10
Interest Payable	79,038,075.00	Closing Stock	0.00
Grants & Subsidies	9,234,291.00	Saleable Stock	17,113,410.00
Education Fund	0.00	Deficit Stock	154,042. 11
Professional Edn. Fund	260,683.84	Damaged Stock	1,697,017.95
Member Relief Fund	100,000.00	Deficit Stock	0.00
Employees' Security Deposit	2,474,000.00	Adjusting Heads Due to	231,494,960.02
Employees Provident Fund	11,679,294.00	Net Loss for the Year	0.00

(Continued)

Table 4. (*Continued*)

Liabilities		Assets	
Particulars	**Amount (Rs.)**	**Particulars**	**Amount (Rs.)**
Dividend Payable to Members	7,629,046.29		
Dividend Payable to Govt.	0.00		
Establishment & Contingency	0.00		
Reserves & Provisions Rent Year	15,000,000.00		
Group Deposit Scheme	222,258,000.00		
Members Welfare Scheme Fund	0.00		
Adjusting Heads Due by	47,584,781.23		
Undistributed Profit of Previous Years	0.00		
Net Profit for the Year	*6,465,387.BS*		
Total	**5,182,393,168.66**	**Total**	**5,182,393,168.66**

place for running the project. This is the first venture in the state. As the bank is an institution standing up for rural economic development, produces from farmers are collected and sold through the Rural Haat and a supermarket. Every week on Saturdays, farmers, SHG groups, women ventures assemble at this place for display and selling of farm and non-farm produces.

3.2.3 *Njattuvela Chantha*

Every year, at the beginning of the monsoon, the bank organises "Njattuvela Chantha" for the benefit of farmers, SHG groups, members, etc. The venue of the programme is a 15,000-square-feet area adjacent to the HO premises. This place is now converted to a Rural Haat. The participants of the programme are Kerala Agricultural University, Kerala Veterinary University, Kavungal Agencies, Haritha Agritech, and nurseries situated in the nearby area. An exhibition-cum-sale of different products from the farm and non-farm sectors is arranged. Vegetable seeds and plants are distributed, enabling cultivation in the upper floors of RC buildings using grow bags. Duration of the programme is from five to seven days. During the inaugural session, students and teachers of 12 schools from the surrounding areas of the bank are invited and vegetable plants are given to them free of cost. Two or three days of seminars were also conducted on various subjects beneficial to a farmer in the areas of agriculture, dairy, horticulture, poultry, etc. Through this programme, the bank aims to mold the society for self-cultivation of vegetables and other indigenous products and also follow natural food habits.

3.2.4 *Green Mythri supermarket*

This is a unit working from two floors in an air-conditioned environment spanning about 6,000 square feet. It was established on 2 November 2013. The features of the supermarket are as follows:

- Products are offered below maximum retail price (MRP).
- Importance is given for organic products.
- A loyalty card is given to clients and the benefits of their purchases during a year is accumulated in points (one rupee for 100 points) and given in kind on the occasion of the Onam festival. This helps to increase sales.
- Credit facility up to INR 5,000 for one month is offered to members.
- All the products from farmers, SHGs, etc. are collected and marketed through the supermarket, so that the interests of members are protected.
- The bank can give employment to 50–60 persons in the locality. The average sale is nearing INR 4 lakh per day with 650–700 customers visiting. In short, the brand name is established. The scale of volume and number of clients visiting the premises of the supermarket is gradually increasing.
- As a part of diversification, Green Café, Matsyafed Fish Mart, Meat Section & Co-op Mart (for collecting vegetables from farmers at favourable prices, branded cooperative consumable goods) were also established.
- Business turnover of the supermarket shows steady growth concerning sales and number of customers visiting in premises over the last seven years.

3.2.5 *Women's empowerment programme*

Functional equality is the right of women. The banks believe that women should have the freedom to travel as much as men. Women are supposed to live as social beings. So, the bank introduced loans for two-wheeler vehicles to women under liberalised norms that enable them to commute to their jobs and participate in social activities.

3.2.6 *Recharging of wells*

Social commitment is one of the principles of cooperation. The bank was facing scarcity of water for even drinking in some parts of its area of operation. As a helping hand, the bank adopted a colony where most of the inhabitants are from the underprivileged Scheduled Castes (SC) group. Sixty-five wells were recharged in the colony intending to improve water for drinking, sanitation, and irrigation sufficient for vegetable cultivation.

3.2.7 *Excellence award*

Each year, school/college students and students from professional colleges in the area are recognised by giving awards for their best performance in final exams. The bank believes that their participation in the future will help the institution to grow to new heights.

Well read programme 2018: Under this programme, the bank provides the necessary financial support to nearby schools increasing the reading capacity of students. At present, the bank is providing monthly magazines and other reading materials. From the beginning of 2018, more support is extended to strengthen the library collection in these schools. The bank has selected nine schools for this purpose. Under this programme, institutions can create strong relations with the youth.

Training to SHGs JLGs, and staff members: The bank is housed in a five-storied building with centralised air-conditioning; each floor occupies about 3,000 square feet of area. The bank has an auditorium of 400–450 seating capacity. This auditorium is used for conferences and other public functions, whereas another hall with a 50–60 seating capacity (a mini auditorium) is available for training and small programmes. Training to staff, SHGs, JLGs, etc. are frequently conducted here.

Coconut complex (work in progress): A coconut procuring and process-ing unit is almost nearing completion. It is expected to be finalised by end of this year. For this purpose, 2.14 acres of land was acquired about 3 kilometres away from the HO. This project is particularly meant for the benefit of coconut cultivation. Coconut drying and processing and con-verting copra to pure coconut oil of export quality are expected to be undertaken in this unit. With 70–75% of the oil marketed through super-markets, the remaining portion in business is a concern in the district. As a part of this, a detailed project report is submitted to NABARD seeking financial help of nearly INR 6 crore bearing an interest of 4%. By fulfill-ing this project, the bank can give employment to 70–75 persons directly and indirectly.

Subhiksha Keralam project: As a part of the Subhiksha Keralam project, the bank is extending financial help to SHGs and ordinary members of the bank. Under this, financial help is provided to integrated vegetable farm-ing, goat farming, poultry farming, aquaculture (fish farming), etc. The bank has distributed over 2.32 crores for this purpose.

Online education: With the outbreak of COVID-19, economically back-ward students need help with online teaching. The bank provided televi-sions (TVs) and smartphones, and also introduced a new low-interest scheme for purchasing TVs, laptops, smartphones, and tablets.

Award and recognition: The bank received the second best performing PACS award in the state by National Cooperative Development Corporation (NCDC) for the year 2018. Fulfilling responsibility to the society, particu-larly weaker sections, the bank is constructing a medical attention centre in their land situated nearby the HO building complex. This centre includes dialysis units, labs, and medical stores within its area of opera-tion. As evidence of its financial strength, the bank is also enclosing the last three years' trading, profit and loss (P&L), and balance sheets. Since

2001, the bank is continuously working on profits for offering dividends to members.

Dyuti: To develop skills, mold good character in students/youngsters in the society, and bring their potential/attachment towards the best for the institution in the future, the bank is conducting classes/training programmes. So far, the bank has already conducted many of such programmes.

COVID-19 award claimed by Kerala bank: The districtwise first prize is awarded to the bank for the remarkable activities done at the time of COVID-19. Thus, as a cooperative institution, the bank is fulfilling the economic, cultural, and social needs of the society. Table 5 presents more details about the cooperative bank.

Table 6 and Figure 1 show the organisational structure of the credit cooperative. The board of directors selected for the period 2018–2023 is shown in the table.

The Peringandur Service Co-operative Bank, No. 297, was registered as Mutual Aid Co-operative Society in 1931 with unlimited liability by the then Cochin State Co-operative Registrar and its HO was at Ambalapuram. The first board of directors took charge in 1932. Sri. Manakkulam Kunjunni Raja was the first elected President and Sri. Ayyappath Raman Menon was the first Secretary. At first, the bank started functioning at

Table 5.   Details of the cooperative bank.

Established	:	1932
Post Office	:	Athani
Taluk	:	Thalappilly
District	:	Thrissur
Village	:	Minaloor
Head Office	:	Athani
Branch	:	Athani, Parlikad & Peringandur
Liability	:	Limited
Audit Classification	:	A Class
General Classification	:	Class one super grade

Table 6.   Board of Directors from 2018 to 2023.

1	Shajan M.R.	:	President
2	Udayakumar K.R.	:	Vice President
3	Jose K.V.	:	Board member
4	Dr. Pradeepkumar K.	:	Board member
5	Binoy Mohan (Kannan Ellikkottil)	:	Board member
6	Muraleedharan V.	:	Board member
7	Unnikrishnan K.P.	:	Board member
8	Mohanan M.R.	:	Board member
9	Vinod M.S.	:	Board member
10	Ajitha Mohandas	:	Board member
11	Nithya M.S.	:	Board member
12	Shereefa Hassan	:	Board member

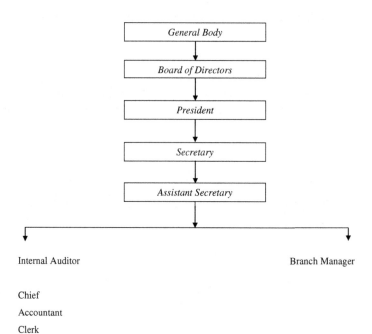

Figure 1.   Organisational structure.

Ambalapuram (Peringandur Village). In 1954, the government converted the bank into an agricultural cooperative bank. In 1957, when the Parlikad Co-operative Society became defunct, the government merged it with the Peringandur Agricultural Co-operative Bank. In 1967, the government converted the bank as a service cooperative bank and participated in its share capital. Now, the bank has completed 89 years of successful operation. The area of operation of the Peringandur Service Co-operative Bank consists of the entire Peringandur, Minaloor, and Parlikad villages, as well as Mundathicode village (southern side of Athani–Pudhuruthy Road).

The major objectives of Peringandur Service Co-operative Bank Ltd. as per the bye-laws are as follows:

- to conduct banking business, i.e. accepting deposits and lending money;
- to assist in development of agriculture and thus help members of the bank to attain better living standard;
- to start outlets for delivering quality products to members and the general public;
- to construct and rent out godowns for storing the produce of farmer members and operate Neethi Medical Store;
- to purchase and sell fertilisers, farm inputs, and consumer goods;
- to conduct MDS business;
- to organise and assist micro-level SHGs.

Peringandur Service Co-operative Bank Ltd. has three branches functioning in Athani, Peringandur (near a medical college) and Parlikad. The work timing of the branches is 9.30 a.m. to 4.30 p.m., and the transaction time is up to 3.30 p.m., while the HO at Athani works from 8 a.m. to 8 p.m. in two shifts. The function of the bank is connected through Internet banking. The total staff strength is 21. Apart from this, nearly 75 employees are working on daily wages in trading units such as supermarket, Neethi store, and fertiliser depot. For details about the cooperative bank, please see Table 7–11.

3.2.8 *Milestones*

Peringandur Co-operative Society was registered in 1932 with unlimited liability. The bank started functioning in 1933. The first managing

Table 7.   Status of the present board.

Date of election	:	2 December 2018
Charge taken on	:	3 December 2018
Date of expiry	:	1 December 2023
Year of last audit	:	2020–2021
		(Under process)
Audit classification	:	Class 1 Super Grade

Table 8.   Investment details.

S. No.	Type	Balance	Interest Receivable
1	TDCB Athani FD	573,472,837	3,994,298
2	Tdcb LT deposit tcr	10,000,000	
3	MCCH Security FD	11,666	846
4	Kerala Feeds Security	37,194	7,139
5	ACS Fund FD	9,400,057	825,542
6	PF FD	2,493,000	12,975
7	Rubco FD	57,282,517	3,337,455
8	Staff Security FD	180,500	37,528
9	Consumer Federation	2,500,000	0
10	Savings A/C. Etc.	10,690,408	28,961
11	Current Account	11,979,341	0
12	Treasury	150,000	0
13	TDLC	2,635,000	36,330
Total		**680,832,520**	**8,281,074**

committee was framed with Sri. Manakkulam Kunjan Raja as the first President of the society. The first deposit (INR 100) was made by Manakkulam Mukundaraja. In the year 1934, the bank was affiliated to District Co-operative Bank, Thrissur. The society shifted to its building in 1948 and appointed the first paid secretary in the year 1950. With time, in the year 1954, the society became an agricultural cooperative bank. The society celebrated the golden jubilee in 1983. The introduction of computerisation self-help groups and action plans for bank development started in the year 1999. The society started its first branch and became profitable after covering all losses in 2001. The bank started its branch at Parlikad in 2005. The bank started refrigerated vans with the assistance of the state horticulture mission for procurement of sales goods in 2015. The society started a consumer store, Green Café under Green Mythri supermarket and green loom. Matsyafed Fish Mart, Meat Mart, and Vegetable Marketing were started in 2020. The bank was recognised with an award by Kerala Bank during COVID-19 for its remarkable activities during the pandemic.

3.3 Kizhathadiyoor Service Co-operative Bank, No. 1995, Pala

The financial crises in 1925–1926 and 1930–1934 in the princely state of Travancore badly affected the backbone of the agricultural sector throughout the state. The price of agricultural produce was reduced to half. The value of land came down and sales came to a standstill. To save the farmers from this situation, an association of farmers and other affected parties was formed in the name and style of "Kizhathadiyoor Sadhujana Sevaka Paraspara Sahaya Sanghom" and registered with the Registrar of Thiruvithamcore Paraspara Sahaya Sanghom under Section 9, regulation 10 of 1089 ME on 3 July 1934, with Register no. 1995.

With the liquidation of Pala Central Bank, the deposits in the society have shown steady growth.

Since the deposit was increasing steadily, the society was compelled to give loans to its members to avoid the accumulation of money for which the bye-law of the society had to be amended. Hence, in the general body meeting, the society decided to register as per the Travancore–Cochin Co-operative Societies Act 1961 with the name and style of "Kizhathadiyoor Service Co-operative Bank Ltd.". The society obtained registration with register no. 1995 on 23 March 1961. The area of operation of the bank is the municipal limit of Pala Municipality having an area of 15.93 square kilometres. The bank is proud to say that out of the total population of 22,056 of the municipality, 16,754 are A-class members of the bank.

Table 9. Profit and loss statement.

	Profit		Loss	
1	Interest on deposits and borrowings	164,929,232.00	Gross profit brought from trading A/c	3,031,169.53
2	Establishment charges	11,591,562.00	Interest on lending's	213,070,124.39
3	Contingencies	23,549,024.19	Miscellaneous (Int. on deposit)	43,012,204.08
4	Depreciation fund	4,600,710.80	Miscellaneous	13,833,954.77
5	Reserve for overdue interest	141,166,451.35	Reserve for adj. heads	139,797.95
6	Res for bad and doubtful assets	19,941,265.00	Reserve for overdue interest	101 648,045 00
7	Land recoupment fund (10/10)(2011-12)	822,352.00	Res for bad and doubtful assets	10 582,958 00
8	Provision for RUBCO investment (15%)	1,000,000.00	Provision for Future Loss	9,500,000.00
9	Res for MDS payment from own fund	3,307,000.00	Res for MDS Payment from Own Fund	3,496,000.00
10	Reserve for Member OD excess payment	70,602,568.00	Reserve for Member OD Excess payment	48,350,885.00
11	Res for van recoupment fund (6/10)	144,215.00	—	

Total	441,654,380.34	Total	446,665,138.72
Profit of the year (carried down)	5,010,758.38	Loss of the year (carried down)	–
Grand total	446,665,138.72	Grand total	446,665,138.72
Loss of the year (brought down)	–	Profit of the year (brought down)	5,010,758.38
Net loss as per P & L account of the previous year	–		
Net profit	5,010,758.38	Net loss	–
Total	**5,010,758.38**	**Total**	**5,010,758.38**

Table 10. Trading including profits and losses.

Sl. No.	Debit Particulars	Amount	Credit Particulars	Amount
1	Opening stock	12,337,749.99	Sales 212,102,535.85	
2	Purchases 183,074,410.96		Less returns 849,354.66	211,253,181.19
3	Less returns 1,552278.34	181,522,132.62	Trade income	3,017,347.29
4			Closing stock	11,029,412.37
5	Direct charges on purchases	28,408,888.71	Add deficit stock	
6			Add damaged stock	
7			Add Dead Stock	
8	**Total**	222,268,771.32	**Total**	225,299,940.85
9	Gross profit carried to P & L account	3,031,169.53	Gross loss carried to P & L account	
10	**Grand total**	225,299,940.85	**Grand total**	225,299,940.85

Table 11. Operational statement of proposed medical store (amount in lakhs).

S. No.	Particulars	2019–2020	2020–2021	2021–2022	2022–2023	2023–2024	2024–2025	2025–2026	2026–2027
1.	Purchases	380	400	430	475	525	550	580	600
2.	Sales	420	440	475	520	575	600	635	660
3.	Margin (10%)	38	40	43	47	52	55	58	60

Notes:

1. All the figures shown above are prepared based on Neethi Medical Store functioning at Thrissur Medical College Campus.
2. Starting figure is taken as 50% of the sale of existing Neethi Medical Store Unit and gradually increasing in the coming years.
3. Margin is worked out at 10% as against 11–12% arrived in the existing unit.

3.3.1 *Health services*

Neethi Medical Store: The bank had entered the field of sale of medicine at a time when the established private medical shops and hospitals continued to exploit the health conditions of the common man by realising the printed MRP price plus applicable taxes. The bank had opened the first Neethi Medical Store at Pala on the very same day Consumerfed had opened its first Neethi Medical Store outlet in Kerala, i.e. on 1 November 1998. Under this scheme, medicines were made available to the customers at a price 15–50% below the MRP. Due to the rush and continued requests of the customers, a second Neethi Medical Store was opened in 2006. The total daily sale of the Neethi Medical Stores taken together works out to INR 3.50 lakh. The bank is proud to say that out of the total medical sale of INR 5.50 lakh in the city, 64% pertains to the medical stores. From the date of opening to 31 March 2020, the bank has provided a discount of INR 12.74 crore to esteemed customers.

Insulin warehouse: To supply quality insulin to the retail medical shops at an affordable rate, the bank had opened Insulin Wholesale Warehouse at Pala. The bank is supplying insulin to various medical shops throughout the district at a cheaper rate. This warehouse opened in the cooperative sector compelled the medical shops to sell insulin to the customers with the increased benefit of discounts of up to 20%.

Prime Minister's Bharatheeya Janaushadhi Pariyojana (PMBJP) Medical Shop: The Government of India had initiated a scheme for providing quality medicines at an affordable price for all, particularly the poor and disadvantaged masses through exclusive outlets named "Jan Aushadhi Medical Store" to reduce out-of-pocket expenses in healthcare. Even though the opening of the "Jan Aushadhi Medical Store" may affect the sale of medicines in the Neethi Medical Store to a large extent, the bank was of the view that priority should be given to the toiled masses who were unable to afford the purchase of medicines from the multinational companies. Hence, the bank had opened two PMBJP Medical Shops in the city on 1 July 2016.

"Oushadhi" outlet: To provide high-quality Ayurvedic medicines at a reasonable price, adhering to classical Ayurvedic text, under the direct supervision of the Ayurvedic physicians, the bank had opened an outlet of

"Oushadhi", the largest producer of Ayurvedic medicines belonging to the public sector in the country.

3.3.2 *Kisco Diagnostic Centre, Pala*

The services offered by diagnostic centres are essential in the healthcare sector. The private sector labs established in this field were collecting abnormal fees for clinical and pathological investigations at their whims and fancies. Hence, to save the general public from the inhuman exploitation of the private labs, the bank had decided to open a fully equipped diagnostic centre at Pala. This is an ultramodern diagnostic centre with comprehensive facilities for laboratory imaging, investigations, and other diagnostic facilities under one roof. The bank had made available advanced technologies to provide information that is critical to the diagnosis and ultimately the treatment of all diseases. At its core is a highly skilled team of medical professionals including physicians, radiologists, qualified lab technologists, lab technicians, and lab assistants. The bank's service portfolio includes advanced laboratory, high-end ultrasound scanner, fully automated biochemistry analyser, hormone analyser, haematology analyser mammography, dental OPG, digital X-ray, full spine–full leg X-ray, and electrocardiogram (ECG). The fee levied is 20–50% less than that of private labs in this field. The bank has facilities to have more than 1,350 types of tests. The bank is proud to say that the accuracy in tests provided is attracting 450–500 customers daily. From 14 June 2010, the date of opening of the diagnostic centre, till 31 March 2020, the beneficiaries were provided with a rebate to the tune of INR 9.24 crore.

Kisco Diagnostic Centre, Erattupetta: A second diagnostic centre under the name and style of "Kisco Diagnostic Centre, Erattupetta" was opened on 1 November 2012. This centre was opened to benefit the people of hilly ranges of the district, mostly farmers and other toiling masses. From the date of inception to 31 March 2020, the beneficiaries were provided with a rebate of INR 2.52 crore.

Kisco–Cenmark Diagnostic Centre, Ramapuram: A third diagnostic centre was opened by the bank on 1 July 2016 jointly with Pala Central Marketing Society at Ramapuram, which is exclusively an agrarian area.

Vaikom Taluk Urban Welfare–Kisco Diagnostic Centre, Vaikom: A fourth diagnostic centre was opened by the bank jointly with Vaikom Taluk Urban Welfare Co-operative Society at Vaikom, the majority of the population of which are coir workers, fisherman, and other economically backward classes. Till 31 March 2020, the beneficiaries were provided with a rebate of INR 39.13 lakh.

Computed tomography (CT) scan centre: The bank has established a CT scan unit with 18 slice CT scan machine (reconstructed to 32 slice), the first of its kind in the taluk. From the date of its opening on 4 December 2012 till 31 March 2020, the centre has allowed a rebate of INR 1.02 crore to the beneficiaries.

Dialysis unit: Dialysis allows people to prolong their life by regularly filtering waste from their bodies. Several kidney patients do not undergo dialysis not because they do not want to prolong their life but due to the cost involved in dialysis and additional expenses required for their journey from home to hospital and vice versa. The bank, considering the pathetic situation of the patients, established a dialysis unit at Pala on 4 February 2012. Here, the bank is levying a fee of INR 650 only from patients for each dialysis even though the actual expenses for dialysis works out to INR 1005. Till 31 March 2020, the bank has allowed a rebate of INR 34.58 lakh to the beneficiaries. In addition, on several occasions, the bank has also issued dialysis kits free of cost to dialysis patients.

Telemedicine facility: The bank has arranged telemedicine facilities in association with Rajagiri Super Speciality Hospital, Aluva. Through this, the customers who want to consult the doctors at the Rajagiri Hospital for diagnosis and continued treatment can have the same without travelling a long distance and without waiting in a queue.

Kisco Clinic: The bank has provided to its customers and the general public free of cost the services of two physicians for their healthcare. This has helped thousands to avail healthcare without any expenses.

Ambulance service: The bank has initiated an ambulance service at Pala in the year 1990, the first of its kind in the town. Now, a handful of ambulances run by private persons, institutions, and hospitals are available in the town. The people of Pala even now are showing preference to this ambulance service as it is the cheapest one even now.

3.3.3 *Commercial services*

Agro Shop: For promoting agriculture, the bank had established an Agro Shop through which agricultural seeds, manure, and agricultural implements are made available to the farmers at moderate rates. The bank is also functioning as a franchise of "Raidco", an agro-industrial development cooperative, manufacturer of agricultural implements.

Soil-testing laboratory: The most widely conducted soil tests are those carried out to estimate the plant-available concentrations of plant nutrients to determine fertiliser recommendations in agriculture. To promote agriculture in the working area of the bank as well as the nearby panchayats which are mostly agri–horti in nature, the bank with the assistance of the Government of Kerala established a soil-testing laboratory. Water samples are also tested here for analysing the contaminants in water.

Consumer store: The bank is running a consumer retail store for the benefit of the members and general public for the sale of good quality and unadulterated consumer goods at a comparatively cheaper rate.

Furniture shops (2): The bank is running two furniture shops in the working area for the sale of good quality wooden furniture and beds at moderate rates. The furniture showroom is functioning as an agent of Kerala State Rubber Co-operative Ltd.

Cotton (textile shop): The bank is running a textile showroom under the name and style of "Kisco Cottons" with a price suiting the common man. The shop is good and provides value for each rupee paid.

Optical showroom: The bank is running an optical showroom from where lens and frames of reputed companies are made available to the customers at moderate rates to have perfect pairs to suit the face.

Business centre: The bank is running a business centre where photostat, lamination, spiral binding, mobile charging services, etc. are made available to the customers at a cheaper rate. Tea, coffee, and snacks are also served here.

Kisco dairy farm: Considering the observation made by the honourable Supreme Court of India on the widespread supply of contaminated milk in the country, the bank has established a dairy unit with the object of providing pure cow milk and allied products to the public. Here, the milk is processed and packed following pasteurisation and homogenisation so that the nutrients and taste of the milk are intact. The products include curd, buttermilk, ghee, sip up, and paneer.

Eco shop: The bank took initiative in establishing an eco shop with the sole object of supplying "safe to eat" vegetables to the common man in light of increasing cancer and other diseases. With the help of the Agricultural Department, Government of Kerala, the bank could form a society of farmers. Now, the society is collecting organic vegetables and "safe to eat" vegetables from the farmers at a fair price and selling them to the general public at an affordable price. The eco shop is running successfully.

Co-op Vegetable Fresh: The bank is running a Co-operative Vegetable Fresh Outlet for fresh and organic vegetables collected from the farmers at a minimum support price fixed by the Government of Kerala and selling them to the customers at a cheaper rate than in the open market.

3.3.4 *Educational services*

Kisco Career Heights: With the avowed object of providing quality training and coaching for various competitive examinations, the bank in association with M/s Career Heights, a partnership firm of eminent professors and faculties in the district has established an institution with the brand name "Kisco Career Heights" which is stationed in the HO building of the bank. The salient feature of Kisco Career Heights is that courses for various competitive examinations are being offered to the students at a concessional and affordable fee. The students coming from a poor financial background are given concessions with a motive to promote their ambition.

Women empowerment: Women constitute an integral part of the socio-economic life and they actively participate in the socio-economic development of the nation. With the motive of empowerment of women, 54 SHGs of women were formed and registered under the bank and they are functioning successfully with the financial support and assistance from the bank. A few units are focused on the fields of agriculture and small industries, such as soap manufacture and curry powder production. In addition, a few units of SHGs of men are also registered with the bank and functioning successfully.

3.3.5 *Cultural activities*

Kisco Library: A library is housed in the HO building of the bank with more than 12,000 books. It provides all the current periodicals along with a large number of reference books on all topics and the works of almost all famous English and Malayalam writers. The library is used by many competitors for the IAS/IPS competitive examinations. The library has been declared as the best performing library in the cooperative sector by the Government of Kerala.

Saphalam 55+: The bank in association with Dementia Care has formed an association of retired public servants to utilise their expertise for the development and the socio-economic well-being of society.

The society is involved in various programmes of the local bodies with professional skill and advising social organisations in their various activities for the development of the society. The society is organising various cultural programmes such as debates and lectures in connection with various topics of international and national importance.

Saphalam monthly magazine: The bank with the association of Saphalam 55+ is publishing a unique magazine, with the name *Kisco Saphalam Monthly*, the only monthly published by a cooperative society in Kerala.

Pala Narayanan Nair Award: Pala Narayanan Nair was a great poet, scholar, and Professor of Malayalam language and literature. Even though he was a resident of Pala for several years, the cultural organisations and local bodies of Pala failed to honour him suitably. To honour this eminent personality and to commemorate him, the Board of Directors of the Bank has decided to proclaim an award every year honouring eminent personalities in the field of literature. The recipients of the award for the previous years are S/S Dr. Pudussery Ramachandran, Chemmanam Chacko, Sakhariah, Ezhacherry Ramachandran, and C. Radhakrishnan.

3.3.6 *Other social services*

Kisco Palliative Unit: The bank had formed a charitable society under the name and style "Kizhathadiyoor Palliative and Social Service Society K.201/10" with the avowed object of providing free medicine and medical equipment for cancer patients, bedridden, and other eligible and needy. It is worth mentioning that within 10 years of existence, this unit could provide medicines and equipment worth INR 25 lakh. The Board of Directors and staff of the bank are the members of the society and the source of funds for the society is the monthly subscriptions by the members and donations from well-wishers. It is a privilege to state that an 80(G) exception has been granted for the donation made to this charitable society.

Another charitable service provided by the bank is the "Annamekal Project", a scheme for providing free food for the poor and starving with the noble objective that everyone in the locality should eat at least once in a day. The bank is also providing financial help to needy patients by providing free medicines.

Meenachil River "Punarjani" (rejuvenation of Meenachil River): The river Meenachil is the main source of drinking water for the residents of four Municipalities: Erattupetta, Pala, Ettumanoor, and Kottayam, as well as several panchayats of the district. A study of water samples collected from 44 points revealed that the bacteriological quality of the Meenachil river is very poor. The presence of faecal indicator bacteria, *Escherichia coli*, and potentially pathogenic bacteria, Vibrio cholerae, Vibrio parahaemolyticus, and salmonella enteric were detected. This sheds light on the fact that raw sewage is dumped into the river. Urban run-offs and effluents of rubber factories appear to be important sources of faecal contamination in the river.

To save the river and its ecological integrity, a community under the leadership of the bank, "Meenachil Aar Punarjani" (Rejuvenation of Meenachil River) was formed coordinating with eminent personalities of all walks of life, and a campaign to save the river was initiated. This initiative got momentum and now several organisations in various parts of the District were formed for the very purpose. A widespread campaign, "Save Meenachil River" is conducted throughout the District and as the first phase, thousands of people joined hands in cleaning the river and its tributaries wherever possible. This programmes has to be continued till the river is saved from the threat of contamination.

Blood bank: In association with the Rotary Club of Pala and Marian Medical Center, the bank has established a full-fledged blood bank at Pala in the premises of Marian Medical Centre. This is the only blood bank in Meenachil Taluk.

Educational assistance: The bank has provided educational assistance to 24 economically backward but talented students to fulfil their educational aspirations. The bank has promised assistance to them for their higher studies to the maximum they want. Out of the 24 students, a few are studying medicine and engineering.

Housing: It is a privilege to state that the bank has donated a house to the victim of the "Endosalphan" affected area in Kasaragod. The bank has provided a second house for a homeless family with two grown-up daughters living under a shelter by the side of a road without proper security.

Again, the bank has met the expenses of constructing two houses for the homeless poor identified and recommended by the resident's associations in the operation area of the bank.

The expenditure incurred by the bank in this regard is INR 20 lakh.

Adoption expenses: The bank is meeting all expenses of the inmates, both children and the aged, of "Snehalayam", an orphanage, and

"Mariasadanam", an institution looking after mentally challenged women and their children. The adoption expenses incurred by the bank on this account is INR 2,035,338.

Blood donors' forum: The donation of blood is the most important and valuable service in human life. As a part of discharging social commitment in the healthcare sector, the bank has formed a blood donors' forum in association with "Bullet Club", an association of youngsters dedicated to serving the poor and needy people.

Janasevana Kendras: Janasevana Kendras have been designed as a single-window facility where citizens can make various government-related transactions under one roof with ease and without delay. With the object of providing more services to customers and the public at large, the branches of the bank started functioning as Janasevana Kendras.

Kisco and Matsyafed Fish Marts: Reports from various laboratories confirm that the fish available in the market for sale is applied with preservatives such as Formalin which are dangerous to the health of human beings. To make available fresh fish without harmful preservatives injurious to human health, the bank in association with Matsyafed, a cooperative for fishermen under the control of the Government of Kerala, is running a fish stall in the town.

Relief to flood victims (2018 and 2019): In 2018, severe floods devastated the entire state of Kerala, badly affecting the economy of the state. Agricultural lands were destroyed, and crops and markets were fully submerged in water causing huge economic losses to farmers and traders. Hundreds of thousands of people were shifted to relief camps and compelled to stay there for weeks. The recurrence of floods in 2019 swallowed up a major portion of the district including the area of operation of the bank. The after effects of the flood are the loss of jobs and livelihoods of the people. In this dire situation, the bank had supplied ready-made textiles amounting to INR 148,575 in the relief camps. The staff and management of the bank also donated INR 3,914,266 to the Distress Relief Fund of the Honourable Chief Minister of Kerala.

Further, in connection with the 2019 flood, the bank had supplied textiles amounting to INR 545,000 and food kits amounting to INR 50,000 to the victims.

COVID-19 — Community kitchen: The COVID-19 pandemic was initially detected in January 2020 in the state of Kerala. The subsequent lockdown ordered by the government terrified the people and they were forced to stay at home. Due to the loss of jobs and income, thousands were fearing starvation. To save the people from starvation, the bank in association with Abhayam Charitable Trust and the financial help of several generous individuals opened a community kitchen at Pala. About 600 needy people were served cooked food twice daily for three weeks.

4. Conclusion

Kerala's credit cooperative sector has caught the attention of different countries for building strong and sustainable cooperatives. The success of the banks is keenly watched. The integration of information technology platforms and financial and human resource systems helps provide good services to the people. Kerala has consistently improved its performance indicators (Franke & Chasin, 2000). This study selected three case studies. Kodiyathoor Service Cooperative Bank is one of the leading cooperative banks in the state and was awarded as the best cooperative bank in Kozhikode. At present, the bank is one of the best cooperatives. The bank has currently 25,000 members with a capital of INR 443 lakh. The bank has diversified into different activities to assist the rural people. Kizhathadiyoor Service Co-operative Bank gives more priority to services to the people, which is also key to the development of the society. Due to diversity in services, Kizhathadiyoor Service Co-operative Bank cannot be placed in the second position among the few leading cooperative banks in Kerala. Peringandur Service Co-operative bank is one of the credit cooperatives that has attained a net profit of more than INR 1 crore. The bank contributed to different diversified activities and disbursed agriculture loans to farmers ensuring food security and self-reliance. The bank has started new projects, including Coconut Lab, Poly House, Neethi Lab, Doctors Clinic, New Neethi Medicals, and Community College. Though this study makes a unique contribution by highlighting the sustainable practices of the banks, it is to be noted that this research is limited to the Kerala state of India. The environments and practices may show variation among the Asian countries. More exploratory studies on the cases of cooperative banks will certainly pave a way for the credit societies in Asia towards sustaining the credit cooperative sector.

References

Filene (2011). Credit Union Financial Sustainability, A Colloquium at Harvard University, Filene Research Institute Report Number 231.

Franke, R. W. & Chasin, B. H. (2000). Is the Kerala model sustainable? Lessons from the past, prospects for the future. In G. Parayil (ed.), *Kerala: The Development Experience, Reflections on Sustainability and Replicability*, London: Zed Books, 256 pp.

Henock, M. S. (2019). Financial sustainability and outreach performance of saving and credit cooperatives: The case of Eastern Ethiopia. *Asia Pacific Management Review*, 24(1), 1–9.

Meyer, R. L. (2002). Track record of financial institutions in assisting the poor in Asia, Retrieved 8 September 2021 from https://think-asia.org/bitstream/handle/11540/4154/2002.12.rp049.track.record.pdf?sequence=1.

Véron, R. (2001). The "new" Kerala model: Lessons for sustainable development. *World Development*, 29(4), 601–617.

Chapter 7

Kibbutz in Israel: From Equal Sharing to Privatisation

A. Allan Degen[*,‡] and Lily Degen[†]

Ben-Gurion University of the Negev, Beer Sheva, Israel

†Eucalyptus 13, Omer, Israel

‡degen@bgu.ac.il

Although socialist communities also existed in the United States and Europe in the 19th and 20th centuries, Martin Buber asserted that the kibbutz was the most impressive of these experiments in communal living — "an experiment that did not fail". Over 50 years after Buber made this statement, the verdict is still out on the success of the kibbutz movement (Schultz, 2021).

Abstract

The first kibbutzim were established in the early 1900s as communes of utopian socialism based on economic, social, and political equalities among the members. They were conceived as rural communities, wholly engaged in agriculture, without employing outside labour. All property was owned collectively, and all members received the same wage independent of their work. Leadership positions were rotated every three years, and any decision affecting the kibbutz had to be discussed by the general assembly. Meals were eaten together in a communal dining hall, and education stressed altruistic, socialist and Zionist values. By 1950, two years after the establishment of the state of Israel, approximately 67,000 Israelis, or 7.5% of the country's population, resided in kibbutzim.

Kibbutzim played a key role in Israel's agricultural development and in its defence and political leadership. Early kibbutzim were often positioned strategically along borders and outlying areas to defend the country. Many top politicians and military and industry leaders, particularly in the 1950s and 1960s, were from kibbutzim. Industry was introduced in the 1920s, and by the 1960s, its income surpassed that of agriculture. In the 1980s, a financial crisis brought most kibbutzim to near bankruptcy. Kibbutzim had borrowed heavily to expand housing and industry, and with changes in political leadership and government policies, they could not repay the loans. Large numbers of skilled people left and many changes were made. In the "renewed kibbutz", privatisation was implemented and members started earning salaries based on their positions, with many members working outside the kibbutz. Industries were sold in part and only 49% remained in sole ownership by the kibbutz. Outside people were brought in to manage industries, with the most qualified people hired for key positions. Kibbutz houses were rented and land was sold to non-kibbutz members to build homes. By demonstrating flexibility, kibbutzim managed to survive the financial crisis. By 2008, there were more people joining the kibbutz than leaving it, a trend continuing today in the renewed kibbutz. About 15% of the kibbutzim maintain equal sharing among members.

Keywords: experimental lifestyle, communal living, innovative child-rearing, democratic community, equality of gender rights, agriculture and industry, rotating leadership

1. Israel: Geography and Demographics

Israel (Hebrew: יִשְׂרָאֵל; Arabic: إِسْرَائِيل), officially known as the State of Israel (Hebrew: מְדִינַת יִשְׂרָאֵל, *Medinat Yisra'el*), with Jerusalem (31°47'N; 35°13'E) as the proclaimed capital city, has a very unique location (between latitudes 29° and 34° N, and longitudes 34° and 36° E.) in the world (Figure 1). Although officially situated in Asia, Israel sits at the crossroads of three continents — Europe, Africa, and Asia. Israel shares its border with Lebanon in the north, Syria in the northeast, Jordan in the East, and Egypt in the south, and Palestinian territories of the West Bank lies to its east and the Gaza Strip to its west. The country has a long coastline on the Mediterranean Sea in the west and touches the Red Sea (Gulf of Eilat/Aqaba) on its southernmost point. Israel is divided into the following six main administrative districts, known as *meḥozot* (Hebrew: מחוזות; singular:

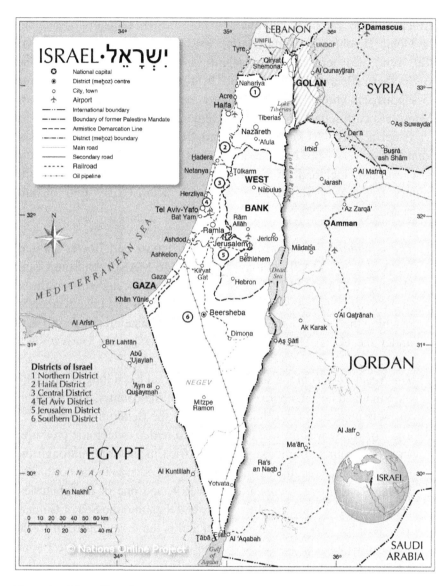

Figure 1.   Map of Israel.

Source: UN Cartographic Section (Nations Online Project).

maḥoz) (district capital in parentheses): (1) Northern (Nazareth), includes the Golan Heights; (2) Haifa (Haifa); (3) Central (Ramla); (4) Tel Aviv (Tel Aviv); (5) Jerusalem (Jerusalem), includes East Jerusalem; and (6) Southern (Beersheba) (Figure 1). The districts are further divided into 15 subdistricts known as *nafot* (Hebrew: נפות; singular: nafa), which are themselves partitioned into 50 natural regions.

Israel is only 470 km in length and 135 km in width at the widest point, and covers 22,072 square kilometres, with the Golan Heights and East Jerusalem included. However, in spite of its relatively small size, the country has a very varied topography, characterised by four distinct landscapes:

(1) *The mountains in the north* include the Upper and Lower Galilee, (peak at 1,208 MASL), Mount Carmel (546 MASL), and the Golan Heights (2,814 MASL). The Golan Heights are located east-northeast of the Sea of Galilee (also known as Lake Tiberias and Lake Kinneret), reaching the Syrian border, and has been administered as part of Israel under the Golan Heights Law passed by the Israeli *Knesset* since 1981.

(2) *The Negev Desert* in the southern part of Israel has a long border with the Sinai and covers approximately 60% of the country. The Negev is sparsely populated but is home to most of the Bedouin in Israel.

(3) *The Rift Valley* was formed by a long fissure due to tectonic pressures and runs from Mozambique in East Africa in the south through the Red Sea and the length of Israel and ends in Lebanon in the north. The Jordan River flows southward in the Rift, and one of its tributaries, Dan River, flows into the Hula Valley and then into the Sea of Galilee. This lake lies 209 m below sea level and is the main source of freshwater in Israel. The Jordan River continues south through the Jordan Valley until it reaches the Dead Sea. This sea is extremely saline (Figure 2), with a salinity of 34.2%, and at 400 m below sea level, is the lowest point in the world (Figure 3). The border between Israel and Jordan runs through the Dead Sea, from which both countries extract minerals, in particular potash. The Rift Valley continues south, forming the Aravah, till it reaches Eilat, a port on the Red Sea.

Figure 2.   Salt crystals on shore of Dead Sea. *Photo credit*: A. Allan Degen.

Figure 3.   Dead Sea: lowest point on Earth. *Photo credit*: A. Allan Degen.

The Aravah is an extreme desert with a mean annual rainfall of 25 mm and summer air temperatures commonly above 45°C.

(4) *The coastal plain* runs parallel to the Mediterranean Sea and extends up to 40 km inland. More than half of Israel's population lives in the

coastal plain, which contains the main major urban centres, deep-water harbours, and most of the country's industry, agriculture and tourist facilities.

In 2018, the population of Israel reached 9,021,000 people, of whom 74.2% were Jews, 20.9% Arabs, and 4.8% others, and it is estimated that, in 2021, there will be 9,338,740 people. The number of Jews in Israel comprise approximately 45% of the Jews in the world and, of the Jews residing in Israel, 75% were born in Israel and 25% immigrated to Israel (called *aliyah*, meaning going up) by way of the Law of Return. By this law, all Jews and their ancestors in the world are granted the right to live in Israel and become Israeli citizens. Of the Jews in Israel, about 44.9% are Sephardi (includes Sephardi and Mizraḥi Jews), 44.2% are Ashkenazi, 3.0% are Beta Israel, and 7.9% are others, which include Cochin Jews, Bene Israel, and Kariate Jews. Sephardi, meaning Spanish, are Jews who originated mainly in Spain and also in Portugal; whereas, Mizraḥi, meaning eastern, are Jews who arrived from the Middle East and Central Asia, and generally had lived under Muslim rule for many generations (Danon, 2018). Ashkenazi is applied to all Jews who originated in Europe, Beta Israel came from Ethiopia, and Cochin Jews and Bene Israel came from India. The Arabs are mainly Muslims, although there are also Christian Arabs. By religion, 74.2% follow Judaism, 17.8% Islam, 2.0% Christianity, 1.6% Druze, and 4.4% other religions. Jerusalem is of special importance to Judaism, Islam, and Christianity, the three Abrahamic religions, as the Western Wall and the Temple Mount, the Al-Aqsa Mosque and the Church of the Holy Sepulchre are all found in the Old City (Figure 4). In Judaism, the practice of religion varies widely, ranging from secular (*ḥiloni*) to ultra-orthodox (*ḥaredi*). In addition, Sephardi and Ashkenazi Jews pray differently, have many different traditions, attend different synagogues, and each has its own chief rabbi. Muslims are mainly Sunni, although there are some Shia, Ahmadiyeh, Sufi, Shazaliyeh, and Alawite. Circassians in Israel are non-Arab, predominantly Sunni Muslims. The Druze religion developed from Ismaili Islam; however, they do not identify themselves as Muslims but practise a secretive religion and call themselves *Ahl al-Tawhid* (People of Unitarianism or Monotheism). Among the Christians,

Figure 4.   Jerusalem with the wall in front and the Dome of the Rock Mosque in the centre. *Photo credit*: A. Allan Degen.

more than 75% are Arab Christians, while there are also Greek Orthodox, Russian Orthodox (Figure 5), Aramean, Armenian, Assyrian, and Copt Christians. In addition, the Baha'i is a monotheistic religion in which the centre is located in Haifa. The followers of this religion are guided by three principals: the unity of God, the unity of religion, and the unity of humanity.

Hebrew is the official language in Israel; Arabic was a second official language till 2018, when the Israeli *knesset* (parliament) designated it as a language of "special status in the state". English was the official state language during the British Mandate and is still used widely today. Road signs include English, alongside Hebrew and Arabic (Figure 6), official documents are often written in English, media use English subtitles and English is commonly used in universities. The other languages spoken in Israel include Russian, French, Amharic, and Spanish. Literacy rate in Israel stands at 97.8%, and 49% of the 25–64 age group has attained tertiary education. This latter percentage ranks third among the 37 Organisation for Economic Co-operation and Development (OECD) countries, which average 35% overall (OECD, 2016).

Figure 5.   Russian orthodox Church in Jerusalem; *Photo credit*: A. Allan Degen.

Figure 6.   Road sign warning drivers to be aware of camels near the road in English, Arabic, and Hebrew; *Photo credit*: A. Allan Degen.

In 2020, the estimated gross domestic product (GDP) in terms of purchasing power parity (PPP), which reflects the differences in cost of living and inflation rates of countries, totalled USD 372.3 billion and averaged USD 40,336 per capita; whereas, the nominal GDP totalled USD 410.5 billion and averaged USD 44,474 per capita, which ranked 31st of 193 countries in 2019 (IMF, 2020). In 2019, Israel had a human development index (HDI) of 0.919, which is considered a very high level and ranked 19th of 189 countries, and in 2018, had a Gini index of 34.8, which is considered a medium rank. HDI is a composite index that includes life expectancy, education, and per capita income, while the Gini index represents the income or wealth inequality within a nation. In September 2010, Israel became the 33rd member to join the OECD. Israel, with a score of 73.8, ranks second of 14 countries in the Middle East and North Africa and 26th of 184 countries in the freedom economic index. "Economic freedom is the fundamental right of every human to control his or her own labour and property. In an economically free society, individuals are free to work, produce, consume, and invest in any way they please. In economically free societies, governments allow labour, capital, and goods to move freely, and refrain from coercion or constraint of liberty beyond the extent necessary to protect and maintain liberty itself. The index covers 12 freedoms — from property rights to financial freedom" (Economic Freedom, 2021). In 2017, Israel exported goods totalling USD 60.6 billion which included mainly machinery and equipment, software, cut diamonds, agricultural products, chemicals, and textiles and apparel; and imported goods totalling USD 66.8 billion, which included raw materials, military equipment, investment goods, rough diamonds, fuels, grain, and consumer goods (World Factbook, 2021). The World Economic Forum's Global Competitiveness Report ranked Israel 16th (Schwab, 2017), whereas the World Bank's Ease of Doing Business ranked Israel 54th in the world.

2. Prior to the Establishment of the State of Israel

There has been a presence of Jews in Israel since biblical times. Abraham came to Canaan in approximately 1700 BCE and bought a burial plot for his wife Sarah at the *Cave of Machpela* (Hebrew: מְעָרַת הַמַּכְפֵּלָה, Me'arat HaMakhpela; cave of the double tombs or cave of the double caves) in

Hebron at a cost of 400 shekels in silver. It was important for Abraham to pay the full price of the land so that he owned the property. Abraham was also buried at the *Cave of Machpela* as were Isaac, Abraham's son; Rebecca, Isaac's wife; and Jacob, Isaac's son. About 900 BCE, after King Solomon's reign, the land was divided into the Kingdom of Israel in the north and the Kingdom of Judah in the south. King Solomon had built the first temple which was destroyed by Nebuchadnezzar II, King of Babylonia, who also exiled the Jews in 586 BCE. Cyrus the Great, a Persian, conquered the land and allowed the Jews to return in 538 BCE, when the second temple was built. The Macedonians, under Alexander the Great, conquered the land, including Judea, in 332 BCE. In 70 CE, the Romans captured Jerusalem, destroyed the second temple and expelled many of the Jews. In the 7th century CE, with the rise of Islam, the Muslim Arabs conquered the land, including Jerusalem. The Crusaders invaded and conquered Jerusalem in the First Crusade, in 1096–1099, massacring many Muslims and Jews who fought side by side. Sultan Saladin defeated the Crusaders in 1187 and took control of Jerusalem and most of the surrounding land. Saladin invited the Jews to return to Jerusalem; many did and settled there. In 1260, the Mameluks took control, eradicating any remaining crusaders and made life difficult for the Jews with anti-semitic (anti-*dhimmī*) actions. They stayed in power till 1516, when they were defeated by the Ottomans. The Ottoman Empire ruled till 1917, when it was defeated by the British. The British received the mandate to administer what was called Mandatory Palestine.

3. Establishment of the State of Israel, Wars and Peace Treaties

Many Jews immigrated to Israel before the establishment of the State. The first *aliyah* to Israel took place between 1881 and 1903, with 25,000 to 35,000 Jews who were escaping pogroms from Eastern Europe and Russia. Pogroms are violent riots aimed at destroying Jews. At this time, and prior to the first *aliyah*, a small number of Jews from Yemen also immigrated to Palestine. With funding mainly from the Rothschild Family, Jews in Palestine established settlements and purchased 350,000 dunams of land. It was in this period that Theodor Herzl, an Austro-Hungarian

Jewish writer, published *Der Judenstaat* (The Jewish State) in which he presented his ideas on establishing a Jewish state as a safe refuge for European Jews. Herzl was credited with founding Zionism and, in 1897, chaired the First Zionist Congress held in Basel, Switzerland. A statement issued from the Congress declared, "Zionism seeks to establish a home for the Jewish people in Eretz Israel secured under public law".

The second *aliyah* took place between 1904 and 1914 mainly due to the pogroms in Kishenev, Moldavia. Approximately 40,000 Jews immigrated to Palestine and, like the first *aliyah*, most of the immigrants were non-Zionist orthodox Jews, who came to Israel to escape economic hardships and persecution due to anti-Semitism. However, there were also some Zionist-socialists, who were instrumental in establishing the kibbutz movement. In 1917, the Balfour Declaration was sent to Baron Rothschild by Arthur Balfour stating the intention of creating a Jewish State in Palestine. The League of Nations granted Britain the Mandate to Palestine in 1922, and this included the activation of the Balfour Declaration. Jews comprised approximately 11% of the population at this time, with Muslim Arabs comprising most of the rest. The third *aliyah* took place between 1919 and 1923 and the fourth *aliyah*, between 1924 and 1929, when approximately 100,000 Jews immigrated. The fifth *aliyah*, of approximately 250,000 Jews from Europe and Asia, took place between 1929 and 1939 because of the rise of Nazism and increased anti-Semitism. In 1946, the Jews reached 31% of the population in Palestine. On 29 November 1947, under General Assembly Resolution 181, the United Nations voted to partition British-ruled Palestine Mandate into a Jewish state and an Arab state. On 14 May 1948, one day before the British ended its mandate in Palestine, David Ben-Gurion, head of the Jewish Agency, declared that "the establishment of a Jewish state in Eretz-Israel (Land of Israel), to be known as the State of Israel" (Figure 7).

The day following the declaration, Egypt, Transjordan, Syria, and Iraq, with support from Yemen, Morocco, Saudi Arabia, and Sudan, launched the 1948 Arab–Israeli war. The war lasted 10 months and after the cease fire, Israel controlled the land under Resolution 181 and almost 60% of the land designated for Jordan under the partition plan. Jordan controlled the West Bank, including Jerusalem, and Egypt controlled Gaza. Approximately 700,000 Palestinians were expelled or fled Israel

Figure 7. David Ben-Gurion (First Prime Minister of Israel) publicly pronouncing the declaration of the State of Israel, 14 May 1948, Tel Aviv, Israel, beneath a large portrait of Theodor Herzl, founder of modern political Zionism, in the old Tel Aviv Museum of Art building on Rothshild St.; photo © Rudi Weissenstein.

Source: Ministry of Foreign Affairs, Public Domain, https://commons.wikimedia.org/w/index. php?curid=33261039.

and became Palestinian refugees, whereas 156,000 Palestinians remained and became citizens of Israel. This war has been labelled as the *Nakba* (the catastrophe) by the Palestinians. In 1949, Israel was voted in as a member of the United Nations. During the first three years of the State of Israel, the number of Jews doubled from 700,000 to 1,400,000 as Holocaust survivors and Jews from Arab countries made *aliyah* to Israel. From the beginning, Israel was led politically by the Labour Party under the leadership of David Ben-Gurion, and the kibbutz movement had a leading role in the new state. Since 1948, approximately 3.3 million Jews immigrated to Israel and of this total, 1.46 million (44.3%) arrived from 1990 onward. In 2019, 33,250 Jews immigrated to Israel, slightly less than half were from Russia (CBS, 2020).

In 1956, Gamal Abdul Nasser nationalised the Suez Canal, which was owned primarily by France and Britain. Egypt had closed the Straits of Tiran and the Gulf of Aqaba to Israeli shipping since 1950. This crisis led to the second war between the Arabs and Israelis, called the Suez War. With the backing of France and Britain, Israel defeated the Egyptian forces and captured the land till the Suez Canal and opened shipping through the Gulf of Aqaba. Under pressure from the United States and Russia, Israel was forced to withdraw, and a United Nations Emergency Force (UNEF) was stationed along the border between Egypt and Israel. As part of the agreement, Israel was guaranteed that the Straits of Tiran would remain open. However, in 1967, Nasser closed the Straits of Tiran to Israeli shipping, mobilised Egyptian forces, and had the UNEF removed. This led to the third Arab–Israeli war, named the Six-Day War. Israel defeated Egypt and captured Sinai and Gaza Strip. In addition, Israel captured the West Bank, including Jerusalem from Jordan, and the Golan Heights from Syria. This provided Jews with access to holy sites in Jerusalem, which had been denied by Jordan since the creation of the State of Israel. Approximately 300,000 Palestinians fled the West Bank and 100,000 Syrians fled the Golan Heights. The fourth Arab–Israeli war was in 1973 on Yom Kippur, a holy day of prayer and fast for Jewish people, and was named the Yom Kippur War. Israel was attacked by Egypt, under the command of Anwar Sadat, and by Syria, under the command of Hafez al-Assad; Israel was led by Golda Meir, Israel's fourth prime minister and a member of Kibbutz Revivim. Israel was caught unprepared for this attack, but after suffering many casualties, the Israeli army advanced into Syrian territory in the north and crossed the Suez Canal into Egypt in the south. The Israeli army established a presence on the west bank of the Suez Canal and encircled the Egyptian Third Army. A disengagement treaty between Israel and Egypt was signed on November 1973 and between Israel and Syria on May 1974. The new border between Egypt and Israel was set at the Mitla and Gidi passes in the Sinai and a UN peace keeping force was stationed between the countries. In 1978, under the Camp David Accords and brokered by US President Jimmy Carter, Egypt received control of the whole Sinai Desert and, in return, recognised Israel's right to exist. In 1979, Israel, under Likud Prime Minister

Figure 8.   President Jimmy Carter shaking hands with Egyptian President Anwar Sadat and Israeli Prime Minister Menachem Begin at the signing of the Egyptian–Israeli Peace Treaty on the grounds of the White House; photo © *U.S. News & World Report.*

Source: United States Library of Congress, Public Domain, https://commons.wikimedia. org/w/index.php?curid=2821924.

Menachem Begin, and Egypt, under President Anwar Sadat, signed a peace treaty, which established normal diplomatic relations between the two countries (Figure 8).

Following continued skirmishes between Israel and the Palestinian Liberation Organization (PLO) operating in Southern Lebanon, the First Lebanon War started in 1982, when Israel invaded Lebanon, almost reached Beirut, and surrounded the PLO. The PLO members, under Yasser Arafat, were allowed to leave and set up operations in Tunisia. The Israeli army withdrew from Lebanon by 1985. The Second Lebanon War started in 2006 when Hezbollah, a militant organisation supported by Iran, fired rockets at Israeli settlements from Southern Lebanon. The war, which left many casualties and displaced people, lasted for 34 days. A United Nations Security Council Resolution, approved by both the Lebanese and Israeli governments, called for disarmament of Hezbollah, withdrawal of the Israeli Defense Forces (IDF) from Lebanon, and the deployment of Lebanese Armed Forces and a United Nations Interim Force in Lebanon (UNIFIL) in the south. Most Israeli troops left Southern Lebanon by October 2006. In addition to the wars with surrounding Arab countries, there were also violent riots in the West Bank, Gaza, and within Israel called *intifadas*. The first *intifada* started in December 1987 and ended in 1993, a time when the Oslo Accords were signed. The second *intifada* lasted from September 2000 to 2005. Rocket fire between Gaza, mainly Hamas under Ismail Haniyah, and Israel has been a continual occurrence over the years, with large outbreaks in 2008, 2012, 2014, and 2021.

In October 1994, a peace treaty, brokered by US President Bill Clinton, was signed between the Hashemite Kingdom of Jordan, under King Hussein, and the State of Israel, under Prime Minister Yitzhak Rabin, in which land and water disputes were settled and cooperation in tourism and trade were encouraged. Recently, normalisation agreements brokered by President Donald Trump were signed between Israel and four Arab countries. The agreements were under the framework of the Abraham Accords Peace Agreements: Treaty of Peace, Diplomatic Relations and Full Normalisation. In August 2020, the United Arab Emirates (UAE) was the first Persian Gulf country to normalise relationships with Israel: "The nations agreed to approve bilateral agreements on 15 areas of mutual interest, including finance, trade, aviation, energy, telecommunications, health, agriculture and water" (Riechmann *et al.*, 2020). The agreement was announced by Prime Minister Benjamin Netanyahu for Israel and Abu Dhabi's Crown Prince Mohammed bin Zayed Al Nahyan for UAE. Direct flights between the countries have been initiated. At the signing was Bahraini Foreign Minister Abdullatif al-Zayani representing Bahrain's King Hamad, who pledged "to advance diplomacy, mutual cooperation and regional peace" with Israel (Riechmann *et al.*, 2020). In October 2020, an announcement was made that Sudan and Israel will normalise relationships and end the state of belligerence between their nations. The leaders also agreed that delegations will negotiate agreements of cooperation in economic and trade relationships as well as in agriculture technology, aviation, migration issues, and other areas for the benefit of the two peoples. The agreement was signed between the countries in January 2021. In December 2020,

Morocco, under the leadership of King Mohammed VI, agreed to "resume diplomatic relations between Morocco and Israel and expand economic and cultural co-operation to advance regional stability" (BBC, 2020). Morocco became the sixth Arab country to normalise relationships with Israel and, here too, direct flights between the two countries have been initiated.

4. First Kibbutzim and Ideology

The first kibbutzim were established by Ashkenazi *olim* (immigrants) from Eastern Europe in the early 1900s. This was during the Ottoman Empire at the time of the second *aliyah*. Most kibbutzim, however, were established during the British mandate in the 1930s and 1940s, before the creation of the State of Israel in 1948 (Abramitzky, 2011). Many hardships were involved in starting the first kibbutzim — swamps had to be drained and malaria, typhus, and cholera were widespread. In addition, the settlements were attacked and robbed frequently by Bedouin living in the vicinity. By combining resources in a commune, it was possible for the *olim* to survive the adverse conditions.,

The first form of a kibbutz in Israel was created in 1909 at Umm Juni on the southwest end of the Sea of Galilee on land purchased by *Keren Kayemet Leisra'el* (the Jewish National Fund). Seven Zionist-socialist men from Russia, who immigrated to Palestine during the second *aliyah*, settled on the commune. Although regarded as relatively successful, the commune disbanded after one year. A group of 12 teenage immigrants from Russia, 10 men and two women, known as the "Hadera Commune" (Figure 9), leased the land in 1910, and called the commune *Kvutzat* Degania (meaning, team of cereal grains). Degania (later called Degania Aleph) became to be recognised as the "Mother of the *kevuzot*" and was used as a blueprint for kibbutzim (Figure 10). By 1914, there were 50 members (CIE, 2021). The members wanted a small commune, so when numbers began to rise, another *kvutzah*, Degania Bet, was established in 1920 on land provided by Degania Aleph (Figure 11). Degania Bet was considered the first organised kibbutz and one of its founders, Levi Eshkol, was the third prime minister of Israel. In 1932, Degania Bet allotted a tract of land for the establishment of Kibbutz Afikim. All three kibbutzim exist today: Degania Aleph with over 500 people, Degania Bet

Figure 9. Some members of the Hadera Commune.

Source: https://israeled.org/degania-alef-established-as-first-kibbutz-in-israel/.

Figure 10. People working on Kibbutz Degania Aleph; photo © Yaakov Ben Dov: The Israel Internet Association.

Source: PikiWiki Israel 52619 kibbutz degania.jpg — Israel free image collection project, Public Domain.

Figure 11.   Degania Alef and Degania Bet at Lake Kinneret; photo © Ben Herzberg. *Source*: Public Domain, CC BY-SA 3.0, https://commons.wikimedia.org/w/index. php?curid=1278656.

with over 650 people (Orni & Gilboa, 2008; NJOP, 2018) and Afikim with approximately 1,500 people (ICBS, 2019).

The early kibbutzim were established by *olim* with very strong egalitarian beliefs by "putting the commune before the individual". For many kibbutz members, the ideology started before their arrival in Palestine when they belonged to a Zionist-socialist group, such as *Ha'shomer Ha'tza'ir*, in Eastern Europe. The kibbutz was envisioned as a commune of utopian socialism, based on an egalitarian society according to the principles, "from each according to his ability, to each according to his needs" (Fogiel-Bijaoui, 2007). It was conceived as a rural community, wholly engaged in agriculture, without employing outside labour (Spiro, 2004; Moscovitch & Achouch, 2015). The hiring of outside workers was looked upon as "exploitation" (Abramitzky, 2011). Economic equality was achieved by collective ownership of all property, which included land, housing, and producer and consumer goods. All members of the commune received the same wage or personal budget, independent of the work they did or skills they possessed. Political equality was implemented by rotating leadership positions every three years and any decision affecting the kibbutz had to be discussed and approved by the general assembly (Palgi & Getz, 2014). Leadership positions did not receive special privileges and most members preferred not to be elected to these positions. Meals were eaten together in a communal dining hall, and education was provided by a collective education system on the kibbutz (Figure 12). Education was intended to instil altruism and socialist and Zionist values, as well as "encouraging high work ethics and norms, cooperation, an extended-family approach, caring about the collective more than about oneself, and having meaningful service in the army" (Abramitzsky, 2011). Traditional higher education was discouraged, as was attaining the *bagrut* diploma (high school diploma). In fact, college education was not permitted and

Figure 12.   Degania Elementary School; photo © קוסמוס תל אביב.

Source: PikiWiki Israel 5734 school at Deganya.jpg, https://commons.wikimedia.org/wiki/
Category:Degania_Alef#/media/File:PikiWiki_Israel_5734_school_at_Deganya.jpg.

any member wishing to study outside the kibbutz had to obtain permission. As expressed by Zilbersheid (2007), "Israeli kibbutzim constituted a radical transformation of human nature into a new, better nature: private property and exploitation were abolished; organisational aspects analogous to the state were also abolished; and labour was partially turned into non-instrumental activity. The Israeli welfare state created a supportive framework for the utopian experiment in the kibbutzim by reducing to power of the free market". All male members received the same clothing, as did all female members (Spiro, 2004). When members handed in their clothes to be washed, they would not receive the same set of clothes in return. Gender equality was stressed as part of the kibbutz ideology. To allow women to work freely, children were raised together in children's houses according to ages. Children slept together in a children's house in most kibbutzim (Bettelheim, 1969). In fact, some members believed the children belonged to the kibbutz and not to a family. Nonetheless, gender inequality existed, and some of the traditional male–female roles were evident. Agriculture, looked upon as productive and prestigious, was done almost entirely by men, while services, such as kitchen duties, laundry (Figure 13), and childcare, all seen as non-productive activities, were done almost entirely by women (Fogiel-Bijaoui, 2007). Men usually were in charge of the secretariat of the kibbutz and women were under-represented in the committees. It should be pointed out, however, that about 75% of the *olim* arriving in Israel were men and, consequently, most of the kibbutz members were men.

By 1950, two years after the establishment of the state of Israel, approximately 67,000 Israelis, or 7.5%t of the country's population, resided on kibbutzim. Kibbutzim played a key role in Israel's agricultural development and in its defence and political leadership. Early kibbutzim were often positioned strategically along borders and outlying areas to defend the country. Many top politicians and military and industry leaders, particularly in the 1950s and 1960s, were from kibbutzim. At first, members led a spartan existence without extra frills, such as make-up for women, fancy clothes and air-conditioning in the homes. Housing consisted of the bare minimum, usually just sufficient for sleeping accommodations. This lifestyle continued until the early 1970s when

Figure 13.   Laundress: A woman washes laundry on Kibbutz Rodges (1930–1940).
Source: The Archive of the Religious Kibbutz, PikiWiki website, https://jwa.org/media/
laundress-kibbutz-rodges-ca-1930.

"the generation of kibbutz founders was still dominant in kibbutz management and kibbutz life was carried on with restraint, privately and conservatively, without undue expenses devoted to raising the standard of living" (Askenazi & Katz, 2009). However, the second generation of kibbutz members, the children of the founders, did not share the same rigid philosophy of equal sharing as their parents. They preferred more privacy and better living conditions, which included more household furniture and appliances and some private land (Ashkenazi & Katz, 2009). In addition, industry started developing in kibbutzim in the 1920s and 1930s, and by the 1950s and 1960s, with the rise of industry in Israel, income from industry increasingly became an important source of income in most kibbutzim (Figure 14) and surpassed income from agriculture (Moskovich

Figure 14.   Factory and salesroom of mattresses from "Polyron" at Kibbutz Zikim; photo © Jaim Sivan.

& Achouch, 2015). New technologies were developing in Israel and in kibbutzim, in particular in the use of plastics in the field of irrigation equipment (Figure 15) (Almaliach, 2009).

5. Financial Crisis of the 1980s and Recovery of Kibbutzim

The standard of living was always higher in kibbutzim than in the rest of Israel. Many kibbutzim borrowed heavily from the banks in the 1970s and 1980s to satisfy the requests of members, in particular to improve housing and to expand industries. It was easy and cheap for kibbutzim to borrow money because inflation, which reached a peak of 445% in 1984, was very high and loans were often not linked to the rate of inflation. More importantly, kibbutzim were supported by the Labour Party, which traditionally helped kibbutzim with easy loan repayments and many subsidies.

Figure 15.   Irrigation equipment sold at "Netafim" at Kibbutz Hatzerim. The kibbutz has sales worldwide designing irrigation systems; photo © A. Allan Degen.

However, the Likud Party, under Prime Minister Menachem Begin, formed the government in 1977, and government policies no longer favoured such support for kibbutzim (Moskovich, 2007). In 1985, Israel instituted the "Price Stabilization Act", causing the rate of inflation to fall substantially (Ashkenazi & Katz, 2009) and interest rates on loans to increase to high levels. Many government subsidies, which were once offered to the kibbutzim, were removed, and with the sudden shift in the economic policy to stabilise prices, many kibbutzim found themselves with huge debts they could not repay. Eventually, some of the loans were erased and others were modified, but living standards in many kibbutzim fell considerably (Abramzky, 2011). Close to a third of the kibbutzim were almost bankrupt, and over 20% of the members, many of the younger generation, left kibbutzim between 1983 and 1995 (Abramitzky, 2009; Ben-Rafael, 2011; Casakin & Reizer, 2017). Individuals applying to enter the kibbutz during this period had less skills and earned 20% less than the average Israeli population. To control this "negative flow" of members, kibbutzim, in 1985, established a special centralised organisation which screened individuals and did not accept those with especially low education or skills (Abramizky, 2011). Kibbutzim were forced to negotiate new terms for their debts with a government that insisted on market-oriented reforms. Some debts were financed by wealthier kibbutzim (Ashkenazi & Hess, 2009), while members that remained on the kibbutzim called for reforms (Russell *et al.*, 2011).

Consequently, from 1990, kibbutzim underwent major changes due to the new economic status and shifted from a socialist to a more capitalist orientation (Palgi, 2002; Moskovich & Achouch, 2013). The transformation in the "renewed kibbutz" took place in three key areas (Ben-Raphael, 1997; Casakin & Reizer, 2017): "(1) administration, which involved the shift of a community management style to a separation between management, and community living in the kibbutz; (2) the privatisation process, which facilitated the personal and financial independence of the members such that economic rights were transferred in a variety of areas like education, home maintenance, pensions, and health with kibbutz members allowed to use private funds for personal needs; and (3) segregation of the collective system, which was reflected in the inclusion of new residents, the selection of external workers for jobs in local industries, and the construction of new housing, infrastructure, and services".

Kibbutzim attempted to maintain as many communal values as possible but, to ensure their sustainability, "were forced to adopt principles of the capitalistic neo-liberal economy" (Palgi & Getz, 2014). As part of the privatisation process, members were advised to start private bank accounts so that they could transfer funds which remained from their personal allowances (Ashkenazi & Hess, 2009). Some kibbutzim introduced other major reforms, such as abolishing the traditional dining hall. According to the report of the Public Committee for the Kibbutzim (also known as the Ben Rafael Committee) in 2003, "60% of the kibbutzim were practically insolvent, and 80% of them could not repay their debts" (Ben-Rafael, 2011). In addition, the kibbutzim faced a demographic crisis. There was a rise in number of people living in kibbutzim till 1990 and decline afterward. Two of the main changes that took place were the reorganisation of the communal way of life by way of privatisation and the granting of permission for newcomers to join the kibbutz in differentiated statuses. As of 2004, the majority of kibbutzim adopted a "safety net" model, whereby members keep some fraction of their earnings and shared the rest with their fellow members.

The relaxation of the strict principle of self-labour by kibbutzim enabled employment of more outside workers, especially in seasonal agricultural work and in industry. This process was encouraged by kibbutz members who preferred employment of their choosing, and the percentage of members working outside the kibbutz rose (Palgi & Orchan, 2007). In 2011, about 40% of kibbutz members worked outside the kibbutz, up from about 25% in 1994 (Palgi & Getz, 2014). Kibbutzim rented houses, especially, but not only, to people who worked in the kibbutz as paid labourers, which provided additional income to the kibbutz (Greenberg *et al.*, 2016).

Privatisation had set in, with the most far-reaching changes as follows: (1) the implementation of non-equal salaries to individual members; (2) dividing kibbutz shares among members; and (3) allowing members the right of home ownership (Palgi, 2002, 2006; Ben Rafael & Topel, 2009; Getz, 2017). With the differential salary among members, the "kibbutz deducted high progressive community taxes which were used as a safety net for the members. In addition, all members had to pay a fixed tax for municipal expenses such as gardening, garbage disposal, and road/pavement construction". Kibbutzim adopting the differential salary method were considered as a "renewed kibbutz" according to Israeli legal regulations (Manor, 2004; Ben-Rafael & Topel, 2011, Russell *et al.*, 2011). Consumption services, which were traditionally distributed freely according to need, were now purchased (Arbel, 2013). In this way, members could choose the services wanted, making it a more efficient system. Towards the end of the 20th century, kibbutzim sold land at the periphery to enable the building of homes adjacent to the kibbutz, whose residents would not be kibbutz members (Charney & Palgi, 2013).

After the departure of many young and qualified members, kibbutz industries began to hire external professional managers (Almaliach, 2009). Profitability became the main concern for kibbutz industries, eroding some of the aims and principles of the original kibbutzim. In the past, the Kibbutz General Assembly (KGA) made decisions for industries. However, the frequent rotations of plant managers caused a lack of continuity in policy and was inefficient. Today, industries are run by elected board of directors, comprising kibbutz members and outsiders, who make the decisions, and members receive reports (Palgi, 2006). The board of directors decide on the managers, many of whom are outsiders and who are hired for longer tenures (Raz, 2009). The old managerial style, which provided kibbutz members with preferential appointments to positions, was disbanded. Under the new policies, the trend is not to favour kibbutz members and workers for positions and workers can be fired, even kibbutz members. The industry is much more selective in the hiring of people for the positions, with the new appointment slogan, "The right person for the job in the right place".

In essence, industry was separated from the kibbutz and acted as an independent economic entity, with equality among all workers. Kibbutzim sold shares of their industries on the stock exchange and formed partnerships with non-kibbutz firms (Moskovich & Achouch, 2015; Moskovich, 2020). By 2018–2019, only 49% of the industries was owned by a single kibbutz, 30% had shared-ownership with non-kibbutz entities, 13% had shared ownership with other kibbutzim, and 8% had shares traded on the stock market (Kibbutz Movement, 2020).

6. Kibbutzim Today

Abramitzky (2011) reasoned that there were three reasons why an equal-sharing arrangement in a commune was unlikely to be successful: "First, high-ability members have an incentive to exit equal sharing arrangements to earn a wage premium — so-called 'brain drain'. Second, low-ability individuals have an incentive to enter equal-sharing arrangements so that they can be subsidised by more-able individuals — so-called adverse selection. Third, in context of equal sharing, shirking and free-riding are likely to be prevalent". However, in testing his premise, it was found that in all years, kibbutz members work longer hours than the population average and more so for richer kibbutzim. Therefore, shirking work could be ruled out. And some kibbutzim maintained the equal-sharing policy, albeit a minority of the kibbutzim. Kibbutzim have survived because of their flexibility, and it appears that changes will be made in the future should there be a need.

Figure 16. Kibbutz Ziqim showing a typical kibbutz entrance with a gate that can be controlled remotely by a code known by all members; photo © Jaim Sivan.

Although the kibbutz underwent many changes, even upheavals, over the years, the general design of the kibbutz remained the same. Each kibbutz has a main entrance (Figure 16) and a main circular road leading to the homes, industries, and agriculture, which returns to the exit of the kibbutz (Figure 17). Many kibbutzim accept temporary volunteers, and some run combined kibbutz *ulpan* programmes, which teach the Hebrew language to new *olim* and volunteers. A number of young Israelis are establishing urban kibbutzim, called *irbutz* (*ir* means city). Members live communally in a developing urban area and work to strengthen the neighbourhood population and improve the surroundings. They retain their own assets but often have meals and holiday celebrations together. These kibbutzim are associated with Israel's national kibbutz movement.

All kibbutzim belong to the Kibbutz Federation, which is run democratically, and kibbutz representatives meet to decide on policies and budgets (Palgi, 2006). Of 264 kibbutzim, 249 (94.3%) are from *T'nuah HaKibbutzim* (*Takam*) and 15 (5.7%) are from *Kibbutzim Ha'Dati* (religious kibbutzim). Prior to 2000, kibbutzim were divided into the *Te'nuah Ha'kibbutzim Ha'Meuchdet*, (60%), *Kibbutzim Artzi* (32%), and *Kibbutzim*

Figure 17. A map of Kibbutz Ziqim at the entrance of the kibbutz. To the right, past the dotted lines are houses that were built by non-members after purchasing land from the kibbutz. On the left is the dairy operation of the kibbutz; photo © Jaim Sivan.

Ha-Dati (8%). The *Artzi* group was formed by a leftist Eastern European group called *Ha'shomer Ha'tzair*, and these kibbutzim held a higher degree of socialist ideology than the others. In 2000, *Artzi* and *Takam* united.

Kibbutzim are formally registered as communal associations — *Aguda Shitufit*. Prior to 2005, to be recognised as a kibbutz by the government, the settlement had to be based on collective and equal ownership, as well as on common production, consumption, and education. However, with the changes in the structure of the kibbutz, in 2002, the Israeli government appointed a committee, with Eliezer Ben Rafael as chair, to redefine the kibbutz. The committee's recommendation was accepted in

2004 on the classification of two types of kibbutzim as follows (Ashkenazi & Katz, 2009): "(1) The 'Communal Kibbutz': A cooperative society that is a separate settlement, organised on the basis of collective ownership of assets, self-employment, and equality and cooperation in production, consumption and education; and (2) The 'Renewed Kibbutz': A cooperative society that is a separate settlement, organised on the basis of collective partnership in assets, self-employment, equality and cooperation in production, consumption and education, that maintains mutual guarantee among its members, and whose articles of association include some or all of the following: (1) relative wages according to individual contribution or seniority; (2) allocation of apartments; and (3) allocation of production means to its members, excluding land, water and production quotas, provided that the cooperative society maintains control over the means of production and that its articles of association restrict the negotiability of allocated production means". In 2020, of a total of 264 kibbutzim, 39 (15%) were communal kibbutzim and 225 (85%) were renewed kibbutzim (Shlomo Getz, *personal communication*).

In 2008, there was a greater number of people joining than leaving the kibbutz; this was the first time in 20 years that this positive balance occurred and the trend has been continuing with the renewed model. Today, different kibbutzim admit people under three basic classifications. Some kibbutzim admit newcomers only as potential full members, in line with the traditional communal kibbutzim. Some kibbutzim have introduced a partial member status in which the admitted individual is economically independent of the kibbutz. These individuals do not transfer their income to the kibbutz and pay the kibbutz based on the services they use. A third status is a permanent resident in the kibbutz municipality who is not a kibbutz member. In 2018, approximately 179,100 people lived in kibbutzim, less than 2% of the Israeli population, with more than 70% in the periphery. According to districts, 87,200 (48.7%) lived in the North District, 18,100 (10.1%) in the Haifa District, 4,100 (2.2%) in Yehuda and Shomron District, 500 (0.3%) in the Tel Aviv District, 26,500 (14.8%) in the Central District, 4,800 (2.7%) in the Jerusalem District, and 37,900 (21.2%) in the South District. Approximately 6% of the kibbutzim have up to 200 people, 15% have 200–399 people, 26% have 400–599 people, 21% have 600–799 people, and 32% have greater than 800 people. Of the people on the kibbutz, 35% are members, 23% are children, 10% are special (potential members, etc.), and 32% are non-members (Kibbutz Movement, 2020).

In a 2018–2019 kibbutz report, 24% of the kibbutzim were considered to be in excellent financial status, 43% in good financial status, 28% in average financial status, and 5% in weak financial status. Industry earned 46.8 billion shekels, had more than 250 factories, and employed 26% of the kibbutz work force, with outside workers making up more than 45% of the workforce (Moskovich & Achouch, 2017). Agriculture earned 30.5 billion shekels, with 12.5 billion shekels (42%) from livestock and 17.9 billion shekels (58%) from fruits, vegetables, flowers, and crops. In livestock, poultry earned 6.2 billion shekels (20% of total agriculture), cattle earned 4.5 billion shekels (15%) (Figures 18 and 19), sheep/goats earned 1.1 billion shekels (4%), and others earned 0.7 billion (3%). Fruits earned 6.8 billion shekels (22% of the total agriculture), vegetables earned 5.8 billion shekels (19%), flowers earned 1.9 billion shekels (6%), citrus fruits

Figure 18.   Sign in front of the dairy operation at Kibbutz Zikim stating that there are 528 cows, 417 female calves, 183 male calves, and 16,832 kg milk daily; photo © Jaim Sivan.

Figure 19.   Dairy cows being fed at Kibbutz Zikim; photo © Jaim Sivan.

earned 1.3 billion (4%), and field crops earned 2.1 billion shekels (7%) (Kibbutz Movement, 2020). The kibbutz sector accounts for approximately 48% of the overall agricultural production of the country with similar holdings of the livestock sector and crop production. Moreover, they account for 91% of the national production of open field crops that require the cultivating of large agricultural areas. The contribution of kibbutzim to the national economy amounts to approximately 40% in agriculture, 9.2% in industrial output, 7.2% in industrial export, and 10% in tourism (Reitan *et al.*, 2019; Kibbutz Movement, 2020).

Almost all members of the kibbutzim voted to accept the model of the renewed kibbutz. Some members, mostly older people, opposed the new model as they felt it would compromise their principles and harm their quality of life (Ashkenazi & Hess, 2009). "The original Degania members may well have considered the current privatisation of kibbutzim to be a failure. Today, only 15 percent of kibbutz income is from agriculture, and most of the physical agricultural work is done by foreign workers — an idea which would have been anathema to the original kibbutzim. A substantial amount of kibbutz income still comes from industry, but now kibbutzim are also running commercial services that are increasingly profitable. Kibbutz-run commercial tourism has been particularly successful, and many kibbutzim boast beautiful guest houses and hotels" (Schultz, 2021). Much of the egalitarian ideology has been eroded. However, kibbutz members still elect members who are responsible for community management, and they still participate in discussions at kibbutz assemblies and in votes for making decisions relating to the management of the services. In addition, there is still cooperative ownership of land which has remained common property in the kibbutz. Somehow, despite all the changes, the feeling of equal sharing still permeates throughout the kibbutz.

Acknowledgements

We thank all the kibbutz members who provided me with information on the kibbutzim, in particular Jaim Sivan from Kibbutz Zikim and Avi Rosenstreich from Kibbutz Be'eri. We also thank Shlomo Getz (Institute for Research of the Kibbutz and the Cooperative Idea, University of Haifa, Haifa, Israel) and Ella Wasserman for data and material on kibbutzim.

References

Abramitzky, R. (2009). The effect of redistribution on migration: Evidence from the Israeli Kibbutz'. *Journal of Public Economics*, *93*(3–4), 498–511.

Abramitzky, R. (2011). Lessons from the kibbutz on the equality–incentives trade-off. *Journal of Economic Perspectives*, *25*(1), 185–208.

Almaliach, T. (2009). *The Kibbutz Industry 1923–2007 — Economic and Sociological Study*. Yad Ya'ari, Israel, Daliah [in Hebrew].

Arbel, S. (Ed.) (2013). *Kibbutz Movement Yearly Report: Data for 2011*. Tel Aviv, Israel: The Kibbutz Movement.

Ashkenazi, M. H. & Katz, Y. (2009). From cooperative to renewed kibbutz: The case of Kibbutz "Galil", Israel. *Middle Eastern Studies*, *45*(4), 571–592.

Bettelheim, B. (1969). *The Children of the Dream*. NY: Macmillan Co.

BBC (2020). Morocco latest country to normalise ties with Israel in US-brokered deal. Retrieved from https://www.bbc.com/news/world-africa-55266089.

Ben-Rafael, E. (1997). *Crisis and Transformation: The Kibbutz at Century's End*. NY: Suny Press.

Ben-Rafael, E. (2011). Kibbutz: Survival at risk. *Israel Studies, 16*(2), 81–108.

Ben-Rafael, E. & Topel, M. (2011). Redefining the kibbutz. In Palgi, M. & Reinharz, S. (eds.), *The Kibbutz at one Hundred: A Century of Crises and Reinvention*. NJ, USA: Transaction Publishers, pp. 249–258.

Casakin, H. & Reizer, A. (2017). Place attachment, residential satisfaction, and life satisfaction: Traditional and renewed kibbutz. *Journal of Human Behavior in the Social Environment, 27*(7), 639–655.

CBS (2019). Central Bureau of Statistics, Population in the Localities. Retrieved from https://en.wikipedia.org/wiki/Afikim#cite_note-Israelpopulations-1.

CBS (2020). Central Bureau of Statistics, Media Release, Immigration to Israel 2019. Retrieved from https://www.cbs.gov.il/en/mediarelease/pages/2020/immigration-to-israel-2019.aspx.

CIE (2021). First Kibbutz in Israel Is Established, Center for Israel Education. Retrieved from https://israeled.org/degania-alef-established-as-first-kibbutz-in-israel/.

Charney, I. & Palgi, M. (2013). Sorting procedures in enclosed rural communities: Admitting "people like us" into renewing kibbutzim in northern Israel. *Journal of Rural Studies, 31*, 47–54.

Danon, D. (2018). *What Do You Know? Sephardi vs. Mizrahi, Katz Center*. University of Pennsylvania. Retrieved from https://katz.sas.upenn.edu/resources/blog/what-do-you-know-sephardi-vs-mizrahi.

Economic Freedom (2021). Index of Economic Freedom, The Heritage Foundation. Retrieved from https://www.heritage.org/index/about.

Fogiel-Bijaoui, S. (2007). Women in the Kibbutz: The "Mixed Blessing" of Neo-Liberalism. *Nashim: A Journal of Jewish Women's Studies & Gender, 13*, 102–122.

Getz, S. (2017). *A Survey of Changes in the Kibbutzim*. Kibbutz Movement and the University of Haifa Institute for Study and Research of the Kibbutz and the Cooperative Idea, Haifa [in Hebrew].

Greenberg, Z., Cohen, A., & Mosek, A. (2016). Creating community partnership as foundation for community building: The case of the renewed kibbutz. *Journal of Community Practice, 24*(3), 283–301.

ICBS (2019). Israel Central Bureau of Statistics. Retrieved from https://www.cbs.gov.il/he/mediarelease/DocLib/2019/134/11_19_134b.pdf.

IMF (International Monetary Fund) (2020). World economic databases. Retrieved from https://www.imf.org/en/Publicatios/SPROLLs/world-economic-outlook-databases#sort=%40imfdate%20descending.

Kibbutz Movement (2020). *Annual Review #17. Data for 2018-2019*. Saint John, NB, Canada: Chooka Media Group.

Manor, R. (2004). The "renewed" kibbutz. *Journal of Rural Cooperation, 32*(1), 37–50.

Moskovich, Y. (2020). Management style in kibbutz industries. *Management Research Review, 43*(6), 691–715.

Moskovich, Y. & Achouch, Y. (2013). From collectivism to capitalism: Cultural change in a kibbutz factory in Israel. *Journal of Rural Cooperation, 41*(1), 80–95.

Moskovich, Y. & Achouch, Y. (2015). Metamorphosis of a kibbutz industry: An Israeli case study. *EuroMed Journal of Business, 10*(2), 181–197.

Moskovich, Y. & Achouch, Y. (2017). Family home culture and management-employee relationships: Comparing two kibbutz factories. *Journal of Co-operative Organization and Management, 5*, 95–107.

NJOP (2018). The Story of Degania. Retrieved from https://njop.org/the-story-of-degania/.

OECD (2016). Education at a Glance 2016: OECD Indicators. Retrieved from https://read.oecd-ilibrary.org/education/education-at-a-glance-2016/israel_eag-2016-63-en#page1.

Orni, E. & Gilboa, S. (2008). *Deganyah*, Encyclopaedia Judaica, 2nd Ed. Retrieved from https://www.jewishvirtuallibrary.org/deganyah.

Palgi, M. (2002). Organizational change and ideology: The case of the kibbutz. *International Review of Sociology, 12*(3), 389–402.

Palgi, M. (2006). Pitfalls of self-management in the kibbutz. *International Review of Sociology — Revue Internationale de Sociologie, 16*(1), 63–7.

Palgi, M. & Getz, S. (2014). Varieties in developing sustainability: The case of the Israeli kibbutz. *International Review of Sociology, 24*(1), 38–47.

Palgi, M. & Orchan, H. (2007). *Opinion Poll in the Kibbutzim*. Haifa, Israel: Institute for Research on the Kibbutz and the Cooperative Idea.

Raz, A. (2009). Transplanting management participative change, organizational development, and the glocalization of corporate culture. *The Journal of Applied Behavioral Science, 45*(2), 280–304.

Reitan, A., Rubin, O. D., Rubin, A., & Kimhi, A. (2019). Privatization, demographic growth, and perceived sustainability: Lessons from the Israeli renewing kibbutzim. *Sustainable Development, 27*(6), 1076–1084.

Riechmann, D., Lee, M., & Lemire, J. (2020). Israel signs pacts with two Arab states: A "new" Mideast? AP News. Retrieved from https://apnews.com/article/bahrain-israel-united-arab-emirates-middle-east-elections-7544b322a254ebea1693e387d83d9d8b.

Russell, R., Hanneman, R., & Getz, S. (2011). The transformation of the kibbutzim. *Israel Studies*, *16*(2), 109–126.

Schultz, R. G. (2021). The Kibbutz Movement. My Jewish Learning. Retrieved from https://www.myjewishlearning.com/article/the-kibbutz-movement/.

Schwab, K. (2017). The Global Competitiveness Report 2017–2018. World Economic Forum. Retrieved from http://www3.weforum.org/docs/GCR2017-2018/05FullReport/TheGlobalCompetitivenessReport2017%E2%80%932018.pdf.

Spiro, M. E. (2004). Utopia and its discontents: The kibbutz and its historical vicissitudes. *American Anthropologist*, *106*(3), 556–568.

World Factbook (2021). Explore all countries — Israel. Retrieved from https://www.cia.gov/the-world-factbook/countries/israel/.

Zilbersheid, U. (2007). The Israeli Kibbutz: From Utopia to Dystopia. *Critique*, *35*(3), 413–434.

https://doi.org/10.1142/9789811253799_0008

Chapter 8

Entrepreneurial Model for Sustaining Cooperatives with Special Reference to Dairy Cooperatives

Ashok Kumar Gupta[*,§], Anindita Baidya[†,¶], and Subhanwesha Mahapatra[‡,‖]

Group Head – Cooperative Training National Dairy Development Board, Anand, Gujarat, India

†*Senior Manager – Cooperative Training National Dairy Development Board, Anand, Gujarat, India*

‡*Senior Manager – Cooperative Training National Dairy Development Board, Anand, Gujarat, India*

§*akgupta@nddb.coop*

¶*abaidya@nddb.coop*

‖*subhan@nddb.coop*

Abstract

The dairy sector is undergoing huge changes in the present times. On the one hand, consumers are demanding wider choices of milk and milk products, and on the other, the dairy industry at the grassroot level is standing at a threshold between two generations, where the newer generation would take up dairying as a livelihood when it sees in it profit and promises of a better life. In India, dairying, as a small/medium-scale enterprise, has been instrumental in bringing socio-economic change by ensuring year-round income, self-employment options, enhancing nutrition status, and providing platform for developing leadership and managerial skills. However, in many areas, milk producers still face challenges of getting timely and quality input services.

The backbone of this highly complex industry is the milk producer. It is important to encourage young dairy entrepreneurs who could take up dairying as a profession and command a better life for self as well as facilitate growth for the society at large. The smart entrepreneurs can provide innovative and cost-effective solutions in a decentralised value chain. This can be an alternative to currently functional centralised value chain. It can be achieved by establishing a system to identify, groom, and handhold the aspirants in ventures in well-researched and localised business propositions which are cost-effective, efficient. An enterprise cannot be just perceived as an income-generation activity. It is far more-reaching than just earning money. The dairy entrepreneurship needs to thrive as an ecosystem where an individual or a group can play important roles in various units of the system and support each other in backward and forward linkages with innovations and services in breeding, feed and fodder, use of ICT in the value chain, tools and implementations, and decentralised quality-complied dairy product manufacturing. The enterprises, especially social enterprises, are vehicles of change where the social entrepreneurs can lead the society by taking the development process in their own hands and not depending merely on benefactors.

Keywords: dairy, entrepreneur, cooperatives, business, marketing

1. Introduction

The Earth is a complex system of interrelationships among the air, water, soil, animals, plants, and microbes. Prigogine calls it a nonlinear, dynamic system capable of performing in far-from-equilibrium conditions (Nicolis & Prigogine, 1989). From the age of Enlightenment to the stage of the Industrial Revolution, nature was dominantly perceived as a resource and a means to achieve economic goals.

Similarly, any enterprise in itself depends on many interdependent factors which contribute to each other directly or indirectly and as a whole influence the enterprise. Thus, an enterprise in itself can said to be an ecosystem or ecological niche, which has social, financial, and institutional factors interacting with each other. These factors can either be facilitating or inhibiting factors which affect the future path of the venture.

In India, cooperative business model is the back-bone of dairy industry. Efforts in capacity building throughout the dairy value chain have been instrumental in bringing socio-economic change by ensuring year-round income, self-employment options, enhancing nutrition status, and providing platform for developing leadership and managerial skills. However, in many areas, milk producers still face challenges in getting timely and quality input services.

Following are the challenges faced by the Indian dairy sector:

1. **Selection of cattle breed:** Choice of good lactating cattle breeds can minimise many future risks at the very initial stage. Most of the farmers are unaware about breed selection and lack the knowledge of genetic history of breeds. Furthermore, they induct new animals from distant regions or wherever available rather than select the breeds most suitable to the local climatic conditions.

2. **Managing lactation period of animals:** Lack of understanding and developing animal breeding plan to minimise the dry period and ensure continuous supply of milk throughout the year is another pertinent issue.

3. **Investment in feeding:** For a farmer, the investment on feeding is decided on his/her calculation of the income from milk. However, from the animal's health perspective, nutrition is crucial for ensuring good production. So, there is always a tussle between these two.

4. **Traditional feeding practices:** Traditional Indian feeding system consists of roughage-based feeding system. This system restricts the nutrition base feed for productive milch animals. Prevention of this system is only possible if green fodder supply to animal is ensured year round. There is always a dilemma between the scientist's recommendation of feed conversion and a farmer's perception of economising the cost of feed.

5. **Knowledge of dairy farming:** Most of the new dairy farm owners need to develop adequate knowledge of dairy animal management and farm management practices. Also, automation with modern tools and implementations has not been very effective yet. Therefore, if the new dairy farmers lack hands-on knowledge on dairying, s/he may have trouble in reaching profitability.

6. **Hygiene conditions in farm:** Improper shelter to cattle and leaving them exposed to extreme climatic conditions affect the hygiene and

productivity of the animals. Unsanitary/unhygienic conditions of the cattle shed and milking yards lead to mastitis in animals. Unhygienic milk production leads to reduction in quality and subsequent spoilage of milk and other products.

Disposal of animal waste on time is also a concern in clean milk production practices. Quality issues due to contaminants carryover in milk: Somatic cell counts, antibiotics and pesticide residues, aflatoxin availability in feed and fodder raise concerns over supplying clean and adulteration-free milk to the consumers of the dairy products.

7. **Marketing and pricing:** City dwellers, who need fresh quality milk, or hotels, restaurants, hostel, P.G areas, caterers could be targeted as potential customers. This will minimise costs and earn more revenue. Perception of the farmers, towards commercial dairy enterprise as an alternative to other occupation need to be built along with marketing facilities, expanding customer base and extension services in proper feeding and animal health case so that Fat and SNF contents are maintained. This will help in reducing the production cost and thus will make dairying remunerative.

8. **Balancing Lean Flush Ratio:** A substantial quantity of marketable surplus is procured by private players. While the milk payment to the primary producers is competitive during lean season, they many a times refuse to buy extra milk during the flush months. During such times, the producers turn to the cooperatives. This increases the load on Cooperatives' processing facilities and thus results in increasing milk powder stock, which again impacts the milk price in the market.

2. Opportunities for Innovation in Dairy Value Chain

The drivers of demand for milk in India are population growth, urbanisation, and increasing per capita income. The consumption of milk has been rising, commensurate with the increase in purchasing power of people, changing food habits and lifestyle, and demographic growth. In our largely vegetarian population, milk with its many benefits is the one and only source of animal protein. Further, factors such as increased consumer interest in high protein diet and increasing awareness and availability of dairy products through channels such as organised retail chain are also driving the growth.

With the increase in per capita income and awareness about benefits of quality food products, the consumption of milk in rural areas has also increased reasonably. At present, there are about 2,000 towns in India, many of which converted from rural to semi-urban areas ("rurban"). These towns provide excellent opportunity to extend POI network to reach the consumers seeking healthy living. The milk-consuming population has been consistently rising in the country both in rural and urban areas. According to Consumer Expenditure Survey (CES, 2011–2012) of NSSO, about 78% and 85% of the rural and urban populations, respectively, reported consumption of milk in the country. While share of food expenditure in total household expenditure has been declining over the years, the share of milk expenditure to total food expenditure has risen over the past few decades not only in the case of urban population but also in the case of rural population. Share of milk expenditure to total food expenditure during 1993–1994 was 18% and 15% in urban and rural populations, respectively, which increased to 20% in the urban and 19% in the rural populations in 2011–2012.

As per an estimate done by Department of Animal Husbandry & Dairying, consumption (handling) of processed and packaged milk and milk products will increase from 20% in 2015–2016 to 50% in the organised sector in 2023–2024 (Vision 2022–2023). This growth in above factors indicates that the demand for milk and milk products will rise consistently in the future.

3. Entrepreneurial Design Approach

Peter Drucker stated that the entrepreneur always searches for change, responds to it, and uses it as an opportunity. In the event of a change, the entrepreneur views it as an opportunity rather than a problem. Drucker also makes it clear that entrepreneurs don't require a profit motive. Entrepreneurs mobilise the resources of others to achieve their entrepreneurial objectives, while administrators use their existing resources and their job descriptions which actually constrains their visions and actions.

World is now global and exponential due to technological achievements largely sustained by Moore's law. This law dictates price-performance doubling time, which is now squeezed from the standard 2 years to 18 months. Gordon Moore, Co-founder of Intel, 50 years ago, observed that there was a potential for computer power doubling every two years by placing more transistors in the microchips. This doubling was also illustrated to price and performance. This law is now replicated successfully in almost all business and needs to be contextualised in the dairy sector of India. However, adoption of entrepreneurial approach in establishing an organisation is more difficult than having an enterprise. But since established organisations have good resource base, capital, dedicated customer base, data, employees, suppliers, and infrastructure, they can be in a better position to transform new ideas into concrete value-creating successful services. It needs careful nurturing of the identified potential interventions.

The human brain processes many millions of bits per second, but only a fraction of the signals reach consciousness. Some of the key filters that sort out signals are human biases. Usually, humans are overoptimistic about the future and basically think that things are going to be better in the future than in the past.

Knowing this becomes interesting when dealing with the individual immune system barriers to change and innovation. We human beings have fundamentally different risk profiles, which is the first of three crucial parameters defining individual immune system.

Not every individual is a born entrepreneur and a risk-taker. Human risk profiles are, among other things, controlled by the chemical activities of our brains, which make us more or less open to seeking out risk or stability. The majority of us are programmed, or "wired" as brain researchers call it, to seek out stability and status quo. Only a few think of changing the environment and bring in innovation. However, this behaviour can also be changed by providing system-oriented institutional and capacity-building support. By establishing a system to identify, groom, and handhold entrepreneurial aspirants, the success rate in starting anything new could be enhanced.

Innovation is in the eye of the beholder a reimagining of the categories that transforms value proposition. It achieves functionality, convenience,

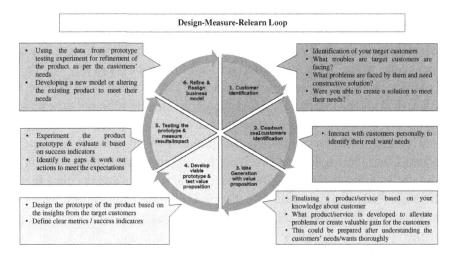

Figure 1.   Design-Measure-Relearn Loop.

reliability, price, or user experience. Efforts should be made for value creation and value capture from the various options that might be crafted within each of the six stages mentioned in Figure 1.

The application of the above design helps in acquiring three core processes:

1. It favours experimentation over-elaborate planning.
2. It prioritises customer/user feedback over intuition.
3. It emphasises iterative design over traditional big design up-front development.

Aspiring entrepreneurs need to carefully craft a business plan by focusing one value-creating service, one process worth optimising, one potentially transformative experience, and then do everything to become champions. Identification and adoption of innovative technological/business processes have always helped businesses grow. Today, it is a critical facilitator for businesses as well for economies. It has a profound role in ensuring optimisation and efficiency.

4. Illustrate the Business Hypothesis

Whenever any aspiring entrepreneur says, "I have a brilliant idea that can change the world", it is required to redefine his/her business proposition, and the aspirant entrepreneur wants to pursue this idea because s/he faced a certain problem and could not find a readily available solution. S/he now thinks that the solution (idea — yet to even arrive at a "proof-of-concept" (PoC) stage) is only way to solve this problem. What is more, s/he also believes that the whole world is dying for this incredible value position. Usually, aspirants have a solution to a technical problem and presume that there is a ready market waiting for their solution. The truth, unfortunately, is far from it. Wanting to solve a problem without listening to the "voice of the (potential) customer" is a sure recipe for failure. This is not to undermine the brilliance and technical capabilities that the individual and the team may have in building a very good product or service. However, most entrepreneurs (especially those who start off without any work experience or exposure to the real world of business) come to discover the harsh reality after having put at stake a considerable amount of time, money, efforts and career opportunities, hoping that they will become a unicorn very soon. When we observe some of the aspiring professional dairy farmers, we could learn that:

- the youth usually jumps into the enterprise without studying the feasibility, thus making huge investments on "infrastructure" rather than concentrating on personal care of animals;
- at times, people feel that remote management would be possible, they feel they can run a profitable business remotely with one recruited manager at the farm. This becomes disastrous with time. In the words of successful entrepreneurs, one has to personally get involved in it.

Many a times, aspirants dream of selling various milk products without exploring the market; this may again be disastrous. The following is a framework developed and answering questions in each component of the business model describes the size of an opportunity, the problem to be solved, and the solution that new idea/enterprise will lead to success (Table 1).

Table 1.   Key Questions for assessing the Business Model.

Key Partners	Key Activities	Value Proposition	Customer Relationship	Customer Segments
Key partners?	Key activities the	Values which are to be	How do get, retain, and grow	For whom is the
Key suppliers?	value propositions	delivered to the	customers?	value being
Key resources	require?	customer?	Which customer relationships	created?
which are	Distribution channel!?	Customers' problems	have established?	Our important
being acquired	Customer	which we are trying to	How are they integrated with rest	customers?
from partners?	relationships?	solve?	of business model?	Our customer
Key activities of	Revenue streams?	Bundle of product and	Cost involved?	archetypes?
the partners?	**Key Resources**	services we are		
	What key resources do	offering to each	**Channels**	
	value propositions	segment?	Through which channel do	
	require?	Customer needs, which	customer segments want are to	
	Distribution channels?	are being satisfied?	be reached?	
	Customer	What is the minimal	How do other companies reach	
	relationships?	viable product?	them at present?	
	Revenue streams?		Which ones work best?	
			Which one is most cost-efficient?	
			Are we integrating them with	
			customer routine and how	

Cost Structure

What are the most important costs inherent to business
model?
Which of the key resources are most expensive?
Which of the key activities are most expensive?

Revenue Streams

For what value are customers willing to pay readily?
For what do the customers currently pay?
The revenue model?
The pricing tactics?

Source: Osterwalder, A. and Pigneur, Y. (2010). *Business Model Generation: A Handbook for Visionaries, Game Changers, and Challengers*, The Strategyzer Series. Wiley.

5. Exhibiting Heightened Sense of Accountability

Furthermore, there are so many youths blessed with the ability to dream, and if they are trained and mentored properly, they can achieve their dream. They have a very high level of confidence in their own abilities and a belief that anything is possible. Aspiring youth can be exposed to entrepreneurship which can enable them to develop creative thinking, ability to usher a task to the end, willingness to take up challenges and risks, networking, and problem-solving abilities. When these traits are encouraged, they lead them to develop their innate skills. If such youth are encouraged to converge matching their aspirations, it will result in positive result and bring about positive change. It is therefore to pursue a vision, acquire newer skills, using scarce resources efficiently, and drawing in partners and collaborators, successful entrepreneurs require demonstrating a set of attributes.

It is imperative that social entrepreneurs have characteristics of high IQ, EQ, as well as AQ.

IQ or Intelligence Quotient: The intelligence, facts, knowledge, and trivia that one usually possesses.

EQ or Emotional Quotient: The emotional understanding and capability of a person to understand others that helps with differing situations and people.

AQ or Adversity quotient: The AQ is one of the probable indicators of a person's success in life. It is useful to predict attitude, stress, perseverance, and response to changes in environment.

- **Social intelligence and emotional quotient in developing entrepreneurial leadership:** Entrepreneurship is an approach in which individual/group entrepreneurs develop, fund, and implement innovative solutions tested on effectivity and efficiency parameter and that improves or eases the lives of the target people/consumer. To be a successful entrepreneur, one should have some specific competencies, such as good IQ, i.e. analytical skills, ability to relate multiple things, logical reasoning, and ability to store and recall information. At the same time, s/he should also have a good EQ, i.e. *self-awareness* which includes emotional awareness, self-assessment, and self-confidence; *self-regulation* which includes self-control, trustworthiness, conscientiousness, adaptability, and innovativeness; *self-motivation* which includes drive, commitment, initiative, and optimism; *social awareness* which includes empathy, service orientation, developing others, leveraging diversity, and political awareness; and *social skills* which include influence, communication, leadership, stress management, change management, conflict management, and cooperation.

- In addition to the above characteristics, a successful entrepreneur should also have a good social quotient (SQ) or social intelligence (SI). *Social intelligence (SI) is ability of a person to tune into other people's emotions and read the subtle behavioural cues to choose the most effective response in a given situation.* SI is an essential feature because every interpersonal interaction has an emotional subtext to it. And most of that emotional undertone gets manifested less through words and more through the nonverbal behaviours, such as postures, gestures, facial expressions, vocal tones, or for that matter, the way one has shaped one's environment.

- **Developing entrepreneurial leadership with adversity quotient:** Entrepreneurs and leaders are often seen as two sides of a coin as they share many distinctive but common characteristics: able to motivate, visionary, creative/innovative, risk-taking, goal-oriented, patient, flexible, and persistent. Both IQ and EQ are important in shaping a successful leader. However, AQ offers a vital piece to the puzzle that is often overlooked. AQ is a measure of a person's resilience. AQ is all about staying in power. It means taking hits, falling down and getting up, and being stronger than before. A leader with a high AQ is more likely to face up to the challenge. AQ will demonstrate its usefulness in times of great challenges. Higher a leader's AQ, better the chances are of his or her success in a challenging situation. A leader, who are able to once again take charge of situation even after a failure is a valuable asset to any organisation.

Highly successful entrepreneurs have a high AQ, the ability to recover from setbacks. Entrepreneurs with great determination never give up even when the going gets tough. Delays and obstructions never deter them.

Their tenacity and persistence help them to recover from setbacks. They strongly believe hard work can help in overcoming any obstacle. They believe they have the capacity to control their circumstances, and they are highly motivated to change adversity into opportunity by taking action. Instead of giving in to feelings of frustration and anger when they encounter obstacles, they can see beyond the roadblocks and visualise a better future. Their optimistic attitude helps them attain the desired business outcome. They take personal accountability for the consequences of their choices and actions, and doing so mobilises them to act. They strongly believe that their setbacks and failures are the result of a lack of effort on their part, and they are willing to do whatever it takes to fix things. This compels them to double their efforts, try new options, and push forward when faced with adversity.

National Dairy Development Board (NDDB) has acquired experience in grooming and nurturing aspirants youths in the field of artificial insemination, providing advisory services to the farmers by local resource person or DSC Secretary, dairy farming, etc. During the implementation of National Dairy Plan over eight years, NDDB trained 77,500 youths to sustain their livelihood. The training duration varied between 15 and 125 days. Table 2 provides some details.

Considering the growing demand for milk in India, the youth can be involved and groomed to take up social entrepreneurship in dairy. They need to be provided adequate training and handholding support on scientific dairy animal management, entrepreneurial traits, and ethical business practices. Dairy cooperative business model will be able to effectively harness the humanness and creativity. Dairy cooperatives developed the

Table 2.   Training for skill enhancement of village youth.

S. No.	Name of the Training	Duration	No. of Participants Trained
1.	Artificial Insemination (AI)	45	6,500
2.	Local Resource Person (LRP)	15	40,000
3.	Dairy Cooperative Society (DCS) Secretary	26	30,500
4.	Dairy Entrepreneurs	12	500
5.	**Total**		**77,500**

understanding that business humaneness contributes to long-term business performance excellence which brought in ethics, values, and relatively democratic functioning.

Furthermore, social entrepreneurship can be developed as a useful platform for evolution into social leadership. The aspiring youths can be groomed and nurtured on the traits of social entrepreneurs to become social leaders to sustain the cooperative nature of the industry. The empathy, idealism, enlightened self-interest, and managerial skills in dairy cooperative can be combined with a larger vision, a sense of mission, and the skills of social leadership of the youth.

6. Developing Social Entrepreneurship Model

The first step will be mobilising and identifying young aspiring youth willing to take up innovative ventures in animal husbandry and dairying. Grooming of individuals may help them to pick an idea that has a strong value proposition around which a viable and defendable business plan can be formulated. The processes adopted for nurturing or grooming the entrepreneur are as follows:

1. **Crystallising an idea:** It enables the participants to identify their interest — what they are good at and what gives them joy. Based on this, they can evaluate various ideas and transform them into reality in the form of a profitable and scalable venture.
2. **Feasibility assessment on designated success parameters:** Aspirants learn how to evaluate the feasibility of the various ideas under consideration through appreciation of market requirements and situations, costing and pricing, customer aspirations, future prospects in terms of revenue generation and scalability, IPR issues if any, and ensuring compliances of FSSAI.
3. **Build value and customer loyalty:** It makes the aspiring entrepreneurs understand how to create value through appreciation of integrated product design involving innovations and creativity in dairy value chain. In addition, it will help in recognising the importance of different stages of market and its maturity and impact of the competing forces.

7. Designing Innovative Scalable Interventions in Dairy Value Chain

Agriculture and animal husbandry operate in an ecosystem where there are complex factors which determine the profitability of the venture. Today's dairy sector needs to encourage the aspiring youth to bring in innovations and creativity in all the factors of ecosystem, such as tools and implementations, use of ICT, and research and demonstration in feed and fodder. It comprises farmer-level intervention after carefully assessing the existing dairy value chain in the region and exploring the scope of technology induction, value addition, or evolving innovative processes in relation to clean milk production in the context of hygiene and sanitation, breeding, nutrition, cow comfort, and health management and farm management. Entrepreneurs with similar activity may form a "Producer's Common Interest Group" (PCIG), and all the activities may be consolidated under the umbrella of Animal Husbandry and Dairy Producer Organisation (AH&DPO). Each PCIG can have a confined area of business operations (approximately 20–30 km depending on the mobility, ease of business, and sphere of requirements from the users. Each of the enterprises will provide creative solutions in backward or forward linkages to each other, as required.

Some of possible options of AH&DPO are described as follows:

1. Animal Feed and Fodder:
- **Preparation of area-specific mineral mixture/cattle feed preparation as per local needs and quality parameters:** There are areas where assured cattle feed and mineral mixtures are not available to the farmers and they have to depend on the fluctuating supply in the market. The AH&DPO can take up the activity of preparing cattle feed and mineral mixture under specified guidelines. The milk union, if existing in the area, will have to specify the standards and continuously monitor the quality and necessary compliances.
- **Green fodder production and conservation to meet own and local demand for fodder at competitive market rate:** In most of

the agrarian households, land is limited and the natural tendency is to engage the land for food/commercial crops. In this situation, farmers have to depend on the market for green fodder.

The AH&DPO can engage in the following two activities:

- Cultivation of green fodder as per the geography and season in leased land and distribution/sale of the same to the milk producers.
- Fodder densification and distribution.

In both the activities, AH&DPO can coordinate with existing dairy cooperative societies (DCSs) in the area. In case DCSs are not functional in the area, the AH&DPO can directly contact the farmers.

2. **Artificial insemination as skill-based entrepreneurial activity to provide quality services to clients along with heifer rearing for providing authentic high-yielding breed:** The entrepreneurs of AH&DPO can carry out animal insemination (AI) activities in the area. Along with this, awareness creation on the importance of scientific animal breeding will be carried out by this dedicated team. Furthermore, some of the entrepreneurs may venture into heifer rearing for the suitable good-breed animals in the region. This will help increase the number of improved high-yielding breeds.

3. **Farmers' training centre as entrepreneurial activity to professionalise learning on dairy extension interventions:** Progressive dairy farmers in a region can setup micro training centres (MTCs) and help the farmers in the region to learn about dairy farming through various demonstrations. The MTCs can also function as a platform for dairy extension services on scientific animal management practices.

4. **AH and dairy infrastructure and machinery innovation and product development:** Enterprising youth may be mentored in a wide range of innovations in dairy infrastructure and machinery, such as fodder implements, silage machineries, low-cost cattle feed and mineral mixture machines, processing, and packaging. Innovations suitable to the local area may be encouraged. Either well-performing DCSs or some interested entrepreneurs can opt for processing of indigenous

milk products, which can amalgamate local wisdom of the product along with mechanisation and quality assurance. The milk unions can buy the product if it suffices the quality compliances laid down by the milk union.

5. **Milch animal rearing and cow dung slurry management:** Farmers who are already practising good animal husbandry practices can organise into AH&DPO or well-performing, interested DCSs can also take up the proposed activity. In addition, the group can take up slurry management practices which will add to the livelihood of the farmers. The initiation of this activity will depend on the readiness of the farmers, processing facility, and profitability.

It is very important to leverage innovative, technology-based interactive solutions for the enduring challenges faced by Indian farmers in relation to the dairy sector. The institution-building processes need to be facilitated by an agency to work out the multiple solutions to support aspirant youths in co-developing new technologies and developing mutually beneficial business ties in the dairy sector. The social entrepreneurs need to be assisted in adapting innovative technologies as per the requirements of the Indian diary sector and partnering to jointly exploit the resulting commercial opportunities. The social entrepreneurship approach will encourage youths to find innovative, inclusive, low-cost diagnostics and predictive solutions for dairying in rural areas. This will be a multisectoral approach by building a joint vision and consensus among different institutions as partners.

The social entrepreneurship model will be able to effectively harness the humanness and creativity of the rural youth. As the intervention is totally stakeholders-oriented, it can lead to humanising the business. Furthermore, social entrepreneurship can be developed as a useful platform for evolution into social leadership. The aspiring youth can be groomed and nurtured on the traits of social entrepreneurs to become social leaders to sustain the cooperative nature of industry. The empathy, business orientation, enlightened self-interest, and techno-managerial & entrepreneurial skills can be nurtured among milk producers of the region with holistic vision, a sense of mission, and social leadership.

Social entrepreneurs need to be mentored in a well-designed step-wise incubation so that the aspirant can be well aware of the entire ecosystem. This can be an interdisciplinary process and should have the following steps:

- develop understanding about entrepreneurial traits among the individual members and needs of social entrepreneurship in animal husbandry and dairying.
- illustrate entrepreneurial business acumen to assess existing dairy value chain.
- explore techno-economic model and feasibility assessment of proposed interventions.
- build business continuity plan by preparing and testing financial assessment and business plan in enterprise expansion areas.

One of the ways for this can be creating centres of excellences where the youth can have exposure, incubation, and orientation to take forward social enterprises in which they become confident. These centres of excellence for nurturing and grooming aspirant youths should be developed in different regions in each state. State dairy federations can take up this task by supporting progressive milk unions in the state. This will ensure area-specific and need-based enterprises, relevant to the area and also be the bedrock for developing future social leaders.

8. Expectations of the Aspiring Entrepreneurs

During training programmes at NDDB, Anand, aspiring dairy entrepreneurs have shared their excitation from the ecosystem to go ahead in the noble work of fostering social enterprise. This includes:

- technical support in gaining skill and knowledge in the enterprise,
- understanding of ecosystem,
- liaison and handholding
- sharing success stories so that they can draw inspiration.

9. Conclusion

The future lies in the hands of the young generation. This young and energetic group can function as the instruments of change. Therefore, enterprises cannot be just perceived as an income-generating activity. It is far more reaching than just earning money. Enterprises, especially social enterprises, are vehicles of change, where the social entrepreneur can lead the society in taking the development process in their own hands and not depending merely on benefactors.

It is important to remember that every enterprise in embedded in a web of social relations, values, and norms. A value-driven enterprise which is not merely income-oriented but driven by the ethos of a community-driven change, led by an entrepreneur, can ensure meeting aspirations in the changing times.

The cue can be drawn from the dairy cooperatives where financial independence is achieved along with a remarkable change in the community life. The leadership allows it to find its inner strength. The income earned is aggregated and utilised in a way that could serve the needs of the people. The income earned helps to meet the financial needs of the shareholders; it helps the professionals to build a career in the institution, helps in modernising the enterprise, and at the same time, establishes equity and a trust in the market.

In past, dairy cooperatives have acted as effective platform for grooming and supporting entrepreneurs. This is a model where the entrepreneur as well as the dairy cooperative have prospered together, having met each other's aspirations and cushioned the challenges. On one hand, milk and milk products are highly perishable commodity and on the other, the consumer demands its accessibility at their own convenient time. Collectivising the business has proved effective and today looking at the changing scenario and need for de-centralisation of the value chain, the aspirations of the dairy entrepreneurs have to be re-defined for mutual prosperity.

References

Douglas, H. (2020). Cultural innovation: The secret to building breakthrough businesses. *Harvard Business Review*, September–October, 106–116.

Kris, O. (2019). *Transforming Legacy Organisations: Turn Your Established Business into an Innovation Champion to Win the Future*. Padstow, Cornwall, UK: TJ International Ltd.

Limos, M. A. (9 December 2019). *Forget I.Q. and E.Q. Success is about A.Q.* https://www.esquiremag.ph/long-reads/what-is-adversity-quotient-a00293-20191209.

Joshua, G., Scott, E. L., & Stern, S. (2018). Strategy for start-ups: First answer two questions; then explore four paths. *Harvard Business Review*, May–June 2018, 44–51.

Pradip, K. (2017). *Fast Forward towards Civilizational Greatness: Paradigm of Civilization Greatness*. Gujarat: Ahmedabad Management Association Publication.

Ranjay, G. (2019). The soul of a start-up: Companies can sustain their entrepreneurial energy even as they grow. *Harvard Business Review*, July–August 2019, 84–91.

Zalocusky, K. A., Ramakrishnan, C. Lerner, T. N., Davidson, T. J., Knutson, B. & Deisseroth, K. (2016). Nucleus accumbens D2R cells signal prior outcomes and control risky decision-making. *Nature*, 531, 642–646.

Chapter 9

Cooperative Banks: Tracing, Tracking, and Treating the Failures

Anil Kumar Angrish[*,‡] and Sanjeev K. Bansal[†,§]

*Department of Pharmaceutical Management, National Institute of
Pharmaceutical Education and Research (NIPER), SAS Nagar, Sector-67,
Mohali, Punjab, India*

†*Department of Management, I. K. Gujral Punjab Technical University, Main
Campus, Kapurthala-Jalandhar Highway, Kaputhala, Punjab, India*

‡*anil@niper.ac.in, anilkangrish@gmail.com*

§*commerce.ptu@gmail.com*

*Semi-official institutions, in a country so dangerous for banking as
India, should be conducted on the safest possible principles.*
John Maynard Keynes, *Indian Currency and Finance*

Abstract

Cooperative banks are the lifeline of a developing economy like India. In order
to serve the best interests of society, the cooperative banking sector must be
sound otherwise, the very rationale behind their creation will be lost. However,
in India, many cooperative banks have failed to deliver the desired results.
Failure has questioned the functioning of these banks in general. Many a times,
various cooperative banks have failed to pay depositors. There are a number of
reasons behind their dismal performance.

In this chapter, the reasons for the failure of urban cooperative banks (UCBs) have been studied, and an effort has been made to find out the measures undertaken to prevent failures of cooperative banks, including UCBs, and protect the depositors.

Keywords: cooperative bank, urban cooperative banks (UCBs), losses caused, measures undertaken to protect, suggestions

1. Introduction

Failure of banks in India is not a new phenomenon. In 1913–1914, 54 banks were shut down out of which 28 were from Punjab and 11 from Bombay (now Mumbai). In the subsequent period, the location of failures shifted towards Southern India and West Bengal. Close to 1,800 banks failed during the period of 1913–1966. Majority of the bank failures were from Kerala (25%), followed by West Bengal (21%) and Madras (20%). It is pertinent to note that John Maynard Keynes asked for conducting banking in India on the "safest possible principles" way back in 1913, and his words still hold true. The same warning is applicable for cooperative credit institutions which comprise urban cooperative banks (UCBs) and rural cooperatives. UCBs, which are also known as primary cooperative banks, serve customers in urban and semi-urban regions. UCBs are either registered under the terms of a certain state's State Cooperative Societies Act or under the provisions of the Multi-State Cooperative Societies Act, 2002 if the bank's area of operation extends outside that state's boundary. Rural cooperatives provide both short- and long-term credit. Primary agricultural credit societies (PACSs) at the village level, district central cooperative banks (DCCBs) at the district level, and state cooperative banks (StCBs) at the state level make up the framework of three-tier short-term cooperative credit. PACSs do not come under the purview of the Banking Regulation Act, 1949. StCBs and DCCBs, on the other hand, are registered under the State Cooperative Societies Act of their respective states. The Reserve Bank of India (RBI) regulates both StCBs and DCCBs. The National Bank for Agricultural and Rural Development (NABARD) has delegated inspection powers under Section 35 (6) of the Banking Regulation Act to conduct inspection of state and central cooperative banks. State cooperative agriculture and rural development

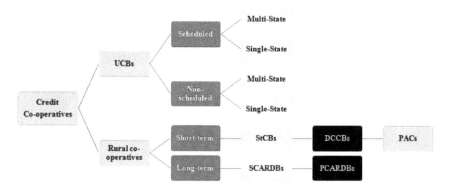

Figure 1.   Structure of cooperative credit institutions in India.

Source: Developments in Co-operative Banking (2016–2017). In *Report on Trend and Progress of Banking in India* (p. 99).

Table 1.   Facts related to cooperative banks in India.

Number of urban cooperative banks (UCBs) as on 31 March 2020	1,539
Number of rural cooperative banks as on 31 March 2019	97,006
Asset size of cooperative banking sector as a percentage of asset size of scheduled commercial banks (SCBs)	About 10%

Source: Report on Trend and Progress of Banking in India, 2019–2020. Reserve Bank of India (pp. 92–112).

banks (SCARDBs) and primary cooperative agriculture and rural development banks (PCARDBs) are two long-term credit delivery cooperatives. Figure 1 presents the structure of cooperative credit institutions in India.

Urban and multi-state cooperative banks in India have more than 8.6 crore depositors who trust these banks with their money that amounts to about INR 4.84 lakh crore in over 1,500 such banks in the country. The importance of cooperative banks is evident from Tables 1 and 2.

In 2020, the Union Finance Minister told Lok Sabha that the financial status was weak for at least 277 UCBs, and about 105 cooperative banks were not able to meet minimum capital requirements as fixed by the regulator. Net worth was negative for 47 banks, and gross nonperforming assets (NPAs) of almost 328 UCBs were more than 15%. Gross NPA ratio

Table 2.   Deposits held by UCBs in major states.

Name of the State	Number of UCBs	Deposits (in crore)
Maharashtra	496	>300,000
Gujarat	219	55,102
Karnataka	263	41,096

Source: Compiled from Urban cooperative banks report nearly 1,000 frauds worth over Rs. 220 crore in past five fiscals: RBI (27 January 2020), *Economic Times*.

of UCBs also deteriorated to 10.36% in September 2020 from an earlier level of 9.89% in March 2020.

One major concern about cooperative banks in India is regarding their failure from time to time. In an article in *ThePrint* dated 10 July 2020, the authors noted that 127 cooperative banks have been shut down by the RBI in the period between 2013 and 2018, i.e. more than 20 banks in a year. In majority of the cases, these banks failed to pay depositors. These banks did not come under media scrutiny as these banks primarily catered to "rural" and "poor" population. It is an area of concern as rural cooperative banks make up 65% of the total asset size of all cooperative banks taken together by the end of March 2020.

The failure of cooperative banks in India is attributed to many factors. Increase in the NPAs is one major reason, which in turn is attributed to poor appraisal and recovery systems. Other reasons include small capital base, non-productive use of funds of cooperative banks, higher financial and management cost, decline in deposits, movement of quality customers to other banks, irregularities and misdeeds of boards and management, and delay in penal action against responsible persons, issues related to wilful defaulters.

2. Literature Review

IBS Center for Management Research (2002) published a case study on cooperative banks scams in India. Mitra (2012), through the case study of Saraswat Co-operative Bank, highlighted the performance of the bank, compared with that of other banks, and listed possible reasons of success which have caused the conversion of Saraswat Co-op Bank to a private bank from a cooperative bank. Nayak (2012) presented his analysis for financial inclusion through cooperative banks. He considered it as a feasible option for inclusive growth. An information booklet published by the Institute of Chartered Accountants of India (ICAI, 2013) provided details about UCBs, their problems, expectations, and remedies thereof. Jayasree and Gangadharan (2017) in their study made an attempt to evaluate capital adequacy of UCBs in India since their inception by the RBI. The authors concluded that about 94% of the UCBs in India satisfied capital adequacy ratio as stipulated by the RBI, thereby pointing out that UCBs are financially strong. Chandshive (2018) carried out a study on growth and performance of DCCBs in Maharashtra. Srivastava and Kumar (2019) in their study identified key factors for failure of UCBs which, in their opinion, can be monitored effectively to prevent any further instances of failure of UCBs in India. Gain and Manikumar (2020) discussed options and opportunities for rural cooperative banks in India with specific reference to development and marketing of banking products and services. Gowtham and Suganya (2020) carried out a study on the performance of two UCBs. Mallick and Das (2020) in their study explained the affiliation among capital adequacy, management ability, and profitability in StCBs. Most recently, in February 2021, the RBI has set up a panel led by N. S. Vishwanathan, former Dy. Governor of the RBI, to study prospects of consolidation among UCBs and chart a roadmap for the sector.

In addition to the above-listed studies, the authors have gone through multiple studies. Those studies covered different aspects such as lending practices of co-op banks, financial inclusion through cooperative banks, and financial performance and efficiency of cooperative banks.

3. Objectives of the Chapter

In order to bridge the gap between existing studies, the present study has been conducted with the following specific objectives:

(i) to find out the number of UCBs which have failed from March 2004 onwards;
(ii) to determine the loss caused by the failure of cooperative banks including UCBs;
(iii) to identify the reasons behind the failure of UCBs;

(iv) to find out the measures undertaken to prevent failures of cooperative banks, including UCBs, and protect the depositors.

4. Research Methodology

The period from March 2004 onwards was chosen because, as of 31 March 2004, 732 out of 1926 UCBs are classified as Grade III or IV, accounting for 38% of the total. This grading signified weakness and sickness. These facts compelled the RBI to prescribe new regulations. In 2005, the RBI conceived the sector's vision paper, which envisioned a multi-layered "regulatory" and "supervisory" approach, as well as the revival of potentially viable UCBs and the non-disruptive exit of non-viable UCBs. This resulted in a process of rehabilitation and consolidation in the cooperative banking sector. The data have been collected from secondary sources, mainly from various RBI reports, speeches, and notifications, among others.

One major change came in July 2021 when the Union Government carved out a Ministry of Co-operation from the Ministry of Agriculture. The newly created Ministry of Co-operation has been placed under the Home Minister.

To determine the loss caused, a representative measure has been used. This proxy measure is the amount of compensation given by the Deposit Insurance and Credit Guarantee Corporation (DICGC) to the depositors due to the failure of cooperative banks. All depositors might not have received the full amount due on account of their deposits as full amount was not insured under DICGC norms.

To identify the reasons behind the failure of cooperative banks, **a sample of those 10 major cooperative banks** which have failed has been taken up and the issues related to failure as evident from press reports and financials of the respective cooperative banks have been identified.

4.1 Number of cooperative banks which have failed from 2004 onwards

To find out the number of cooperative banks which have failed from 2004 onwards, information has been compiled from various reports from the RBI.

Table 3.   Number of urban cooperative banks.

Year	No. of UCBs	Fall in No. of UCBs	Cumulative Fall in No. of UCBs
March 2004	1926	–	–
2004–05	1872	54	54
2005–06	1853	19	73
2006–07	1813	40	113
2007–08	1770	43	156
2009–10	1721	49	205
2010–11	1674	47	252
2011–12	1645	29	281
2012–13	1618	27	308
2013–14	1606	12	320
2014–15	1589	17	337
2015–16	1579	10	347
2016–17	1574	5	352
2017–18	1562	12	364
2018–19	1551	11	375
2019–20	1544	7	382
March 2020	1539	5	387

Source: Based on Chapter V: Developments in Cooperative Banking. In *Report on Trend and Progress of Banking in India*, 2019–2020. Reserve Bank of India (p. 95).

From Table 3, it is evident that the number of UCBs has gone down from 1926 to 1539, i.e. 387 UCBs have been closed/merged during the period between March 2004 and March 2020, which turns out to be 20.09% (Table 4). In other words, every fifth UCB that used to exist in March 2004 is no more in existence by March 2020. This fall in the number of UCBs is the direct outcome of non-disruptive exit of non-viable UCBs and due to consolidation in the sector.

From above, it is evident that majority of UCB mergers (88.24% of the total) took place in three states, namely, Maharashtra (53.68%), Gujarat (25.74%), and Andhra Pradesh (8.82%) only during the period between 2004–2005 and March 2020.

Table 4.   UCB mergers from 2004–2005 to 31 March 2020.

Name of the State	State-wise No. of UCB Mergers	Percentage of Total (%)	Cumulative No. of UCB Mergers
Maharashtra	73	53.68	73
Gujarat	35	25.74	108
Andhra Pradesh	12	8.82	120
Karnataka	4	2.94	124
Rajasthan	3	2.20	127
Chhattisgarh	2	1.47	129
Uttar Pradesh	2	1.47	131
Uttarakhand	2	1.47	133
Telangana	2	1.47	135
Punjab	1	0.73	136
Total	**136**	100%	

Source: Based on Chart V.4 of Chapter V: Developments in Cooperative Banking. "Report on Trend and Progress of Banking in India", 2019–2020. Reserve Bank of India (p. 95).

4.2 Loss caused by the failure of cooperative banks

the number of claims settled by the DICGC is a meaningful measure of the loss caused by cooperative bank failures. The DICGC is a wholly owned subsidiary of the RBI that insures bank deposits. The DICGC Act, 1961, governs DICGC.

The DICGC settled claims of 351 cooperative banks amounting to INR 4,822.33 crore (Table 5). The Deposit Insurance Scheme of the DICGC has rescued thousands of depositors on several occasions. As of 31 March 2020, about 94.3% of all claims settled by the DICGC since its founding related to cooperative banks that were liquidated, amalgamated, or restructured. The number of banks that are liquidated or ordered to be wound up determines the amount of DICGC devolvement. Even when there are defaults, not all claims are paid at the same time. There have been times when those banks have also revived. As of 30 September 2019, the total amount devolved to DICGC was INR 14,098 crore, with INR 3,414

Table 5. Number of cooperative banks registered and insured with DICGC as on 31 March 2021.

Type of Cooperative Bank	Number of Cooperative Banks Registered and Insured with DICGC
State Co-operative Banks (StCBs)	34
District Central Co-operative Banks (DCCBs)	347
Urban Co-operative Banks (UCBs)	1,538
Total	**1,919**

Source: Based on *Annual Report 2020–2021*. Reserve Bank of India (p. 165).

crore in the case of state cooperatives bank and DCCBs and INR 10,684 crore in the case of UCBs which included PMC Bank as well. As a percentage of the Deposit Insurance Fund (DIF), these deposits accounted for around 13.9%. DIF is funded by premiums received from banks that have their accounts insured, interest earned from investments, and cash recovered from failed banks' assets after adjusting expenditures which include payment of depositor claims and related expenses, net of taxes.

During 2020–2021, claims worth INR 993 crore have been processed by the DICGC. Out of this claim, claims to the tune of INR 564 crore pertain to nine cooperative banks only.

As on 31 March 2021 247.8 crore bank accounts are fully protected accounts which forms 98.1% of the total number of bank accounts, i.e. 252.6 crore. Hence, about 4.8 crore (1.9% of the total) accounts are not insured with the DICGC. This percentage is fairly good in comparison to international benchmark of 80%. As on 31 March 2021, total insured deposits are INR 76,21,258 crore (50.9%) of total assessable deposits of INR 1,49,67,776 crore. In other words, 49.10% of the total deposits do not have DICGC cover. An amount over and above INR 5 lakh in one bank account does not have insurance coverage.

Losses, which cannot be measured, include closure of banks and resultant loss of jobs. For example, PMC Bank had 137 branches spread over six states. Moreover, loans given might have turned up to into productive activities had they not failed.

4.3 Reasons behind the failure of cooperative banks

There are many reasons attributed to the failure of cooperative banks (Table 6). Internal control failures, operational risk due to delinquent behaviour by one or more of these banks' employees, regulatory framework issues, inability to combine cooperative principles with professionalism, and a lack of avenues to raise additional capital are all major reasons for cooperative banks' failure. It is hard to distinguish between shareholders, depositors, and borrowers in these banks, so these banks are highly susceptible to abuse by influential persons associated with these banks.

Table 6.   Timeline of failure/crisis pertaining to 10 UCBs.

Name of the Co-op Bank	Licence Cancelled/Merger or Acquisition Allowed/Administrator Appointed by the RBI
Punjab and Maharashtra Co-operative (PMC) Bank	On 24 September 2019, the RBI capped withdrawals and launched investigation. On 18 June 2021, Centrum Financial Services and BharatPe permitted takeover of the bank
Madhavpura Co-op Bank Ltd.	4 June 2012
Amanath Co-op Bank Ltd.	Merger permitted by the High Court in August 2014
CKP Co-operative Bank	2 May 2020
Prudential Cooperative Urban Bank	15 December 2004
Mapusa Urban Co-operative Bank Ltd.	15 April 2020
Anyonya Co-operative Bank Ltd., Vadodara (Gujarat)	3 September 2010
The Urban Co-operative bank Limited, Bhubaneswar	17 February 2014
Seva Vikas Bank, Pimpri	8 June 2021 (RBI appointed administrator and Board of Directors superseded)
Kapol Co-operative Bank	In special general body meeting, merger with Cosmos Cooperate Bank Ltd. on 9 June 2021 approved

Source: Compiled by the authors from various sources duly acknowledged in the references.

To identify the reasons behind failure of UCBs/crisis-ridden UCBs, 10 such failures/crisis-ridden UCBs have been picked (Table 7). These UCBs failed at different points of time but have certain commonalities so far as their failure/crisis is concerned. Timeline of their failure/crisis is given in Table 6.

All above-listed cooperative banks were prominent ones, e.g. PMC Bank was set up in 1984 and by 2019, the bank had 137 branches across six states with deposits of USD 1.5 billion.

Madhavpura Mercantile Cooperative Bank (MMCB) was the largest in the state of Gujarat. It obtained banking licence on 19 August 1994 and within two years, i.e. from April 1996, it became a multi-state cooperative bank. MMCB's banking licence was cancelled by the central bank, i.e. RBI on 1 June 2012.

Amanath Cooperative Bank was established in 1977 to assist disadvantaged Muslims in Karnataka while adhering to Islamic principles, and it became Karnataka's first scheduled UCB and the largest UCB in the state by the year 2000. For the first time, in November 2009, a newspaper from Bengaluru (then Bangalore) accused promoters of the bank of swindling INR 300 crore. And in October 2013, it was decided to merge it with Canara Bank.

CKP Co-operative Bank, established in 1915, was one of the oldest UCBs in Mumbai. In case of CKP Co-operative Bank, as on 31 March 2020, nonperforming loans of INR 153 crore formed 97% of the total loan book of INR 158 crore. Concentration risk was evident as INR 85–90 crore loan was only in the real-estate sector. Deterioration took place over a period. In 2012, outstanding loan book stood at INR 622 crore and over a period, it was able to recover significant amount of the outstanding loans.

Prudential Co-operative Urban Bank was the oldest and largest UCB in Andhra Pradesh. It was set up in 1920. At the time of cancellation of licence of the bank, it had 20 branches with 400 staff. In total, 24 borrowers owed INR 210 crore to the bank.

Mapusa Urban Co-operative Bank was setup in December 1965. In April 2020, it had 193 staff members, 1.19 lakh shareholders, and 2.48 lakh depositors. Management of the bank had the plan to merge it with the

Table 7.   Ten major failures/crisis among UCBs and associated facts.

Name of the Co-op Bank	Persons Blamed and Management Personnel Involved	Major Defaulter/No. of Defaulters	Loss/Fraud to the Bank/Alleged Fraud	Statutory Auditors/Independent Auditors Blamed	Internal Control System Failure
Punjab and Maharashtra Co-operative Bank (PMC)	Waryam Singh, former Chairman of the bank and Joy Thomas, Managing Director	Promoters of HDIL, a realty firm	INR 4,335 Cr.	Yes. Jayesh Sanghani and Ketan Lakdawala, proprietors of Ashok Jayesh & Associates and Lakdawala & Co.	Yes as 44 unsecured loan accounts were replaced by 21,409 dummy accounts
Madhavpura Co-op Bank	Ramesh Parikh, former Chairman of the bank and Devendra Pandya, MD	Ketan Parekh, a share broker	INR 1,357.41	Yes. Name of Manubhai A. Panchal & Co. figured & penalised for 2 years	Loans to 19 of Ketan Parekh's companies without cross verification
Amanath Co-op Bank Ltd	Ayub Khan as the President of the bank, Mohd. Asadulla, GM of the Bank and K. Rahman Khan as Chairman (1988–2002)	Ziaullah Shareef of India Builders, Irfan Razack of Prestige Group	INR 159 Cr.	N.A.	A General Manager created benami accounts and took loans that became NPA
CKP Co-operative Bank	Former Chairman (2011–12) and 21 employees blamed by Prakash Mandhre, CKP employee	55 wilful defaulters and Vijay Vaidya of Nanai Dairy and Avishkar Developers, Dinesh Shah of Labdhi Corporation, and Phulchand Jagdtap of Siddharth Dairy	INR 85.49 Cr.	N.A.	Loan without verification of documents and fake addresses

Prudential Cooperative Urban Bank	Chairman Boorugu Muralidhar, CEO B. Pullaiah and directors Vittal Rao, C B Nair and P R Mohan and seven others	Rajeev Reddy, MD of resort chain Country Club, A S Chowdhary, Chairman of Navabharat Enterprises and J Rameshwar Rao, Chief of MyHome Estates	24 borrowers owed Rs. 210 Cr. to the bank	N.A.	Nonperforming Assets were INR 139.05 Cr. whereas actual amount stood at INR 300.22 Cr., One borrower defaulted and then given loan under another name
Mapusa Urban Co-operative Bank Ltd.	Ashwin Khalap resigned as the Chairman in Sept. 2015 and Chairman, Gurudas Natekar and 13-member board resigned in Sept. 2018	1,512 loan accounts defaulted	Stakeholders and depositors alleged mismanagement but no amount specified	N.A.	N.A.
Anyonya Co-operative Bank Ltd., Vadodara (Gujarat)	Advances to bank directors and relatives amounting to INR 57.85 Lacs (2002–03) — Persons not named	212 defaulters for INR 20.12 Cr. and Co-op Banks (Petrofils MMCB, etc.)	Financial mismanagement and inability to recover loans alleged but no amount specified	N.A.	N.A.
The Urban Co-operative bank Limited, Bhubaneswar	A Senior Odisha Administrative Service officer, Secretaries and former Manager arrested	1,546 defaulters for INR 42.77 Cr.	INR 117 Cr. fraud	N.A.	Loans sanctioned in the name of relatives on forged documents, Collateral valued at three times of original price

(Continued)

Table 7.   *(Continued)*

Name of the Co-op Bank	Persons Blamed and Management Personnel Involved	Major Defaulter/No. of Defaulters	Loss/Fraud to the Bank/Alleged Fraud	Statutory Auditors/ Independent Auditors Blamed	Internal Control System Failure
Seva Vikas Bank, Pimpri	Bank Chairman, Vice-Chairman, and directors named in the F.I.R. regarding multi-crore fraud in July 2019	Over 104 defaulters	Alleged fraud to the tune of INR 500 Cr.	N.A.	INR 6 cr. Loan given to a non-existent person and amount mis-appropriated, loans without valid mortgages or non-existent assets, forged documents used
Kapol Co-operative Bank	Director Hiren Mehta arrested in 2013 who facilitated 3 businessmen in siphoning off INR 14.50 crore	Director of Decent Corporation in INR 14.5 Cr. fraud	INR 50 Cr. loss caused by directors as per an FIR registered in 2016 by the Economic Offences Wing (EOW)	N.A.	Bogus letters of credit, loans on fake documents

Sources: Compiled by the authors from various sources duly acknowledged in the references.

PMC Bank but it was abandoned due to PMC Bank crisis. In April 2020, against deposits of INR 354.97 crore, the bank had own banking assets with a book value of INR 18.28 crore, own banking assets with a market value of INR 73.57 crore, non-banking assets worth INR 13.40 crore, and advances worth INR 50.92 crores. Deposit Insurance Cover stood at INR 282.76 crore taking into account INR 5 lakh insurance cover for each account. Hence, the bank had a surplus of INR 245.84 crore.

Anyonya Co-operative Bank, Vadodara (Gujarat), was the first cooperative bank in Asia. The bank was setup by Vitthalrao Kavthekar under the guidance of Lokmanya Tilak in 1889 as Anyonya Sahayakari Mandali Co-operative Bank. The bank had 29,000 members and more than one lakh depositors. The bank had deposits with other co-op societies, such as Madhavpura Mercantile Co-op Bank (INR 77.20 lakh), Ahmedabad Urban Co-op Bank (INR 1.08 crore), and Petrolfils Co-op (INR 3.09 crore). Erosion in deposits was to the extent of 24.2% as on 31 March 2005 as per the statutory inspection of the bank. Statutory inspections were conducted from 2005 to March 2009. In 2008, the bank made an unsuccessful attempt with Saraswat Cooperative Bank. In February 2010, the bank terminated the services of 46 employees out of 109 to save the bank from liquidation. In October 2011, DICGC paid INR 31.9 crore to the bank's depositors.

Odisha's Urban Co-operative Bank was setup in 1988 and started incurring losses in 2001. The state government provided an assistance of INR 6 crore to revive the bank but it did not work. It got the nod to merge with Pune-based Cosmos Co-operative Bank in January 2013, but it failed to materialise. By October 2019, deposits worth INR 33.87 crore against 11,672 accounts were locked, out of which deposits of INR 29.67 crore belonging to 7,700 depositors was traced, whereas INR 4.2 crore of deposits of 3,972 accounts were yet to be located. Four directors of the bank have been arrested too.

Seva Vikas Cooperative Bank, Pimpri is the most recent entrant in the list of cooperative banks which is facing allegations of fraudulent transactions and misuse of public money. In July 2021, the RBI has superseded the board of directors of the bank and appointed an administrator. The RBI in its written communication pointed out the deteriorating financial position, high NPAs, decline in net worth, and decline in deposits of the bank.

Table 8: Ten Major failures/Crisis among UCBs and associated facts at the time of failure.

Name of the Co-op Bank	Depositors	NPAs or Stressed Loans	Deposit Base of the Bank	Loan Book of the Bank	Accumulated Losses/ Losses in Last Fiscal Before Closure/ Imposition of Strictures	Equity Capital or Net Worth
Punjab and Maharashtra Co-operative Bank (PMC)	>9,00,000	INR 3,518.89 Cr. (31 March 2020)	>INR 11,617 Cr. (March 2019)	INR 8,880 Cr.	INR 6,835 Cr.	INR 5,850.61 Cr.
Madhavpura Mercantile Co-op Bank	>50,000	INR 1,126.55 Cr.	INR 100 Cr. of individual depositors and INR 617 Cr. of 67 Co-op banks	INR 1,126.59 Cr.	INR 1,357.41 Cr.	INR 1,316.50 Cr.
Amanath Co-op Bank Ltd	>240,000	>INR 66 Cr.	INR 400 Cr.	INR 240 Cr.	INR 113 Cr.	INR 7 Cr.
CKP Co-operative Bank	1,33,300	INR 153 Cr.	INR 485.56 Cr. (in November 2019)	INR 158 Cr.	INR 11.71 Cr.	INR 239.18 Cr.
Prudential Cooperative Urban Bank	1,86,765	INR 300.22 Cr.	INR 532.06 Cr. (as on 31 March 2002)	INR 451.71 Cr. (on 31 March 2002)	N.A.	Assets exceeded deposits
Mapusa Urban Co-operative Bank Ltd.	2,48,000	INR 27.97 Cr. (2016–2017)	INR 354.97 Cr.	INR 156.58 Cr. (2016–2017)	INR 64.98 Cr. (2016–2017)	Advances and assets exceeded deposits

Anyonya Co-operative Bank Ltd., Vadodara (Gujarat)	>1,00,000	INR 31.71 Cr. in 2007 and INR 22.4 Cr. in 2010 (September)	INR 86 Cr. (September 2007) and INR 107.3 Cr. in June 2003	N.A.	Operating Profit of INR 47 Lacs in 2010–2011	INR 21.82 Cr. as on 31 March 2005
The Urban Co-operative bank Limited, Bhubaneswar	About 14,000	Gross NPAs at 39.94% and Net NPAs at 31.9%	INR 28 Cr. (June 2012)	INR 39 Cr. (INR 42.77 Cr. in October 2019)	INR 22.57 crore as accumulated loss	INR 16 Cr. (in August 2013)
Seva Vikas Bank, Pimpri	>100,000	RBI letter stated that Gross and net NPAs are at alarmingly high level	INR 823 Crore in 2018 and INR 409 Cr. by 31 March 2021	N.A.	Losses for two consecutively years (31 March 2020 and 31 March 2021)	INR 88.50 Cr. as on 31 March 2018 and INR 50.28 Cr. as on 31 March 2021
Kapol Co-operative Bank	2,50,000	INR 138 Cr. as at March-end 2020 and INR 141 Cr. as at end March 2019	INR 392 Cr. as at end March 2020	INR 150 Cr. as at end March 2020	INR 36 Cr loss in FY20 and INR 30 Cr in FY19	N.A.

Note: In certain cases, figures were not available but percentages were available in the RBI documents.

Source: Compiled by the authors from various sources duly acknowledged in the references.

Table 9.   Division of subjects under the Constitution of India.

Seventh Schedule of the Constitution of India	
List I — **Union List**	Entries 43 and 45 empowers the Union Legislature to make laws
	Entry no. 43: "Incorporation, regulation and winding up of trading corporations, including banking, insurance and financial corporations, but not including co-operative societies." **Entry no. 45:** "Banking"
List II — **State List**	Entry 32 empowers the State Legislature to legislate on the incorporation, regulation, and winding up of cooperatives
	Entry no. 32: "Incorporation, regulation and winding up of corporations, other than those specified in List I, and universities; unincorporated trading, literary, scientific, religious and other societies and associations; co-operative societies."

Source: Extracted from Seventh Schedule of the Constitution of India.

With this, the RBI stated that the present management has failed in discharging its responsibilities and has conducted the bank's business in a manner that is detrimental to the interest of present and future depositors of the bank.

Kapol Co-operative Bank was set up in 1939. Kapols are considered Vaishya or Baniyas from Saurashtra in Gujarat. In the 17th century, the first reported migration of this community to Mumbai took place. Most common last names in the community are Parekh, Kapadia, Doshi, Mehta, and Vora. The RBI put the bank under directions from the close of business on 30 March 2017.

In addition to the above 10 examples, numerous examples exist where senior functionaries of the cooperative banks abused their position. In a recent example, J&K Cooperative Bank Chairperson Mohd. Shafi Dar and others sanctioned an INR 223 crore loan to a non-existent society in the name of River Jhelum Co-operative House Building Society. Anti-Corruption Bureau (ACB) unearthed the siphoned off funds and INR 187 crore had been frozen by 2 June 2020.

4.4 Underlying reasons behind the failure of cooperative banks other than those which are evident in the financials of those banks

4.4.1 *Ambiguity in regulatory framework due to division of subjects under the Constitution*

In view of the above division, the Banking Regulation Act applies to cooperative banks in a modified manner (Tables 8 and 9). The Registrar of Cooperatives in different states exercise control on aspects such as "incorporation", "election of management", "management of cooperative banks", "regulation", and "winding up" of cooperative banks. It is commonly observed that "management", "control", and "operations" of cooperative banks cannot be separated. So, even if the RBI as the banking sector regulator is of the impression that the management is incompetent, mismanaging the affairs of the bank, or abuses the controlling position, then the regulator cannot act against the management or go on to an extent of winding up the bank.

4.4.2 *Supervisory capacity of the RBI*

Given the sheer number of banks and their branches, supervisory capacity of the RBI is limited. The RBI was formed on 1 April 1935 and it was expected to deal with bank failures.

The timeline, shown in Table 10, is important regarding bank failures. It was in 1935 that the RBI came into existence. From 1935 to 1947, the table depicts the failure before independence. In 1969, nationalisation of banks took place. Nationalisation of banks was again enforced in 1980. Thirty-six private banks have been put under moratorium from 1969 onwards. Many banks were merged with comparatively better public sector banks (PSBs), e.g. Global Trust Bank (GTB) was merged with Oriental Bank of Commerce in 2004.

A number of prominent banks failed, and it has been observed that the RBI could not avoid bank failures even when it had the regulatory and supervisory role. In a most recent instance, one founder-director of PMC bank, Charan Singh, alleged that way back in 1993–1994, there

Table 10.   Bank failures before and after
the formation of the RBI.

Time Period	Number of Bank Failures
1913–1934	About 350
1935–1947	About 900
1947–1969	665
1969–2019	37

Source: Tabulated on the basis of information
available in Agrawal (26 February 2018). Banking
crises: An Indian history. *Mint*. Kalyanasundaram
(17 September 2020). Bringing co-operative
banks under RBI may not really help. *Business
Line*.

was a fraud of INR 100 crore and his father wrote a complaint to the RBI
as well, requesting thorough investigation and action, but the regulator
failed to detect the irregularities and the complaint was hushed up. In the
past, the regulator failed to act in the following cases in a timely
manner:

(i) Stock market scam in 1991.
(ii) Indian Bank scam in 1996.
(iii) Global Trust Bank involvement in stock market scam in 2001.
(iv) Stock market scam in 2001.
(v) NPAs accumulation and write-off from time to time.

4.5 Measures undertaken to prevent failures of cooperative banks

The Central Bank has various tools like CRR and SLR to prevent failures,
by taking care of liquidity issues. The RBI also performs the monitoring
role as statutory statements are sought from time to time. The RBI also
carries out inspections at regular intervals.

4.5.1 *Ordinance issued in June 2020 and subsequent changes through Gazette notification of the Banking Regulation (Amendment) Act, 2020 to give more powers to the RBI on Cooperative banks*

On 27 June 2021, the Union Government came up with an Ordinance to reform the banking sector regulator's oversight of cooperative banks. Later on, through a Gazette notification dated 29 September 2020 of the Banking Regulation (Amendment) Act, 2020, more powers were given to the RBI to regulate cooperative banks. Major changes are listed in Table 11.

Table 11.   Recent changes introduced by the RBI on oversight of co-op banks.

Changes Incorporated	Previous Situation	Situation after Amendment
The RBI intervention in failing banks and protection of deposits	Imposition of moratorium and resultant hardship to the depositors	Failing bank may be merged with another bank and existing accounts continue to operate seamlessly
Changes in the Banking Regulation Act and the powers of the RBI	Dual control of the Registrar of Cooperatives and the RBI over the cooperative banks	Banking Regulation Act to have the supremacy over cooperative banks. The RBI empowered to "change the management", "dissolve the co-op bank" and have powers to override the powers of the State Registrar of Cooperatives
Access to financial markets	Cooperative banks were not allowed to access financial markets	Cooperative banks allowed to issue shares, debenture, and other securities. Equity securities will act as a cushion to depositors and these security holders will absorb the losses first

Source: Comparison is based on the Gazette notification dated 29 September 2020 of the Banking Regulation (Amendment) Act, 2020; Patnaik, Ila and Shubho Roy (10 July 2020). How Modi govt's ordinance on cooperative banks can prevent PMC-like scams, protect depositors. *ThePrint*.

4.5.2 *Increased insurance coverage for depositors in all insured banks*

The PMC bank crisis compelled the government to rethink the mechanism to protect all savings of the depositors. The PMC bank being an urban-centric bank had significant presence in Mumbai, the financial capital of the country. The existing Deposit Insurance Scheme in India protected the deposits only to the extent of INR 1 lakh per depositor in a bank under the DICGC Act. Through the Union Budget of 2021 (1 February), the Finance Minister increased this limit to INR 5 lakh per depositor in the bank. Enhanced Deposit Insurance Cover of INR 5 lakh, i.e. five times the earlier deposit insurance coverage, is effective from 4 February 2020. Moreover, as per the recent approval of the Cabinet in the provisions of the DICGC Act, the amount will be paid within 90 days of the failure of the bank. Deposit Insurance Cover of INR 1 lakh remained static since 1993, and the limit was enhanced after a gap of 27 years. Due to increase in the deposit insurance coverage, banks including cooperative banks started paying a premium of 12 paise per INR 100 deposited as against 10 paise per INR 100 deposited earlier.

The increase in the limit to INR 5 lakh per depositor will bring some solace, but still it is not a cover for full amount of the depositor. For example, in the case of CKP Co-operative Bank, as highlighted among the failures earlier, total deposits of 1,130 customers stood at INR 120 crore, so average balance in each account stood more than INR 5 lakh. The rest of the bank's depositors had a balance less than INR 5 lakh, and their total deposits stood at INR 365 crore. A total of 132,170 depositors, i.e. 99.2% of the depositors, got their dues in full. The second major issue is about receipt of deposits by depositors after a long period in many cases. For example, in October 2018, about 45,000 depositors who deposited up to INR 2 lakh in MMCB got their money back after 17 years. It is pertinent to note that even after 17 years; only 52% of individual depositors got their money back. In contrast to this, UCBs, which deposited their money with MMCB, got only 28% of their deposits. MMCB had inter-bank deposits of about INR 800 crore from 250 other banks that included UCBs from Gujarat and Maharashtra. It also held deposits of three public sector banks (PSBs), two private sector banks, and two financial institutions. This posed a systemic risk for cooperative banks in Gujarat.

4.5.3 *Report regarding credit information on all borrowers*

UCBs with assets of INR 500 crore or more as of 31 March of the previous financial year (FY) must submit a report to the RBI's Central Repository of Information on Large Credits (CRILC) detailing "credit information on all borrowers" with an aggregate exposure of INR 5 crore or more. This report must be filed on a quarterly basis.

4.5.4 *To appoint auditors by UCBs, approval of the RBI made mandatory*

In April 2021, the RBI made it mandatory for UCBs to get RBI approval to appoint auditors. Now, auditors have to be appointed for a continuous period of three years with a maximum tenure of six years. One audit firm has been permitted to concurrently audit eight UCBs.

4.6 Suggestions

Suggestions on the basis of issues listed above are as follows:

1. UCBs that want to voluntarily convert themselves into small finance banks (SFBs) may be allowed to do so. In 2015, a similar step was recommended by a committee that was headed by Rama Subramaniam Gandhi, Deputy Governor, RBI (2014–2017), that suggested conversion of UCBs to commercial banks, given the fact that UCBs were primarily setup as "small banks" only. These were expected to render banking services to those who had limited means and those who belonged to the "lower and middle classes". Hence, conversion to small finance banks is likely to make them more accountable. In a recent case, Centrum Financial Services and BharatPe, a fintech start-up, have been allowed to take over PMC Bank and convert it into an SFB. In another case, Shivalik Mercantile Co-operative Bank (SMCB) marked the transition to an SFB. SMCB was the first UCB in India that made a transition to an SFB under the "voluntary transition scheme" and started functioning as an SFB from April 2021.
2. Fixation of responsibility and liability on existing management and regulatory personnel can make significant improvement. For example,

in case of J&K State Cooperative Bank (JKSTB), it was observed that Mohd Mujib Ur Rehman Ghassi, then Registrar of Cooperative Societies, Jammu and Kashmir and Syed Ashiq Hussain, Deputy Registrar of Cooperative Societies, Jammu and Kashmir, had hatched a conspiracy along with others in creating a non-existent society in 2018–2019 for obtaining a loan from JKSTB. ACB filed a charge sheet in the INR 223–crore loan scam.

3. Time-bound resolution of issues is required. It has been observed that it takes many years to settle issues. For example, the RBI cancelled the licence of Chandraseniya Kayastha Prabhu (CKP) Co-operative Bank in May 2020. On 3 May 2014, the RBI capped the withdrawal to INR 1,000 under Section 35 of the Banking Regulation Act. In April 2015, the bank formulated an action plan for the years 2015–2018 that comprised targets regarding recovery of NPAs and a profitability plan. In March 2015, NPAs stood at INR 228.41 crore. In January 2016, withdrawal up to INR 10,000 was allowed for depositors. Net worth of the bank was negative to the tune of INR 147 crore in January 2016 itself. So, from January 2016 to 2020, it deteriorated further to a negative net worth of INR 239.18 crore. In this background, it becomes pertinent that timely intervention and resolution of issues in a time-bound manner can help in the survival and revival of cooperative banks in general. First, the RBI puts a bank under directions, withdrawal limits are imposed on depositors, and staff gets salary during this period. This gives a bank "zombie-like" existence.

4. Fixing the responsibility of statutory auditors in a "time-bound manner" can be an important step. In case of statutory auditors for MMCB, the ICAI as per the directions of the Gujarat High Court removed the name of Chartered Accountancy firm for two years from its membership. When the scam surfaced in 2001, the Central Registrar of Cooperative Societies conducted a re-audit. Various shortcomings were observed. Upon inquiry, it was found that there were 19 counts of professional misconduct. These were serious in nature, e.g. amounts pledged to Ketan Parekh's companies were double than what was allowed at that time. A reference was made to the High Court in 2006. It took almost 11 years for the High Court to

issue directions in this regard. Almost 20 years after the scam, auditors faced the action.

5. Politics need to be separated from economics of cooperative banks. In majority of the cases, one commonality was involvement of political leaders in these cooperative banks. For brevity of this chapter, aspects of politics and economics of cooperative banks have not been covered. Leaders of all political parties were part of one or other cooperative bank.

6. Strengthening operational mechanisms is very much required as evident from the fact that UCBs reported 972 cases of fraud involving more than INR 221 crore during 2014–2015 and 2018–2019 as per one RTI. As many as 181 frauds involving INR 127.7 crore were noticed during 2018–2019 itself. During 2014–2015, 478 cases involving INR 19.8 crore and during 2015–2016, 187 cases involving INR 17.3 crore were noticed.

5. Conclusion

Since March 2004, 387 UCBs have had their licences cancelled or withdrawn, or have been merged with stronger UCBs. Since 2004–2005, 136 mergers have taken place among UCBs, with majority of the mergers (53.68%) in the state of Maharashtra. Other states that had a significant share in the total number of UCB mergers comprise Gujarat (25.74%) and Andhra Pradesh (8.82%). Loss to the depositors in cooperative banks is significant, and a representative measure is the number of claims settled by the DICGC, which protects savings of depositors in case of failure of banks. It has been noted that as of 31 March 2020, about 94.3% of the overall claims settled by the DICGC since its inception were to cooperative banks that were liquidated, amalgamated, or restructured. One major initiative to protect the depositors has been announced through Union Budget of 2021. Through this, a hike has been introduced to INR 5 lakh per depositor in the bank under the Deposit Insurance and Credit Guarantee Corporation Act, 1961 from previous amount of INR 1 lakh per depositor. But this limit has limitations as all depositors will not get their deposits back in full and also. Depositors also do not get their money back in a time-bound manner.

References

ACBL's aim was to save people from moneylenders (3 September 2010). *Times of India.*

Agrawal, A. (26 February 2018). Banking crises: An Indian history. *Mint.*

Amanath Bank's CEO transferred (16 January 2010). *New Indian Express.*

An Information Booklet on Urban Cooperative Banks, their Problems, Expectations and Remedies (January 2013). *Institute of Chartered Accountants of India.* New Delhi.

Andhra CID files case against Prudential Co-Op Defaulters (9 April 2003). *Business Standard.*

Anyonya sacks 46 employees (11 February 2010). *Times of India.*

Annual Report 2020–2021. *Reserve Bank of India* (pp. 153–167).

Anyonya: RBI liquidation begins moves to deal the final blow to ailing bank (12 September 2010). *Indian Express.*

AP government for restarting 2 co-op urban banks (26 May 2004). *Business Standard.*

AP forms Spl Cell to avert fresh Co-op Bank Scams (16 June 2003). *Financial Express.*

Arun T. Dhumale and Ors vs. State of Maharashtra (12 March 2021). Bombay High Court Order in the Writ Petition (Stamp) 95405 of 2020.

Axe falls on Asia's oldest co-op bank (4 September 2010). *Indian Express.*

Badrinath, R. (18 May 2013). Amanath Co-operative Bank crisis escalates after withdrawal curbs. *Business Standard.*

Bandyopadhyay, T. (11 August 2014). How safe is your money with cooperative banks? *Mint.*

Basu, D. (27 October 2019). Lessons from PMC: Why govt is responsible for co-operative bank crises. *Business Standard.*

Bill to bring cooperative banks under RBI control gets Lok Sabha nod (16 September 2020). *Business Today.*

Cancellation of Prudentials licence stirs a debate in Andhra Pradesh (13 December 2004). *Financial Express.*

Chandanshive, S. (2018). Growth and performance of district central cooperative banks in Maharashtra. *International Scholarly Research Journal for Interdisciplinary Studies*, 7(40), 9–15.

Cooperative Bank scams in India (2002). IBS Center for Management Research (ICMR).

Dalal, S. (30 March 2016). Continuing failures in Cooperative Banks. *Money Life.*

David, R. (6 June 2003). New Asia's oldest co-op bank starts recovery drive. *Times of India.*

Deposit Insurance and Credit Guarantee Corporation (DICGC) increases the insurance coverage for depositors in all insured banks to ₹5 lakh (4 February 2020). RBI Press Release: 2019–2020/1878. *Reserve Bank of India.*

Depositors' money is safe, no need to panic: Mapusa Urban Bank (17 April 2020). *Navhind Times.*

Depositors of Mapusa Urban Cooperative Bank to protest on Monday (1 February 2020). *Times of India.*

Dev, V. (28 December 2012). Amanath Bank scam: Karnataka Minorities Commission files complaint against Rehman Khan with Lokayukta. *India Today.*

DICGC sees Rs. 14,100 crore claims amid PMC Bank crisis (29 December 2019). *Business Today.*

EOW probes bank officials accused of swindling Rs. 85 crore (24 August 2016). *Hindustan Times.*

Ex-chairman of J&K Cooperative Bank arrested in Rs. 223 cr loan fraud (3 June 2020). *The Tribune.*

Fasiuddin, S. (6 May 2020). CKP Co-op Bank saga highlights RBI patience and another realty link. *Economic Times.*

Former JKSCB chairman arrested in Rs. 223-cr land scam (3 June 2020). *Outlook.*

Former J&K Cooperative Bank chairman arrested in Rs. 223-crore land scam (3 June 2020). *Financial Express.*

Gadgil, M. (17 January 2019). Depositors ready to take a haircut to save Kapol Bank. Mumbai Mirror, *Times of India.*

Gain, T. S. R. & Manikuamr, S. (April 2020). Developing and marketing of banking products and services by rural cooperative banks in India. *Indian Cooperative Review.* National Cooperative Union of India. Vol. 57, No. 4.

Gerard de Souza (25 September 2019). RBI curbs on PMC Bank punctures revival plans of two Goa banks. *Hindustan Times.*

Ghosh, S. (4 May 2020). Over 1,100 customers to lose out in CKP Cooperative Bank's liquidation. *Mint.*

Ghosh, S. (18 June 2021a). Centrum-BharatPe to take over PMC Bank. *Mint.*

Ghosh, S. (15 February 2021b). RBI panel to weigh consolidation of urban co-op banks. *Mint.*

Govt may table amendment to DICGC Act in monsoon session (16 May 2021). *Mint.*

Gowhar, I. (18 February 2011). Tainted MP moved funds to wife's firm. *Mid-day.*

Gowthaman, C. & Suganya, R. (April 2020). A study on performance of Namakkal Urban Cooperative Bank (NUCB) and Rasipuram Urban Cooperative Bank (RUCB). *Indian Cooperative Review.* National Cooperative Union of India. Vol. 57, No. 4.

Gujarat: 45,000 Madhavpura bank depositors to get their money back (2 October 2018). *DNA.*

Hafeez, M. (15 November 2019). Mumbai: Four held for bank loan scam, duping JNPT staffers. *Times of India.*

HC nod for Canara Bank, Amanath Bank merger (2 August 2014). *Deccan Herald.*

Hope floats for Anyonya bank as PM assures help (16 March 2010). *Times of India.*

Implementation of Budget announcements 2020–2021 (1 February 2021). Department of Economic Affairs. *Ministry of Finance.*

J&K State Cooperative Bank ex-chairman, others charge-sheeted in Rs. 223-cr loan scam (11 August 2020). *The Tribune.*

Haj money stuck in Amanath Bank: Minister (31 July 2013). *Times of India.*

Jafri, S. A. (6 April 2003). Prudential coop bank chairman, 3 directors arrested. https://www.rediff.com/money/2003/apr/05prud.htm.

Jayasree, T. O. & Gangadharan, K. (December 2017). Capital adequacy and financial stability of urban co-operative banks in India: A temporal analysis. Finance India. Indian Institute of Finance. Vol. XXXI, No. 4.

Kalyanasundaram, S. (17 September 2020). Bringing co-operative banks under RBI may not really help. *Business Line.*

Kansara, Y. (3 December 2019). A cry for Professional Management. *Outlook Money.*

Kashyap, H. (25 November 2009). Amanath Bank top brass accused of swindling Rs. 300 cr. *Bangalore Mirror.*

Kelkar, N. (5 April 2020). System Failure. *The Week.*

Keynes, John Maynard (1913). *Indian Currency and Finance.* London: Macmillan and Co., Limited.

Khalap jr quits as head of Mapusa Urban Co-op Bank (10 September 2015). *Times of India.*

Krishnaswamy, A. (3 August 2013). Act against embezzlers, co-op registrar orders Amanath Bank. *Deccan Herald.*

Kumar, C. (2 May 2020). RBI cancels licence of CKP Co-operative Bank; depositors to get up to Rs. 5 lakh. *Business Today.*

Kumar, N. (1 February 2021a). If bank fails, Rs. 5 lakh deposit insurance amount to be available immediately to depositors. *The Economic Times.*

Kumar, N. (27 May 2021b). 49.1% bank deposits are not under Rs. 5 lakh insurance cover: Check if your deposit is protected. *Economic Times.*

Kumar, K. R. (24 June 2021c). Kapol Co-op bank takes first step towards amalgamation with Pune-based Cosmos Bank. *Business Line.*

Khanna, S. (26 November 2004). Little hope of recovery for Home Trade scam-hit banks. *Business Standard.*

Lele, A. (6 January 2021). SMCB becomes India's first urban co-operative bank to transition to SFB. *Business Standard.*

Liquidation of Anyonya bank's movable assets begins (13 November 2013). *Times of India.*

Mahesh, K. (11 April 2012). Defaulters delay Prudential Bank liquidation. *Times of India.*

Mallick, S. & Das, S. (2020). Association between management capacity and profitability of scheduled urban co-operative banks in India. *Indo-Asian Journal of Finance and Accounting, 1*(1), 45–63.

Mapusa bank unveils plan to recover loans (2 July 2021). *Times of India.*

Mapusa bank staff irate as directors tender resignation (5 September 2018). *Times of India.*

Menon, A. K. (24 March 2003a). Vasavi Cooperative Urban Bank closes down in Andhra Pradesh. *India Today.*

Menon, A. K. (9 June 2003b). Loan scandal involving bank officials, politicians rocks Andhra Pradesh cooperative banks. *India Today.*

Mitra, A. (August 2012). Co-operative bank turning to private: A case study on Saraswat co-operative bank. *The Management Accountant.*

MMCB ex-CMD release ordered (7 December 2001). *Economic Times.*

Move to refund urban cooperative bank depositors' money (24 October 2019). *New Indian Express.*

Mukherjee, S. (12 July 2021). New ministry of cooperation creates a buzz. *Business Standard* (p. 4).

Nair, A. (8 June 2014). Madhavpura bank collapse is behind us, says RBI executive director. *Financial Express.*

Narayan, K. (4 June 2021). Explained: Why the NCP opposing RBI supervision of cooperative banks? *Indian Express.*

Nayak, G. (27 December 2019). DICGC faces a claim of Rs. 14,000 crore from co-operative banks including PMC: RBI. *Economic Times.*

Nayak, R. K. (2012). Financial inclusion through cooperative banks: A feasible option for inclusive growth. *Indore Management Journal, 4*(3), 9–17.

No funds available: Depositors at India's PMC Bank survive on loans, charity (26 August 2020). *India Today.*

Odisha's Urban Co-op Bank set to merge with Cosmos Bank (20 June 2012). *Business Standard.*

Patnaik, I. & Roy, S. (10 July 2020). How Modi govt's ordinance on cooperative banks can prevent PMC-like scams, protect depositors. *ThePrint.*

PMC scam effect: Ordinance to bring cooperative banks under RBI regulation notified (28 June 2020). *Financial Express.*

PMC bank depositors may get higher payout as it turns into SFB (9 March 2021). ETBFSI.Com. *Economic Times.*

PMC Bank: Two auditors held. *The Hindu.*

Prudential chairman, directors held (6 April 2003). *Times of India.*

Prudential's staff union moots merger (6 February 2013). *Business Standard.*

Ray, A. (16 September 2020). Banking Regulation (Amendment) Bill passed in Lok Sabha to bring cooperative banks under RBI. *Mint.*

Ray, A. (13 May 2021). RBI cancels United Co-operative Bank's licence. *Economic Times.*

RBI approval mandatory for commercial and urban cooperative banks to appoint auditors (28 April 2021). *The Telegraph.*

RBI annuls Madhavpura Mercantile Co-op Bank licence (8 June 2012). *The Hindu.*

RBI scraps licence of ailing Madhavpura co-operative bank (5 June 2012). *Indian Express.*

RBI cancels licence of United Co-operative Bank over inadequate capital, regulatory non-compliance (13 May 2021). *Business Today.*

Reserve Bank of India cancels the licence of The Urban Co-operative Bank Ltd., Bhubaneswar (10 March 2014). *Press Release of the RBI.*

Reserve Bank cancels the licence of The Madhavpura Mercantile Co-operative Bank Ltd., Ahmedabad (Gujarat) (7 June 2012). Press Release. *Reserve Bank of India.*

Reserve Bank cancels the licence of Anyonya Co-operative Bank Limited, Vadodara (Gujarat) (6 September 2010). *Press Release of the RBI.*

RBI cancels the licence of The Surat mahila Nagrik Sahakari bank Ltd., Surat (Gujarat) (22 October 2009). Press Release. *Reserve Bank of India.*

RBI cancels Surat Nagrik Mahila Bank's licence (22 October 2009). *Times of India.*

Report on Trend and Progress of Banking in India 2016–2017. *Reserve Bank of India.*

Report on Trend and Progress of Banking in India 2018–2019. *Reserve Bank of India.*

Report on Trend and Progress of Banking in India 2019–2020. *Reserve Bank of India.*

Revive Prudential Co-op (15 December 2004). *Financial Express.*

Roy, A. (3 May 2020). More than 90% CKP Co-op Bank depositors to get back money, says RBI. *Business Standard.*

Roy, A. & Lele, A. (26 September 2019). PMC Bank's liquidity profile is good, depositors need not worry: RBI. *Business Standard.*

S. Ahmed (13 December 2013). Co-op bank director arrested for aiding 3 siphon off Rs. 14 cr. *Times of India.*

Sequeira, N. (17 April 2020). RBI cancels Mapusa urban bank's licence. *Times of India.*

Sequeira, R. (13 March 2021). Mumbai: CKP Bank closure in depositors' interest: HC. *Times of India.*

Singh, G. (28 September 2019). Collapsing coop banks and scams: When will we ever learn? *New Indian Express.*

Speech of Nirmala Sitharaman (1 February 2020). *Budget 2020–2021*, Ministry of Finance (Point 92 on p. 25).

Srivastava, A. & Kumar, A. (5 March 2019). When and why cooperative banks fail? The case of urban cooperative banks in India. *The IUP Journal of Bank Management, XIX*(1), February 2020, 58–71. Available at SSRN: https://ssrn.com/abstract=3798151.

TDP walks out on Prudential Bank Issue (15 December 2004). *Business Standard.*

Tere, T. (9 April 2009). Maharashtrian candidates keep 'Anyonya' at bay. *Times of India.*

Thaver, M. (18 November 2019). Maharashtra: EOW investigating frauds in 8 co-operative banks. *Indian Express.*

Vijaykumar, V. K. (3 December 2019). What led to the collapse? *Outlook Money.*

What Ails the Co-Operative Banking Sector? (25 February 2013). *Business Standard.*

Whither the Co-operative Banking? (28 October 2015). Speech delivered by R. Gandhi, Deputy Governor at Maharashtra Urban Co-operative Banks' Conference 2015 at Nagpur on 24 October 2015. *Reserve Bank of India.*

Urban cooperative banks report nearly 1,000 frauds worth over Rs. 220 crore in past five fiscals: RBI (27 January 2020). *Economic Times.*

Vadodara co-op banks face RBI fury over NPAs (18 September 2007). *Economic Times.*

Vora, R. & Lele, A. M. (4 July 2012 and updated on 24 January 2013). Gujarat's urban cooperative banks. *Business Standard.*

20 years on, MMCB auditor faces action (12 November 2017). *Times of India.*

Rs. 85 cr. cheating case against co-op bank ex-chief (25 August 2016). *Times of India.*

99% CKP Bank depositors to get back full money: RBI (4 May 2020). *Times of India.*

24 defaulters sank Prudential (9 December 2004). *Times of India.*

Rs. 223-crore J&K loan scam: 2 more co-op former society officials named in chargesheet (18 November 2020). *Hindustan Times.*

8 cooperative banks go belly up this fiscal (9 October 2011). *Business Standard.*

Web References

1. www.ckpbank.net/Docs/Forms/ACTIONPLANENGLISH.pdf (Accessed on 15 July 2021).

2. https://www.dicgc.org.in/FD_A-GuideToDepositInsurance.html (Accessed on 29 June 2021).

3. https://egazette.nic.in/WriteReadData/2020/222114.pdf (Accessed on 1 July 2021).

4. https://rbi.org.in/Scripts/BS_SpeechesView.aspx?Id=978 (Accessed on 30 June 2021).

Chapter 10

Fishery Cooperatives as a Catalyst for Sustainability

Shakti Ranjan Panigrahy[*] and Archit Kumar Nayak[†]

International Agribusiness Management Institute Anand Agricultural University, Anand, Gujarat, India

[*]panigrahy.shakti@gmail.com

[†]archit.iabm@gmail.com

Abstract

Fisheries is one of the key elements in the sustainable development goals (SDGs) declared by the United Nations General Assembly and presumed to be achievable by 2030. Though this sector has been placed as the 14th agenda of the sustainable goals, other core elements. such as no poverty (SDG 1), zero hunger (SDG 2), good health and well-being (SDG 3), gender equity (SDG 5), responsible consumption and production (SDG 12), and climate action (SDG 13) are also connected with fisheries in one way or another. Where there is water, there is fish. From another viewpoint, fisheries are more than a food source — they have major impacts on livelihood of populace and natural resource management of a country. As fish is under the clutches of the informal sector, co-management through cooperatives, which has an impressive impact in today's business ecosystem, cannot be ruled out. Southeast Asian countries are known for their natural resources that attract tourists either for their ornamental fisheries, coral reefs, mangrove plants, or beautiful islands. In this context, the roles of cooperatives are very much pertinent to managing the ecosystem in a responsible way, through which the ultimate stakeholders and their sustainability can be preserved.

Keywords: co-management, fisheries, sustainable development goal, cooperatives

1. Introduction

Our Hon. Prime minister, Mr. Narendra Modi, once stated that the 21st century will be the century of fisheries, which will establish "food for future" concept both in the national and international spheres. Though earth covers about 71% of the water base, the life below the water reflects the future food security of a nation having enough potential for safeguarding the planet by minimising poverty and ensuring prosperity. The role of oceans and fisheries in this context is very much pertinent. Oceans provide half of the planet's oxygen and fix a quarter of the world's carbon dioxide. Fisheries provide three billion people with about 15% of the animal protein they consume and provide employment to at least 140 million in total. So, sustainability of global fisheries was considered as the

Figure 1.   Sustainable development goals and fisheries.

prime focus point for the sustainable development goals (SDGs) of 2030, an agenda adopted by the United Nations in September 2015 (Figure 1). SDG 14 mainly targets fisheries to emphasise conservation and sustainable use of the oceans, seas, and marine resources as a whole.

The absence of an effective sustainable goal can lead to people securing their livelihood through illegal, unreported, and unregulated (IUU) practices, which will be more exacerbated in an environment of poverty, climate and market volatility, and affordable insurance protectionism. Altogether, it will damage the coastal and marine ecosystems. Besides, fish refuges must be maintained for protecting the critical life cycles of aquatic species. In this context, the role of sustainable fisheries development by an integrative approach through co-management policies can be one of the tools for fisheries development in the coming future.

It was projected that human population will reach the landmark of 9 billion in the year 2050, and the growth rate in this direction will be more in the developed countries. This growth rate will be due to patterns of migration and relocation to the urban sector. In this connection, fisheries will be a sector that will fulfil the demand of food and nutrition of the burgeoning population. Rice and fish are two specific commodities that are consumed largely in Southeast Asia.[1] It was observed that per capita fish consumption in Southeast Asia is around 36 kg, which is around double the world average. Growing demand for fish and improved fish consumption in Southeast Asia is also connected with their geographical locations, where many islands are located and the people of the island are exceedingly associated with agriculture, fisheries, and tourism for their livelihood. Unfortunately, overdependence on free resources disturbs the equilibrium of the inhabitants of these particular areas, thus there is a need to think about responsible fisheries in the coming future. Some of the current practices like overfishing, eutrophication, growing processing industries, climatic change, and technological development point towards the need for sustainable fisheries in Southeast Asia.

---

[1]Lysine content is poor in cereals and rich in fisheries. Combination of rice and fish in food content balance the protein requirements of the consumers. It is a great advantage in South Asian countries where paddy is cultivated as a major agricultural commodities followed by fish production.

1.1 Overfishing of fisheries

The changing demand and supply of fish along with growing processing industries in recent times accelerate overfishing in Southeast Asia, which is a matter of concern for many stakeholders, particularly fishers whose livelihoods have been integrated with fisheries. Overfishing was a myth till 20th century, and it was assumed that any sort of overfishing was managed by nature itself. The increasing trade, subsidies, huge fishing capacity, and technological development have profound effect on the fisheries business environment. Furthermore, promotion of surimi industry in this region improved the capacity of the processing industry. As a result, supply-side intervention increased a lot, causing overfishing through IUU ways. Overfishing not only reduces the fisheries stock of targeted species by depletion of spawning stocks but also have negative impact on non-targeted species. Any non-targeted harvest of fisheries leads to dumping of catch again into the seas that leads to water pollution, eutrophication, and fish migration. Besides, demand for farming fishes, such as salmonid, shrimps, and prawns, and wild fish, particularly tuna, in a particular region increase upon fish supply, which leads to overfishing. Again, the processing industries, such as fish meal and fish oil, affect fish habitat both in inland and marine spheres. The Economic Exclusive Zones (EEZs), which used to be only 12 nautical miles from shore but increased to 200 nautical miles after the adoption of the United Nations Convention on the Law of the Sea (UNCLOS) in 1982, has created significant impacts in many Southeast Asian countries. In a nutshell, more than 10 million tons of fish are lost through overfishing which needs to be addressed in these regions which are supposed to be closely related to the fishers' and fishing communities' livelihoods, and management measures should be considered not only on the resources but also on the socio-economic aspects of the relevant stakeholders.

1.2 Eutrophication of water resource and fisheries

Many developed cities like Rome, London, New York, and even Kolkata have flourished on the banks of rivers. Our civilisation also started near to the water base. Again, Southeast Asia is known worldwide for its beautiful beaches from where they got their incomes by promoting tourism. Unfortunately, disproportionate population growth, industrialisation, chemical-centric agricultural production, urbanisation, ageing of water bodies, and climate change pollute the water ecosystem in these areas through eutrophication, algal boom, alkalinity of water, deoxygenation, and mortality of fisheries. It is the obligation and responsibility of the populace, who are residing at the bank of the water base system in these areas, to adopt the concept of responsible fisheries through a co-management system. Private industries should also come forward to maintain the ecosystem through different measures like corporate social responsibility (CSR) and capturing different market segments to turn wastages to wealth.[2]

1.3 Hike in processing industries and fisheries

Most of the processing industry in Southeast Asia is heavily dependent on the import of fisheries from the developed countries. They need the fish mainly for their local consumption (low-priced small pelagic as well as high-value fishery) or for processing industries. Again, increasing aquaculture feed industries in Southeast Asia region may have impact on both inland and capture fisheries. It leads to overcapitalisation of global capture fisheries in these regions and, many a times, ends up as an issue of meeting the operation and capital costs adequately. Another part of fisheries dependency lies on the wild fisheries rather than the farmed fish. Growing demand of wild fish impacts fisheries ecosystem directly or indirectly. Recently, countries such as Indonesia, Thailand, Philippines, Myanmar, Vietnam, and Malaysia are always in the top rung due to the introduction of new fishing gear technologies as well as post-harvest and processing facilities. Still, fisheries industry in Indonesia is relatively traditional and labour intensive. Low technology, low culture, and lack of systematic approaches in Indonesia are suited to a bottom-up strategy, which may be a prime step for co-management in fisheries production for future sustainability.

---

[2]Water hyacinths are used in casual wear, cocktails, and long gowns. Two fashion designers, Lex Buena and Rommel Del Valle, collaborated to capture this market segment in Philippines.

1.4 Technological development and fisheries

Increasing technological development and urban-centric approach in demographic dividends make the fisheries sector more inclined to grow and flourish where land is a very limiting factor both for human resource and for their need for agricultural food production and future sustainability. When roads, bridges, and other large layouts like check dams are essential, fisheries development need to be rigorously taken care of for sustained production and growth. In other words, it is going to be difficult for fisheries to flourish without the support of intensification and integrated agriculture. At the same time, catch levels in oceanic spheres were most stagnant due to overcapitalised global fishing fleet and many others. It was observed that the mesh size, which was 35 mm in the 1960s, now reduced down to 20 mm or even 8 mm, leading to capture of entire fisheries population unselectively. The effect of technological developmental on fisheries proved to be quite critical, thus careful handling is necessary. It was observed that around 200 fisheries are fully exploited while one-third of them are either depleted or heavily overexploited. Malthusian overfishing[3] for the sake of technological upliftment must be monitored. Either inland fisheries or marine fisheries development is not possible without responsive fisheries or co-management policies like though cooperatives.

1.5 Climate change and fisheries

Climate change in very much pervasive and need to be addressed holistically for gaining any advantage in the fisheries sectors. Changing ocean temperature repels the fish to the temperate zones from the tropics. So, the impact of climate change is not only on the magnitude and direction of water sources but also on abundance and migration of fish stock in the region. Rising sea temperature, sea-level rise, acidification, intense storms, and disturbed marine ecosystem impact capture fisheries and also consumption both at individual and aggregate levels. Once the Southeast Asian region (Figure 2) and the people at the bank of the open water resources become vulnerable to climatic change, it impacts their livelihood directly or indirectly.

---

[3]Malthusian overfishing, whereby fishers are driven by desperation towards indiscriminate use of destructive harvesting technology, such as fine-mesh nets and dynamite, for catching fishes.

Figure 2. Southeast Asia includes countries such as Brunei, Burma (Myanmar), Cambodia, Timor-Leste, Indonesia, Laos, Malaysia, the Philippines, Singapore, Thailand, and Vietnam.

Considering the changing scenarios and their impact as discussed earlier, there is a dire need to strengthen cooperatives in Southeast Asia. Cooperatives help to stimulate responsible fisheries along with collectivisation of resources that brings survivability, growth, and profit of the population that directly or indirectly depend on natural water resources for their livelihood. On the one hand, cooperatives improve the bargaining power of the producers in the market by streamlining effective communication practices and negotiation power; on the other hand, they protect the vulnerable sections of a community, particularly women, by providing them proper means for their social security.

2. Southeast Asia and Fisheries Cooperative Sectors

From the perspective of Southeast Asian countries, the roles of cooperatives in establishing fisheries sectors and their development are manifold. With these considerations, fisheries cooperatives and their impact on socio-economic environment of the populace of the region are discussed under the following three headings:

1. History of fisheries cooperatives in Southeast Asia and the reasons for their slow growth.
2. Role and importance of fisheries cooperatives in the Southeast Asia region.
3. Some of the fishery's cooperatives and strategies.

2.1 History of fisheries cooperatives and other issues

The progress of cooperatives in Southeast Asia from the clutches of colonial rule was very much stymied but found its pace during the period 1960–1980 (Box 1). On one side, increased demand and on the other side, infusion of technology and infrastructure made the progress of fisheries development faster than before. Though in different countries, fisheries development through cooperatives were handled by different agencies, the intensity of development was confined around fisheries and populace that depend on them. Cooperative movement in these sectors was always toddler-like, which was likely due to difficulty in liberating the fishermen from the web of moneylenders, and the nature of the members of cooperatives were more like a wilful defaulter for different formal agencies of the government. There is no doubt that the technological development and rise in infrastructure bring a cohesive developmental pattern in fisheries cooperatives despite the different geographic and demographic constraints, but unorganised pattern of credit flows was always a deterrent for the communities in these areas. When fisheries development in Malaysia was concentrated in the east coast of its peninsular, it was under the control of Philippine Government as to look after other small-scale and traditional coastal fisheries. In Indonesia, fisheries development was more difficult despite modern technological development as many small-scale fishery units were dispersed throughout the many islands of this particular country. Fisheries development in Thailand was regulated by Chinese ancestry as it was predominantly viewed from religious and ethnic perspectives. All these macro environmental scenarios impact on fisheries development through cooperatives. Though fisheries cooperatives started to show their significant impact only after 1960 in the region of Southeast Asia, it was first started in Malaysia in 1948.

Box 1:   Fisheries Developmental Scenario in the Period of 1960–1980

This was the period when fishing activities were dwelling between explosive and aggressive fish-catching behaviours against non-explosive and traditional practices for livelihood management. During the 1940s, the explosive way of fish catching was practised by Japanese, and after that, it was taken into consideration by many intruders in the Southeast Asian region. Again, there was quite a hike in the demand for aquarium species in the international market. This got the momentum due to presence of multispecies fisheries in and around the region. Explosive ways, such as sodium cyanides and dynamites applications for fish-catching activities, spoiled the ocean ecosystem not only inside the water base but also outside the periphery. It was observed in many areas that uprooting of mangroves plants was rampant for further fish production through ponds and use of the wood for household activities. Overall, it was highly felt that to establish an organisation that spoke about community organising, capability building, and environmental education for future sustainability. Fisheries cooperatives were the solutions in this regard that address the issues of inclusive developmental practices through better socio-economic and holistic developmental ways.

The following points were considered for fish cooperative developments by different countries:

- It was accepted throughout the world that cooperative development was the mandate of the respective government, and Southeast Asia, being a more political and economically stable region, must consider cooperative in their developmental process.
- As major revenues come from the natural resources in Southeast Asia, particularly from the sea itself, it was an obligation of the government to channelise the economic rent equally among all the population without any discrepancies. It was only possible through establishment of more people-based structures like cooperatives in these regions. It was also noted that it was not only about fisheries but also about the population that needs to be sustained with basic amenities.
- Through cooperative development, it was possible to empower the populations towards preservation of their natural resources (water, fish,

coral reef, mangroves, etc.) that ultimately generate revenues for their livelihood and subsequently pull themselves out of abject poverty.

- Governments also tried to promote NGOs to stabilise cooperatives, more particularly in Philippines. It was a step to replicate the micro-based rural experience of NGOs for the macro-level scenarios. The roles of NGOs in promoting education through members were praise-worthy because this imbibes responsible fisheries and natural resource management among the members of cooperatives.

- Greater say and improved socio-economic environment through fisher-ies cooperatives make them more empowered for their food and nutri-tional security. It had made them more self-reliant with adequate income generation. Community-based management allocated and protected access rights which was a step towards sustainable fisheries development.

- Government was the sole body that protected local institution to apply their rights through different laws and regulations. It was believed that cooperative development was more a top-down approach than bottom-up. National interests were channelised through cooperatives and later were provided more autonomy to manage their issues at grassroot level.

Some of the critical impediments in the fishery's cooperative develop-ment process in Southeast Asia are discussed as follows:

- Fisheries were localised in a very specific ecological zone and any specific overfishing due to technological advancement impacted on future production. It was observed that technological development (e.g. trawlers) increased the catch size but subsequently reduced the high-value fisheries to miscellaneous low-value fisheries. As a result, interest overrun occurred, which resulted in low-income generation among fisheries communities. Resource depletion along with added pollutants and toxins depleted the ecological environment of the sea.

- Once upon a time, a high degree of illiteracy and poverty among the fisheries communities in the region reflected in their loan recovery status. This resulted in poor cooperative management and their sustainability.

- The region was disconnected from others due to their unique disadvan-tage of geographical isolation. So, it was very much difficult to get sound managers to run the cooperatives. The Malaysian Government tried to fill up some posts in cooperatives through government officials but was not satisfactory enough to handle the issues like international trade and economic management.

- In majority of Southeast Asian regions, marketing of produce was channelised through wholesaler-cum-moneylender. The fishermen bound themselves in a web of obligations. The fish merchants even got the powerful positions in the cooperatives, and their role limited the say of fisheries members and their future growth in these segments.
- Dual types of administrative policies were also another impediment in the regions. Both cooperatives and fisheries were managed by separate ministries. Ministry of cooperatives looked after registration parts and operations were taken care of by ministries of fisheries. Overlapping of activities retarded growth of fisheries cooperatives.
- Reports suggest that government interference and control of fisheries cooperatives were also considered as impediments in these areas.

2.2 Importance of cooperatives in fisheries development

The transformation of traditional base fisheries to community base management system through cooperatives is need of the hour for sustained production practices. It was observed that local control of resources has a better impact on natural resource management. Equal participation and equity in distribution of rent on resource management will definitely add value to the system, and cooperative is the structure that speaks about integrity in inclusive way. Besides, cooperatives have also some specific impacts on socio-economic characteristics of fishery communities for different stakeholders as elaborated in the following:

- Cooperative is a structure that makes alignment of communities who identify their issues and perspectives at same base. Government regulates their control measures in more systematic ways. It was a structure that control explosive ways of fish catching to non-explosive and non-destructive technologies that solicit natural resource management quite effectively through inculcation of responsible fisheries.
- Effective education and training through cooperatives generate responsibilities towards fisheries management. Fisheries breeding practices

got isolation for development and fish stock management can be managed effectively. However, without a structure, this is very difficult as the ocean is a free resource for anyone to take up catching and trade fisheries in the market.

- It was perceived that cooperatives can act as a medium where effective information can be channelised in a better way among all the fisheries communities. Information on fisheries and fish stock management help the members to gain and share more profit from the marine resources equitably, which reduced conflicts and improves satisfaction.

- Cooperatives transform the mindset of their members from use orientation to resource management orientation. At the same time, the structure inculcates knowledge, skills, responsibility, and accountability among the members for safeguarding fisheries along with other resources, such as mangroves and coral reefs.

- Fish cooperatives not only increase the economic benefits by having a greater say in the market but also it propels more individual-centric attitudes among the members that trims down ex-leaders' interference in the structure. Improvement in the status quo of the fisheries members in the cooperatives strengthens fisheries development on the one hand and energised tourism sector on the other hand by maintaining natural resource management in Southeast Asia.

2.3 Fisheries cooperatives: Different strategies for sustainability

When the oceanic ecosystem was disturbed due to changing market dynamics, fisheries cooperative was considered as panacea against the issues of concern. For management perspectives, it is more important to highlight the strategy against the deterrents at the time of turmoil (Table 1). Cooperative was always has its own significance to establish the mandate of government machineries from it's the days of inceptions. When maintenance of fisheries ecosystem was considered, particularly in Southeast Asia, it was more related to fish, forest, and food as a whole. Without considering these three tenets of development, it was considerably difficult to sustain livelihood of those who have been dependent on water resources solely from time immemorial.

Table 1.   Cooperatives: Issues and strategy.

Name of the Fisheries Cooperative	Issues Needed to be Discussed	Strategy Against the Issues
Marine Conservation Project in San Salvador, Philippines	• Members of the group have no experience or expertise in fisheries management • Destructive fishing methods ruined the oceanic ecosystem, more specifically, coral reefs	• To educate the fisheries communities, a Peace Corps volunteering was setup that conceptualised a community-based coastal resource management • Haribon Foundation, an NGO, identified different roles of fisheries communities in resource management • Intensive information campaigns were done to inculcate the values and importance of natural resource management for future sustainability • A local ordinance was drafted by communities, change agents, NGOs, and the government to stop fishing in sanctuary and to use only non-destructive fishing methods
The Mangrove Rehabilitation and Coastal Resource Management Project, Mabini-Candijay, Bohol, Philippines	• Bay has no legal control of management by the fisheries communities. Informal tenurial rights were passed on from generation to generation • Commercialisation of fisheries, fishpond technology, and commercial mangrove cutters ruined the ecosystem. Cutting of mangroves plants also destroyed rice and coconut field in neat to its adjacent areas	• Mangrove management was identified as a major thrust area along with community organising, capability building, environment education, mariculture, and concrete artificial reefs • Redefining of mangrove areas and issues of formal right to fishing communities were granted • An integrated approach was started to connect any conflict issues, resource use, and fish pond development • Areas of marketing of mangrove plants were limited in extent

(Continued)

Table 1.   (*Continued*)

Name of the Fisheries Cooperative	Issues Needed to be Discussed	Strategy Against the Issues
	• Open access to resources and lack of legal provisions increased the illegal fisheries in subsequent days • Lack of leadership on coastal resource management was another issue in those areas	
The Community Fishery Resources Management Project, Malalison Island, Antique, Philippines	• Blast fishing, commercial fishing techniques, and degradation of coral reefs affected the ecosystem	• Issues of territorial right to the fisheries communities • Deployment of concrete artificial reefs to improve fish habitats • Provision of alternative forms of livelihood • Consistent capacity building and empowerment for natural resource management
Coastal resource management in Orion, Bataan, Philippines	• Extensive and explosive fisheries impacted oceanic ecosystem • Increased population size destroyed mangrove plants and hiked fish ponds for survivability • Red tides and El Nino affected fisheries from sea quite a lot • Around 1,500 km^2 was largely polluted due to red tides	• An NGO was established to promote sustainable municipal fisheries, diversify income, and, capacity building programme • Fisheries-based patrolling activities and deployment of coral reefs were set up • Patrolling of volunteers put a check on fisheries through destructive technology • Mangrove establishment and sanctuary development was promoted
Community-based management of Hamil Beel, Bangladesh	• During the time of flood, fisheries migrate from lakes to the rivers like the Jamuna river and the Bangi river	• A cohesive management style was promoted • Fisheries members in groups were motivated to go for substantial savings from their earnings

Table 1. (*Continued*)

Name of the Fisheries Cooperative	Issues Needed to be Discussed	Strategy Against the Issues
	• Siltation, flood, and infrastructural development impacted on fisheries development • Initially by private persons and after that managed by local leaders, the fisheries in these areas are exploited considerably • A fish disease, named as Epizootic Ulcerative Syndrome reduced beel fish production	• It was strongly communicated among group leaders to distribute earnings equitably among members • Members were empowered in different areas like leadership development, bookkeeping, gender awareness, and adult literacy • Credit was provided both for fisheries and non-fisheries activities
Fisheries Co-management in the Ox-bow Lakes of Bangladesh	• Fisheries harvest through lease was granted to private players and cooperatives at a time. Even small poor populace was also allowed to enter for fishing. Hindu temple priests were also being allowed for their service. As lease was for short period and involvement of many people were observed, no one was interested in long-term investment • Poor management, insufficient fingerlings, and limited funds were other issues for the fisheries development	• License was provided to those fisheries personnel who were committed to do investment in future • Fishers were also provided right to manage natural water bodies in their proximity • Lease license system was enhanced to 5–10 years for better management and investment

(*Continued*)

Table 1. (*Continued*)

Name of the Fisheries Cooperative	Issues Needed to be Discussed	Strategy Against the Issues
Fisheries Co-management in the Porapora Lakes of Bangladesh	• Fingerlings were purchased from private players who were providing those at any amount of credit. Fishers due to their lack of knowledge depended on them highly from input to output marketing. As a result, the fate of fisheries was under the clutches of monopoly of suppliers	• New generation of fingerlings traders came from village itself who were fishermen or very close to the fisheries communities. As a result, malpractices and corruptions were stopped at many instants • All members were involved in lake fisheries and they were empowered to guide stocking, harvesting, and marketing of fisheries
Management of coral reef areas in Jemluk Village, Bali, Indonesia	• Subsistence of fishers were limited to village market but demand of ornamental fish was increasing in those areas, leading to explosive capture, and in turn to coral reef degeneration	• Construction of artificial reefs through old tires and concretes were promoted by the groups • Fisheries members were also empowered towards tourism sector for gaining extra subsidiary income • Village fisheries members urged to stop dumping garbage and polluting the water • Members also motivated to clean the beach every month
Fisheries co-management in West Sumatra, Indonesia	• To conserve fisheries resource, food, and nutritional security, income of communities were major issues of concern	• Fishing was prohibited in the closing season • It was the responsibility of the communities for monitoring and surveillance of fisheries • Revues were distributed equitably, extra money was utilised for investment, and penalties for violators were incorporated by the community members

Table 1.   (*Continued*)

Name of the Fisheries Cooperative	Issues Needed to be Discussed	Strategy Against the Issues
Fisheries co-management in Ban Laem Makhaam, Thailand	• Commercial marketing of fisheries and explosive harvesting technique were used that spoiled the ecosystem • Exploitation of mangrove plants for charcoal production was also other matter of concerned	• A participatory approach for rural development was promoted where incidence of poverty was quite high • Awareness was given against destructive fisheries techniques • Leaders of the communities like village headman and their assistants were involved in organising village fisheries communities for better goals and sustainability • External change agents like NGOs and academician were motivated to deliver value and responsible fisheries among the communities
Fisheries co-management in Can Gio, Vietnam	• Exploitation of mangrove forest and charcoal was rampant • Improvements of livelihood of local residents were quite necessary for establishing their socio-economic conditions	• Benefits, responsibilities, and penalties were incorporated equally among all the farming communities in the group • Fisheries households were provided monthly allowance for protecting the forests • Contact holders were also given sufficient authority to stop cutting down of forests

3. Concluding Statement

Fisheries cooperatives in Southeast Asia have the obligation and responsibility to integrate grassroots with paramount implications by which livelihood of communities, who have been depending on natural resources from the time immoral, can be survived and sustained. It is not the responsibility of the government only; rather, it is the participatory approach of public and private that makes the system more inclusive. Literacy of the communities brings empowerment and reduces poverty. Educated members can understand the value of natural resource management and their impact on their livelihood. The role cooperatives in this direction is of considerable importance, and with the support of NGOs, these organisations can try to achieve their ultimate objectives.

Southeast Asian countries are known for their natural beauty. These are the regions where a number of islands are present, which attracts tourists, and through these, fisheries communities garner revenues for their survival. Without protecting the natural resource, it is very difficult to sustain the life of populace who depend on them, so it is much more than simply about fisheries. When the oceanic ecosystem is disturbed, its negative impact will also be observed on the community, either in their food or in their livelihood.

Though on a number of occasions, demand–supply mismatch has occurred, their implications are more severely observed in natural resource management. Ocean is a free resource in itself. So, responsible fisheries need to be strengthened through co-management processes. Again, governments should also come forward to implement different rules and regulations to manage the resources. Without water resources, there will be no fish or any form of fisheries-based livelihoods.

Fisheries cooperatives also impact on the market through collectivisation of resources. These structures generate a bigger say for their produce and provide maximum revenues to its fellow fishermen. The philosophy behind the cooperative development is to develop the mindset of *self-help by mutual help*. It is highly essential in fisheries-based cooperatives as well, where getting profit is not the sole goal but equitable distribution of it is also another prerequisite for running the entities. Again, when required, application of penalty against any violation of rule should also be executed for the betterment of the society.

In a nutshell, Southeast Asia is the hub of natural resources where per-capita fish consumption is double that of the world average. Tourism is at the heart of revenue generation and fisheries productions are their major occupation that affects the socio-economic conditions of the population in this region. Cooperative is that platform where integrated, inclusive, and in time solution-oriented policies can be framed for the sustained livelihood of the fisheries communities.

References

Asche, F., Garlock, T. M., Anderson, J. L., Bush, S. R., Smith, M. D., Anderson, C. M., Chu, J., Garrett, K. A., Lem, A., Lorenzen, K., Oglend, A., Tveteras, S., & Vannuccini, S. (2018). Three pillars of sustainability in fisheries. *PNAS*, *115*(44), 11221–11225.

Ayyappan, S. & Gopalakrishnan, A. (2008). Resilience in fisheries and sustainability of aquaculture. In Souvenir, 8th Indian Fisheries Forum (IFF) at Kolkata during 22–26 November 2008, Kolkata, India, pp. 1–9, 115.

Case Studies of Fisheries Co-management in Asia. (2006). Retrieved from http://pubs.iclarm.net/resource_centre/Fisheries&Coastal_2.pdf.

COPAC (2019). Transforming our world: A cooperative 2030 — ILO. Retrieved from https://www.ilo.org/global/topics/cooperatives/publications/WCMS_713990/lang--en/index.htm.

Howes, M., Wortley, L., Potts, R., Howes, A. D., Neumann, S. S., Davidson, J., Smith, T., & Nunn, P. (2017). Environmental sustainability: A case of policy implementation failure? *Sustainability*, *9*, 165. doi: 10.3390/su9020165.

Ikiara, M. M. (1999). Sustainability, livelihood, production and effort supply in a declining fishery. The case of Kenya's Lake Victoria fisheries. Thela Thesis.

OECD, FAO. (2017). Southeast Asia: Prospects and challenges. Agricultural Outlook 2017–2026, pp. 59–99.

Rice, J. C. & Garcia, S. M. (2011). Fisheries, food security, climate change, and biodiversity: Characteristics of the sector and perspectives on emerging issues. *ICES Journal of Marine Science*, *68*(6), 1343–1353. doi: 10.1093/icesjms/fsr041.

Sakiyama, T. (1984). Fisheries cooperatives in Southeast Asia, an institutional perspective. *Senri Ethnological Studies*. Retrieved from https://minpaku.repo.nii.ac.jp/?action=repository_action_common_download&item_id=3303&item_no=1&attribute_id=18&file_no=1.

Yasaditama, H. I. (2018). Promoting fishery cooperative: Window of opportunity toward sustainable fishery development (Case Study: Karangsong Village, Indramayu-Indonesia). *Journal of Saemaulogy*, *3*(2), 73–96.

Chapter 11

Emerging Triple Bottom Line Approach in Cooperatives: A Special Reference to Micro-Enterprise Development Cooperative Society

Sunita Pati[*,¶], K.K. Tripathy[†,‖], Sneha Kumari[‡,**],
and Nisha Bharti[§,††]

[*]Assistant Registrar Cooperative Society, Government of Orissa, India

[†]Officer on Special Duty in the Ministry of Cooperation, Government of India,
New Delhi, India

[‡]Symbiosis School of Economics, Symbiosis International (Deemed University),
Pune, India

[§]Symbiosis Institute of International Business, Symbiosis International
(Deemed University), Pune, India

[¶]sunita.pati29@gmail.com

[‖]tripathy123@rediffmail.com

[**]snehakumari1201@gmail.com

[††]nisha.bharti@siib.ac.in

Abstract

In terms of the performance of cooperatives, accessibility to loan in microenterprise cooperative societies have led to sustainable performance. The study aims to bring out the factors impacting accessibility to loan, which has implications on sustainable performance. The study reveals the indicators for the sustainable

247

performance of cooperatives concerning Microenterprise Cooperative Society in Orissa. This society provides loans and training to rural women so that they can sustain their performance. The society comprises around 13,000 rural women. The study aims to develop a model and empirically validate the model for sustaining the performance of cooperatives. A sample size of 105 respondents has been taken to test the model. WarpPLS has been used to test the model. The study discusses the indicators that have a positive effect on performance. The study provides a clear understanding of the triple bottom line performance of cooperatives. The chapter tries to assess the impact of accessibility on the triple bottom line performance of cooperatives. Cooperatives have been evaluated for their social as well as economic performance but triple bottom line performance was largely ignored in the literature.

Keywords: loan accessibility, economic development, social development, environment development, performance, cooperative

1. Introduction

Cooperatives remain essential in different aspects of economic growth, such as microenterprise development, entrepreneurship development of rural poor, particularly women, and socio-economic and environmental impact in the societies (MacKenzie, 1992; Nilsson, 1999; Ortmann & King, 2007). Microenterprise is beneficial in the rural areas for generating women empowerment and the creation of a self-help group (SHG) micro-credit mechanism (Sharma *et al.*, 2012). Microenterprise development is related to agriculture activities, livestock activities, and other household activities. On 12 May 2020, a three-lakh-crore package has been provided as collateral for an automatic loan is to be provided for business including Micro, Small, and Medium Enterprise (MSME). MSME has been supported with e-market linkages and fintech to make them self-reliant. Microenterprise has a capital investment of INR 2.5 million in the manufacturing sector and INR 1 million for the service sector. Cooperative societies have the power to uplift the economic condition of rural people, particularly women, through entrepreneurial activities and microenterprise development and give them a sustainable livelihood opportunity (Idris & Agbim, 2015). Despite their importance, cooperatives do not receive much attention from researchers. Micro Enterprises Development Co-operative Society (MDCSL) is one such cooperative which has not gained attention in academic research.

MDCSL is a cooperative society that offers opportunities for micro-enterprise development and sustainable livelihood through the promotion of entrepreneurial activities among rural women in the Balasore District of Orissa. MDCSL has achieved several awards in the district as well as state level for best-performing society in terms of microenterprise development. The primary objective of the society is to develop microenterprise for the members for sustaining their livelihood. Microenterprise cooperatives assist in the form of loan and training programmes for rural women. This has led to the opening up of different livelihood opportunities to the women leading to sustainable performance. There is a need to study the impact of accessibility to society on sustainable performance.

Driven by this need, the study aims to develop and empirically validate the model for studying the impact of loan accessibility in cooperatives on sustainable performance. The present study is a case study. We took a sample size of 105 respondents for the study. The present study is organised into different sections. The study precedes with a literature review followed by the theoretical framework and hypothesis formulation. The next section includes research design, results, and discussion. The last section includes a conclusion and future research direction.

2. Literature Review

This section reviews the researches on the triple bottom line, cooperatives, and microenterprise. The research papers on microenterprise and triple bottom line were selected from Scopus, ScienceDirect, EBSCO, Emerald, and Web of Science database. The search resulted in 86 publications out of which 53 publications have been selected which were directly related to the study. The research papers have been extensively reviewed to derive the theoretical framework.

2.1 Triple bottom line

Triple bottom line comprises social, economic, and environmental aspects. Triple bottom line is a concept coined by John Elkington in 1994 to ensure enterprise-led sustainable development. The triple bottom line is confined to social, economic, and environmental parameters (Kumari & Patil, 2019; Kumari *et al.*, 2020). The concept has been further developed as 3Ps, i.e. people, planet, and process. The revised model of sustainable entrepreneurship comprises social, economic, ecological, and cultural parameters (Majid & Koe, 2012). The economic dimensions deal with the optimum utilisation of resources and the flow of money. The social dimensions include contributions towards society, such as job creation, product development, and human rights. The ecological dimensions include environmental protection. The cultural dimension includes social equity and environmental responsibility. Elkington (1994) in his report has discussed that triple bottom line is driven by market, value, transparency, life cycle technology, partnership, time and corporate governance.

2.2 Evolution of Cooperative

At the end of the 19th century, the issues of rural indebtedness and the consequent conditions of farmers were responsible for creating an atmosphere for the chit funds and cooperative societies. The farmers realised that the cooperative movement is an attractive mechanism for solving common problems relating to credit. In this regard, the first co-op credit society was established in February 1889 at Baroda by Shri. V.L. Kavthekar. The idea behind starting cooperative societies in India for fighting rural indebtedness and supplying rural credit on a cheaper rate was first given by Frederick Nicholson in 1895. The Madras Government appointed Frederick Nicholson in 1895 to enquire into the possibilities of staring agriculture banks in the Madras State.

After an inquiry about the possibilities of agriculture banking, Frederick Nicholson advocated the introduction of cooperative credit societies within the state. The Famine Commission (1898), Dupernex (1900), and Edward Law Commission (1901) appointed by Lord Curzon also recommended cooperative credit societies for farmers in India. On the recommendations of the Edward Law commission, the British government passed the first "Cooperative Credit Societies Act" in 1904, this act allows credit cooperative societies only. After realising the shortcoming of the 1904 Act, the government, therefore, passed a more comprehensive act, known as the Cooperative Societies Act of 1912, which recognised non-credit societies also. The Cooperative Societies Act of 1912 recognised the formation of non-credit societies and the central cooperative organisations and federations. In 1942, the British government passed the Multi-Unit Cooperative Societies Act, 1942 with an object to cover societies whose operations are extended to more than one state. The state patronage of the cooperative movement continued even after 1947, the year in which India attained freedom. Cooperation plays an important role in safeguarding the weak and unorganised sections of the people engaged in various economic activities. It has helped in preventing exploitation from capitalists and in raising economic standards of small farmers, artisans, landless labourers, etc. It has also helped in generating new employment opportunities and enhancing the competitive ability of the poor section of the society.

2.3 Micro-Enterprise Development Cooperative Society

The MDCSL has been formed in the year 2008 with the initiative of a group of experienced social workers who have been involved in NGO work. The need for a cooperative was felt with the understanding that the local people are self-independent and have enough resources for their development (Yunusa *et al.*, 2018). It is also felt that there was a need to organise them into a broader forum, unite them for a single cause, pull their resources, and utilise such resources for the mutual benefit under one umbrella. The activities of MDCSL are spread over 235 villages in five blocks of Balasore District *viz.* Bahanaga, Remuna, Basta, Oupada, and Balasore Sadar Blocks. As of the financial year 2018–2019, 988 women SHGs (Udyoga Bikash Mahila Mandals (UBMM)) were promoted covering 10,905 rural women. The primary objective of the society is to develop microenterprises for members for their self-employment, income generation, sustainable livelihood, and overall socio-economic development (Tietze *et al.*, 2007). The society is engaged in arranging a bulk purchase of inputs and raw materials, such as improved seeds, seedlings, fertiliser, bio-fertiliser, pesticides, fingerlings for pisciculture, and improved variety of poultry chicks, ducks, goats, etc., along with allied agricultural accessories, veterinary care facilities, and services for its members for sustaining livelihood (Kumari & Patil, 2017). The core activities of MDCSL are generating micro savings through women SHGs, preparation of resource-/skill-based enterprise development micro plan for members, provision of microcredit for SHG members as per micro-plan budget, and providing technical support (Shaw, 2004). MDCSL follows a six-pronged

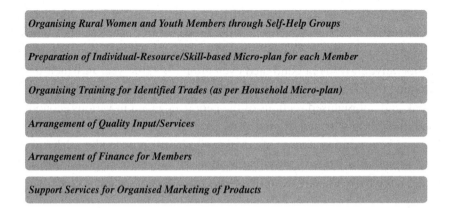

Figure 1. Operational development approach for microenterprise.

operational developmental approach (Figure 1) for microenterprise development of members.

Organising rural women and youth members through self-help groups
Society is responsible for the development of entrepreneurial attitude among rural women and youth, UBMM for women entrepreneurs at the village level and Udyog Bikas Yuva Mandal (UBYM) for youth entrepreneurs at the village level. The society looks after the monthly deposit, share capital, and recurring deposit to develop the creditworthiness of the members.

Preparation of individual resource/skill-based micro plan for each member
The society has done a participatory resource/skill survey of the individual member households. It supports the members in identifying different opportunities for the members and their family, preparation of a household enterprise development microplan, preparation of budget estimate and estimation of credit requirement and assessment of training, and other handholding support requirement.

Organising training for identified trades (as per household microplan)
The society organises training for potential borrowers by experts and subject matter specialists on poultry, goat, pisciculture, mushroom cultivation, vegetable cultivation, etc. at the village level.

Arrangement of finance for members
The society mobilises internal savings and external funds (grant and loan) for financing to UBMM members. It sanctions single-window loans as per the credit requirement of household microplan. The loan disbursement is made at the village level.

Arrangement of quality input/services
Supply of inputs from government-recognised sources and under professional/technical expert guidance is made by the society. There is a provision of doorstep delivery of livestock inputs, veterinary care services, pisciculture, agro-care advisory services, quality agri-inputs: seeds, planting materials, organic fertiliser, bio-pesticides, feeds, preventive and curative medicines, and other services.

Support services for organised marketing of products
Market survey for products produced by rural entrepreneurs, product processing, value addition, packaging, and branding is made by the society. Market linkages to wholesalers, retailers and consumers, bulk procurement, and processing and marketing facilities are also provided by the society.

2.4 Underpinning theory

The cooperatives and SHGs are collectives of members and are based on the concept of social capital. Social capital has gained the most attention across all fields when it comes to economic value. Social capital is the goodwill and trust available within a group of people. Despite the vague nature of the theory, there is a growing consensus among authors for exploring different aspects of social capital. Social capital consists of three dimensions, namely structure (social intentions), relational (trust), and cognitive (common goal) (Nahapiet, 1998). The dimensions result in information sharing, information volume, and information diversity and contribute to performance.

SHGs have a common goal to provide shared representation, interpretation, and system for credit facilities. SHGs are based on the social participation, network building, and collaboration of the stakeholders. Global network involves social relationship and trust with a common cause of restoring the economic standing of the community. Social capital theory in SHGs constitutes the network of association that binds people to form a network and provide assistance in the form of monetary or non-monetary support. Social capital can be gained over a period of time by contributing in different ways to other countries. Thus, social capital is an important component of the proposed framework. This organisation is working with SHGs and promote microenterprises with them. This chapter draws on the theory of social capital. The social capital theory mentions that social capital exists among members. Particularly, when they come in groups like SHGs, their social capital is enhanced, and it helps in increasing the accessibility for various resources. Honig (1998) in a study in Jamaica, concluded that social capital helps microenterprises grow by increasing their accessibility.

3. Theoretical Framework and Hypothesis Development

An extensive literature review was carried out to find out the measures for developing a sustainable framework of MDCSL for microenterprise development. Increased access to microenterprise leads to better performance and sustainability. Access to working capital and microenterprise facilities is considered a building block for sustainability (Al-Mamun *et al.*, 2010). Based on the extensive literature review, the study developed a theoretical framework linking the constructs (Figure 2).

3.1 Accessibility

Accessibility can be defined as the activation potential of available knowledge. Potential means being "capable of development into actuality" and "existing in possibility". This captures the characteristics of accessibility that it is capable of being activated or easily retrieved and then used. Accessibility can be viewed as the "ability to access" and benefit from some system or entity. Accessibility to microenterprise results in the promotion of different business activities among rural women. Access to capital results in an increase in microenterprise assets, resulting in sustainable performance. Accessibility is defined by the size of landholding, adequacy of loan, repayment, and occupation.

3.1.1 *Size of landholding*

The size of landholding is one of the strong parameters for accessibility. As the size of landholding is a deciding factor for the economic condition of the members, it has a link with the accessibility to MDCSL. Microenterprises predominantly require small amounts of capital to start. These microenterprises more than often consist of 1–10 members and engage in activities such as farming, poultry, goatery, and different non-farming activities, e.g. incense stick making and tailoring. Adequacy of loans often leads to accessibility to MDCSL, which is an important parameter. MDCSL provides easy and customised options for the repayment of loans for its members. As most of the members are from economically backward sections and depend on their microenterprises for their livelihood, they need flexible repayment options. So, the repayment of loans leads to accessibility to MDCSL.

3.1.2 *Occupation*

More than 90% of rural women in India are unskilled and restricted to low-paid occupations. Enterprise development is a viable setup to develop economically, socially, and technologically improved quality of life (Sharma & Vandana, 2007). The role of MDCSL is emerging as a promising tool in this context is the area of Balasore District. So, the occupation of members has an impact on accessibility to MDCSL. Based on the knowledge/skill of women members, local resources, and market demand of the area, MDCSL has identified four farming sector trades and two non-farming sector trades for microcredit financing. The producer women do not face any marketing problem and earn a good income for their livelihood. The share capital and various savings deposits of MDCSL members constitute the primary source of funds which is given as loan to MDCSL members for their livelihood enhancement. The loan is considered as an input for production activities or productive services, which will enhance the income of women members and lead them towards a sustainable liveli-hood. Only members are eligible for any loan products from MDCSL. The nature of the loan is microloans, which are critical for the initiation of household-level microenterprises in the farming sector and non-farming sector activities. Such financial services are combined with capacity building support services and institutional development services, which ensures proper utilisation of microloans in productive activities, enhance-ment of income, and overall socio-economic improvement. All such loans are supported by full or partial security deposits which are, in most cases, members' saving deposits along with collective guarantee by other group members.

3.1.3 *Loan adequacy*

Access to financial services is affected by various dimensions such as availability, costs, types, and quality of financial services offered. It is further categorised as reliability (i.e. availability of financial services when needed), convenience (i.e. ease of access to financial services), con-tinuity (i.e. repeated access to financial services), and flexibility i.e. tailor-ing of financial products to the needs of the users (Claessens, 2005). Furthermore, in the context of SHGs, accessibility to finance is studied by various researchers and is related to several factors. Katchova and Barry (2005) pointed out that agriculture credit is highly risky, and financial requirement in agriculture is affected by several factors. Every bank has their procedure to evaluate the loan application, and they consider several factors like credit repayment history, income, and overall financial status (September 2010). In a study by Osano and Languitone (2016), it was found that there is relationship between accessibility and information and availability of collateral. It is important to note that large farmers are bet-ter connected to the financial resources and have better sources of infor-mation. They own land and have options to go for collateral-based loans. In this context, the size of land is taken as one of the parameters for acces-sibility. In a report by IFC (2011), it was pointed out that banks mainly rely on larger farmers for sanctioning the loan. Small and medium farmers face difficulty in accessing loans from formal sources. In a recent study, it was pointed out that accessibility to credit depending on low income and landholdings defeats the purpose of financial inclusion (Henning, 2019). The Rangarajan Committee (2007) also reported that the lack of collateral and weak community network are among the essential reasons for lack of financial inclusion. SHGs are group-based organisations and increase the community network. As this society was largely working for SHGs, adequacy of loan is considered as another critical factor for accessibility. In India, SHG bank linkage programme is one of the important financing programmes. SHG bank linkage programme has the limitation to provide loan up to four times the savings of the SHG. This leads to a limitation on the adequacy of the loan for SHG members.

3.1.4 *Loan repayment*

Repayment of loan facilitate the access to repeat loan to the SHG members. In addition, it is essential to note that the group has to wait for another loan until every member repays the loan. Hence, repayment of loan becomes an important factor for increasing the accessibility of the loan. In a study by PricewaterhouseCoopers in 2019, it was reported that 60% of borrowers have indicated a preference for taking microloans from MFIs compared to banks and other financial institutions. Because of the flexible repayment schedule (PWC, 2019). This led to the inclusion of repayment of loan as one of the criteria for accessibility.

Low amount of loan has been identified as one of the critical problems of SHG bank linkage programme (Ramnathan, 2007; Bharti, 2014). As per the recent state of the sector report released by NABARD in 2019–2020, the total loan size of SHG is 240,994. For an average group size of 12–13 members, the amount of loan comes to 20,000 (NABARD, 2020). This spread is further lower in north and north-eastern areas. In view of this data, the adequacy of loan becomes an important factor for consideration of accessibility. Based on this information, we developed a four-point model for defining accessibility. This theoretical model is presented in Figure 2.

On the basis of the above discussion, we developed the following hypotheses:

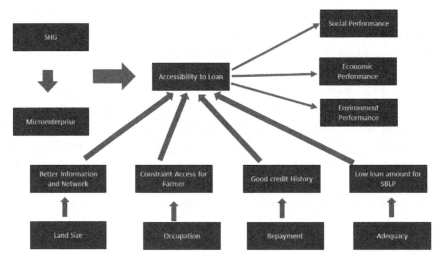

Figure 2.   Theoretical framework.

H1: Size of landholding leads to greater accessibility.
H2: Adequacy of loan leads to accessibility.
H3: Repayment of loan leads to accessibility.
H4: Agriculture Occupation leads to accessibility.

3.2 Linkage between accessibility and sustainability

Microenterprise sustainability involves the application of the triple bottom line into operations (Gualandris *et al.*, 2014; Kumari & Patil, 2019). The society fulfils the customers' demand and gives a profitable outcome for the society in terms of sustainable performance (Sneha, 2017; Danciu, 2013; Raderbauer, 2011).

3.3 Linkage between accessibility to MDCSL and economic development

Microloans provided by society enable those who have no income to set up their small businesses to generate revenue. The society will be able to provide not only sustainable income but also generate employment for others (Kumari, 2017). Income level is an important parameter to understand the economic background. The income of the family greatly influences one's entry into an independent business or professional activity. For example, if the income level of the family is low, a woman avails a loan to raise the adequate financial support to start an independent business or professional activity.

H5: Accessibility leads to economic development.

3.4 Linkage between accessibility to MDCSL and social development

The accessibility to MDCSL helps in the social development of its members. The indicators of social development are social security, use of health kit provided by MDCSL, and member satisfaction.

H6: Accessibility leads to social development.

3.5 Linkage between accessibility to MDCSL and environmental development

Environmental development is determined by the availability of safe drinking water, toilet facility, use of renewable energy like solar light, and use of water purifiers.

H7: Accessibility leads to environment development.

3.6 Impact of sustainability to microenterprise performance

According to the World Bank (2008), training for microenterprise and working capital has a positive impact on economic growth (Gualandris *et al.*, 2014; Danciu, 2013). Economic well-being minimises vulnerability (Al-Mamun *et al.*, 2018). MDCSL is committed to microenterprise development by rural youth and women through promoting SHGs of women members (UBMM) and provisioning microsavings and microcredit in rural areas.

H8: Sustainability leads to performance.

4. Research Design

The study has been conducted in a cooperative society in the Balasore District of Orissa. The area has been well known for cooperatives, SHGs, and microenterprise. In this district, rural women are known to live in poverty. Amid the poverty, the cooperative society has been a source to promote rural women and remove poverty. MDCSL, a cooperative society that promotes rural women through entrepreneurial activities, has been selected for the study. A sample size of 105 respondents from the microenterprise society has been selected for the response. Random sampling has been selected for the study. With a population size of 13,000 rural women in the society, 10% margin of error and 95% confidence level, the sample size calculated is 99 (Singh & Masuko, 2014). Therefore, 105 respondents have been selected as the sample for this study.

The questionnaire has been prepared after an extensive literature review. The questionnaire was pretested by three academic experts and two experts from the cooperative sector. The questionnaire was distributed for data collection. Responses were measured on the Likert scale 1 to 5 with 1 as strongly disagree and 5 as strongly agree. Data were further analysed using partial least-square structure equation modelling, WarpPLS.

4.1 Construct operationalisation

A survey-based instrument has been used to test the model. Exogenous and endogenous constructs have been operationalised as given in Table 1.

5. Results and Discussion

The model has been tested using PLS-SEM. The characteristics of respondents have been tabulated before proceeding to data analysis.

5.1 Characteristics of respondents

The demographic details of the respondents were collected and analysed. The results indicated that almost 37% of respondents lie in the age category of 31–40 years, whereas nearly 29.52% of them are in the age range of 41–50 years. Besides, around 20.95% of the respondents lie in the age

Table 1. Operationalisation of construct.

S. No.	Construct	Indicators	Reference
1	Economic Development	• Microsavings for credit worthiness • Microcredit management at the UBMM level with transparency • Ensuring timely recovery and refinancing as per need of the household enterprise	Mustapa *et al.* (2018); World Bank (2008); Al-Mamun *et al.* (2018)
2	Social Development	• Awareness generation: Women's rights, safe drinking water, women healthcare, solar energy • Promotion of health/sanitation kits by/for SHG members • Marketing of social products (EurekaForbes/TATA Swachh Water Filter, Solar Light, Bajaj Grinder, Induction Cooker, Bharat Gas, Home Appliances, USHA Tailoring Machine SAMSUNG Mobile) • Creation of livelihood models: dairy, goat, poultry, mushroom, fishery, vegetables • Insurance: In case of death, the loan forfeits and savings amount repaid to the nominee • Help in disaster: fire/flood/accidents	Raderbauer (2011)
3	Environment Development	• Waste management. • Toilet construction • Drinking water • Water purifier • Solar light	Adekunle (2011); Danciu (2013)
4	Performance	• Environmental performance • Employee satisfaction • Social reputation	Kaplan and Norton (1992); Gualandris *et al.* (2014); Naik *et al.* (2019); Jeble *et al.* (2019)

group of 50 years and above, but only 12.38% of the respondents are 20–30 years old (Table 2). It was good to see that people above 50 years also have started their own enterprises.

Table 3 shows that the respondents were taken from a wide range of education qualifications, where 45% had passed 10th standard, whereas 15% of the illiterate also took up microenterprise. This clearly indicated that people could see the benefit of microenterprises and were enthusiastic in starting it.

Table 4 shows that around 36% of respondents have no landholdings, i.e. landless. Only 8.57% have more than three acres of land. It is important to note that more than 75% of the microenterprises were promoted by small and marginal farmers only.

Before further analysis of the model, the data have been checked for reliability and normality. The reliability of the data was checked through Cronbach alpha which is 0.75, meaning that the data are reliable (Hair *et al.*, 2010). Normality was checked through skewness and kurtosis. The value of skewness was found to range between +2 and –2 and kurtosis between +7 and –7 (Curran *et al.*, 1996; Dubey *et al.*, 2015; Sneha, 2017).

Table 2.   Age of the respondents.

S. No.	Age	Frequency	Percentage
1	20–30 years	13	12.38
2	31–40 years	39	37.14
3	41–50 years	31	29.52
4	50 years and above	22	20.95
Total		105	100

Table 3.   Education qualification of the respondents.

S. No.	Education	Frequency	Percentage
1	Post-graduation	4	3.80
2	Graduation	15	14.28
3	SSC	22	20.95
4	HSC	48	45.71
5	Illiterate	16	15.24
Total		105	100

Table 4.   Size of landholding.

S. No.	Landholding	Frequency	Percentage
1	More than 3 acre	9	8.57
2	2–3 acre	17	16.19
3	1–2 acre	15	14.28
4	0–1 acre	26	24.76
5	Landless	38	36.19
Total		105	100

A non-response bias test was also performed comparing the early and late responses using paired sample *t*-test (Lai *et al.*, 2013; Lambert & Harrington, 1990; Armstrong & Overton, 1977).

5.2 Common method bias test

The single factor variance extracted using exploratory factor analysis (EFA) was found to be 24.328%, which is below 50% (Table 5). This signifies that common factor bias did not affect the data (Aguirre-Urreta & Hu, 2019).

5.3 Measurement model

Item loadings of the construct was found to be more than 0.6. Average variance error (AVE) was found to be greater than 0.5 and SCR was greater than 0.7, which indicates convergent validity (Fornell & Larcker, 1981). Table 6 shows that the AVE of overall performance is less than 0.5. Since the AVE is smaller (0.4), other construct validity measure of factor loading and SCR is reliable. Incase if the AVE is less than 0.5 but SCR is greater than 0.6, it has been found that the convergent validity is still adequate (Fornell & Larcker, 1981). Discriminant validity was also checked for the data. The square root of AVE of the construct is greater than the squared correlations of the construct.

The results from Warp PLS-SEM software have been used for the analysis of the data. The PLS path coefficients and *p*-values of the model are reported (Figure 3). These path coefficients and *p*-values help to

Table 5.   Total variance explained (Herman's single factor test).

Component	Initial Eigenvalues			Extraction Sums of Squared Loadings		
	Total	Variance (%)	Cumulative (%)	Total	Variance (%)	Cumulative (%)
1	3.892	24.328	24.328	3.892	24.328	24.328
2	1.960	12.252	36.580			
3	1.320	8.249	44.829			
4	1.289	8.059	52.888			
5	1.080	6.748	59.636			
6	0.950	5.939	65.575			
7	0.905	5.659	71.234			
8	0.853	5.331	76.565			
9	0.840	5.250	81.815			
10	0.734	4.586	86.401			
11	0.637	3.983	90.384			
12	0.511	3.192	93.576			
13	0.396	2.474	96.051			
14	0.274	1.710	97.760			
15	0.256	1.600	99.360			
16	0.102	0.640	100.000			

Table 6.   Convergent validity test.

Construct	Number of Items	Number of Revised Items	Factor Loading	SCR	AVE
Economic Development	3	2	0.96 0.90	0.866	0.928
Social Development	3	3	0.781 0.667 0.545	0.70	0.5
Environment Development	4	3	0.724 0.67 0.602	0.705	0.5
Overall Performance	3	3	0.775 0.631 0.442	0.70	0.40

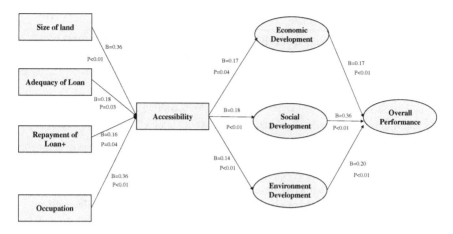

Figure 3.   Results of the model.

understand the relationship between the dependent and independent constructs in the study model. The result shows that the size of landholdings (0.36), adequacy of the loan (0.36), repayment capacity (0.16), and occupation (0.36) have a positive impact on accessibility to Microenterprise Cooperative Society. Size of the land has an impact on accessibility of capital. The members having landholdings in their name get a loan easily. Occupation is divided into agriculture occupation and non-agriculture occupation. The result shows that occupation also plays an important role as the members having farming occupation get access to capital for performing different agriculture activities. Loan repayment has a positive effect on accessibility. Loan repayment comprises prompt repayment and non-prompt repayment. It has been found that the members making a prompt response towards repayment have a better accessibility to capital. As agriculture involves microloans, this is preferable for the members to avail. The accessibility has a positive effect on economic, social, and environmental development (triple bottom line). Accessibility results in environment development (0.14) for facilities such as waste management, safe drinking water, toilets, water purifiers, health kit, and solar lights. The results show that accessibility has a positive influence on economic development (0.17) by providing microsavings for creditworthiness and microcredit management. It also has a strong impact on social development (0.18). The triple bottom line has a strong positive effect on the overall performance of the cooperative society. Since the p-value is less than 0.05,

Table 7.   Key activities of MDCSL.

Development Support Service	• Formation of SHGs (Udyog Bikash Mahila Mandal (UBMM)) • Capacity building of UBMM leaders/members • Household resource-based microplanning • Savings/Credit management training • Forward linkages and handholding support
Technical Support Service	• Livelihood education/Skill training in identified farming sector trades • Skill training/Vocational education in identified non-farming sector trades • Infrastructure development for the supply of quality input at genuine cost, i.e. transit nursery, poultry brooding-house, mobile veterinary care, mushroom-spun production centre • Periodical and emergency technical service to farming sector/non-farming sector enterprise owned by rural women
Financial Support Services	• Microsavings for creditworthiness • Microcredit delivery for household enterprise development • Microcredit management at the UBMM level with transparency • Ensuring timely recovery and refinancing as per need of the household enterprise

all the research hypotheses in the model are accepted. Figure 3 shows the path coefficient of the indicators involved in the model for sustaining the overall performance.

MDCSL is committed to microenterprise development by rural youth and women through promoting SHGs of women members (UBMM) and provisioning microsavings and microcredit in rural areas. The key activities of MDCSL are shown in Table 7.

Table 8 shows that both farming and non-farming sector activities are carried out by the women entrepreneurs. It has been observed that in the farming sector, dairy and poultry are the highest sources of livelihood and in non-farming sector, activities like tailoring and *agarbati* making holds first and second positions, i.e. 16% and 11%, respectively.

5.4 Model fitness and quality indices

The model fitness has been checked using the partial least-square method. The model fitness indicates an acceptable range of the quality indices, as shown in Table 9.

Table 8.   Activities performed by MDCSL.

S. No.	Activity	Frequency	Percentage
1	Dairy	13	12.38
2	Goatery	8	7.61
3	Vegetable farming	7	6.66
4	Prawn cultivation	9	8.57
5	Poultry	11	10.47
6	Grocery	4	3.80
7	Beetle shop	7	6.66
8	Agarbati making	12	11.42
9	Ornament design	4	3.80
10	Tailoring	17	16.19
11	Saree business	5	4.76
12	Woolen garment	8	7.61
Total		105	100

Table 9. Model fit and quality indices.

Quality Indices	Indice Output	Acceptable Range	Ideal
Average block VIF (AVIF)	1.79	if ≤ 5	≤ 3.3
Average full collinearity VIF (AFVIF)	2.157	if ≤ 5	≤ 3.3
Tenenhaus GoF (GoF)	0.265	small ≥ 0.1, medium ≥ 0.25, large ≥ 0.36	small ≥ 0.1, medium ≥ 0.25, large ≥ 0.36
Sympson's paradox ratio (SPR)	0.9	if ≥ 0.7	1
R-squared contribution ratio (RSCR)	0.946	if ≥ 0.9	1
Statistical suppression ratio (SSR)	0.800	if ≥ 0.7	
Nonlinear bivariate causality direction ratio (NLBCDR)	1	if ≥ 0.7	

6. Conclusion

Microenterprise development acts as a catalyst in the social and economic development. MDCSL is playing a vital role in the success of UBMMs. The sustainable livelihood framework involving accessibility to working capital for economic, social, and environmental impact on the members can lead to greater performance of microenterprises. The result of this study is the validation of a model for providing access to intellectual and financial resources for microenterprise development and sustainable livelihood in the Balasore District of Orissa that, if successful, will provide a blueprint for providing services in other poor developing districts as well as states in a sustainable way. The study has attempted to develop a locally inspired model for the provision of services to promote microenterprise, entrepreneurship, self-efficacy and sustainability, and performance through a case study.

7. Limitations and Future Research Direction

The study is confined to the women-run microenterprises in Balasore District and is limited to cross-sectional data. The study has reported the impact of microenterprise in sustainable livelihood and paves the way for further research to be undertaken by linking the big data for performance measurement of the women enterprises.

References

Adekunle, B. (2011). Determinants of microenterprise performance in Nigeria. *International Small Business Journal*, *29*, 360–73.

Aguirre-Urreta, M. I. & Hu, J. (2019). Detecting common method bias: Performance of the Harman's single-factor test. *ACM SIGMIS Database: The DATABASE for Advances in Information Systems*, *50*(2), 45–70.

Al Mamun, A., Nawi, N. B. C., Ibrahim, M. A. H. B., & Muniady, R. (2018). Effect of economic vulnerability on competitive advantages, enterprise performance and sustainability. *Social Sciences*, *7*(4), 54.

Al Mamun, A., Abdul Wahab, S., & Malarvizhi, C. A. (2010). Impact of Amanah Ikhtiar Malaysia's microcredit schemes on microenterprise assets in Malaysia. *International Research Journal of Finance and Economics*, (60), 144–154. From https://papers.ssrn.com/sol3/papers.cfm?abstract_id=1946089 as retrieved on 20 January 2022.

Armstrong, J. S. & Overton, T. S. (1977). Estimating nonresponse bias in mail surveys. *Journal of Marketing Research*, *14*(3), 396–402.

Bharti, N. (2014). Approaches to microenterprise development: Comparison of case studies from Maharashtra. *International Journal of Business and Globalisation*, *13*(4), 519–541.

Claessens, S. & Laeven, L. (2005). Financial dependence, banking sector competition, and economic growth. *Journal of the European Economic Association*, *3*(1), 179–207.

Curran, P. J., West, S. G., & Finch, J. F. (1996). The robustness of test statistics to nonnormality and specification error in confirmatory factor analysis. *Psychological Methods*, *1*(1), 16.

Danciu, V. (2013). The sustainable company: New challenges and strategies for more sustainability. *Theoretical and Applied Economics*, *20*, 7–26.

Dubey, R., Gunasekaran, A., & Ali, S. S. (2015). Exploring the relationship between leadership, operational practices, institutional pressures and environmental performance: A framework for green supply chain. *International Journal of Production Economics*, *160*, 120–132.

Elkington, J. (2004). Enter the triple bottom line. *The Triple Bottom Line: Does It All Add Up*, *11*(12), 1–16.

GPFI & IFC (Global Partnership for Financial Inclusion and International Financial Corporation). (2011). Scaling Up Access to Finance for Agricultural SMEs: Policy Review and Recommendations.

Gualandris, J., Golini, R., & Kalchschmidt, M. (2014). Do supply management and global sourcing matter for firm sustainability performance? An international study. *Supply Chain Management: An International Journal*, *19*, 258–274.

Hair Jr, J. F., Hult, G. T. M., Ringle, C., & Sarstedt, M. (2016). *A Primer on Partial Least Squares Structural Equation Modeling (PLS-SEM)*. Thousand Oaks, CA: Sage Publications.

Hair, J. F., Anderson, R. E., Babin, B. J., & Black, W. C. (2010). *Multivariate Data Analysis: A Global Perspective*, 7th edn. Upper Saddle River, NJ: Pearson Education, 800 pp.

Hair, J. F., Ringle, C. M., & Sarstedt, M. (2011). PLS-SEM: Indeed a silver bullet. *Journal of Marketing Theory and Practice*, *19*(2), 139–152.

Henning, J. I., Bougard, D. A., Jordaan, H., & Matthews, N. (2019). Factors affecting successful agricultural loan applications: The case of a South African credit provider. *Agriculture*, *9*(11), 243.

Honig, B. (1998). What determines success? Examining the human, financial, and social capital of Jamaican microentrepreneurs. *Journal of Business Venturing*, *13*(5), 371–394.

Idris, A. J. & Agbim, K. C. (2015). Micro-credit as a strategy for poverty alleviation among women entrepreneurs in Nasarawa State, Nigeria. *Journal of Business Studies Quarterly*, *6*(3), 122.

Jeble, S., Kumari, S., Venkatesh, V.G. and Singh, M. (2020), "Influence of big data and predictive analytics and social capital on performance of humanitarian supply chain: Developing framework and future research directions", *Benchmarking: An International Journal*, *27*(2), 606–633.

Katchova, A. L. & Barry, P. J. (2005). Credit risk models and agricultural lending. *American Journal of Agricultural Economics*, *87*(1), 194–205.

Kumari, S. (2017). Review on developing a conceptual framework for technology adoption towards sustainability in agro based industry. *SAMVAD*, *13*, 14–19.

Kumari, S. & Patil, Y. (2017). Achieving climate smart agriculture with a sustainable use of water: A conceptual framework for sustaining the use of water for agriculture in the era of climate change. In P. Rao and Y. Patil (eds.), *Reconsidering the Impact of Climate Change on Global Water Supply, Use, and Management*, IGI Global, pp. 122–143.

Kumari, S. and Patil, Y.B. (2019), "Enablers of sustainable industrial ecosystem: framework and future research directions", *Management of Environmental Quality*, *30*(1), 61–86.

Lai, L. C., Cummins, R. A., & Lau, A. L. (2013). Cross-cultural difference in subjective wellbeing: Cultural response bias as an explanation. *Social Indicators Research*, *114*(2), 607–619.

Lambert, D. M. & Harrington, T. C. (1990). Measuring non-response bias in customer service mail surveys. *Journal of Business Logistics*, *11*(2), 5.

MacKenzie, L. R. (1992). Fostering entrepreneurship as a rural economic development strategy. *Economic Development Review*, *10*(4), 38.

Majid, I. A. & Koe, W. L. (2012). Sustainable entrepreneurship (SE): A revised model based on triple bottom line (TBL). *International Journal of Academic Research in Business and Social Sciences*, *2*(6), 293.

NABARD (2020). Annual Report 2019–20. Mumbai, India: NABARD.

Naik, S., Bhandari, J., Pati, S., Bhandari, D., Acharya, M. K., Mane, M. K., & Kumari, S. (2019). Developing a model to study the influence of resource based and social capital theory on performance of sugar cooperative factory: A case study approach. *SAMVAD*, *19*, 20–33.

Nilsson, J. (1999). Cooperative organisational models as reflections of the business environments. *LTA*, *4*(99), 449–470.

Ortmann, G. F. & King, R. P. (2007). Agricultural cooperatives I: History, theory and problems. *Agrekon*, *46*(1), 18–46.

Osano, H. M. & Languitone, H. (2016). Factors influencing access to finance by SMEs in Mozambique: Case of SMEs in Maputo central business district. *Journal of Innovation and Entrepreneurship, 5*(1), 13. https://innovation-entrepreneurship.springeropen.com/articles/10.1186/s13731-016-0041-0.

Raderbauer, M. (2011). Strategic sustainability-strategic implementation of sustainable business practice in Viennese accommodation. Master's thesis, University of Exeter, Devon, UK.

Ramanathan, A. (2007). Financial Inclusion in India through SHG-Bank Linkage Programme and Other Finance Initiatives by NABARD. In Issues Paper presented at Financial Globalization Conference 22–23 November 2007, India.

Rangarajan, C. (2008). Report of the committee on financial inclusion, Government of India, New Delhi. Risk Management Examination Manual for Credit Card Activities, 2007.

September, M. T. (2010). Credit risk management: Loans to high risk agricultural clients in Central South Africa. Master's thesis, University of the Free State, Bloemfontein, South Africa.

Sharma, A. & Vandana, K. (2007). Indian Rural Women and Entrepreneurship. Third Concept, November, p. 51.

Sharma, A., Dua, S., & Hatwal, V. (2012). Micro enterprise development and rural women entrepreneurship: Way for economic empowerment. *ArthPrabhand: A Journal of Economics and Management, 1*(6), 114–127.

Shaw, J. (2004). Microenterprise occupation and poverty reduction in microfinance programs: Evidence from Sri Lanka. *World Development, 32*(7), 1247–1264.

Singh, A. & Masuku, M. (2014). Sampling techniques & determination of sample size in applied statistics research: An overview. *Ijecm. Co. Uk, II*(11), 1–22.

Sneha, K. (2017). Exploration and development of a sustainable agro based industrial ecosystem model with special reference to sugar industry, PhD Thesis, From https://shodhganga.inflibnet.ac.in/handle/10603/191965, retrieved on 4 January 2022.

Tietze, U., Siar, S., Upare, M. A., & Upare, S. M. (2007). Livelihood and Micro-enterprise Development Opportunities for Women in Coastal Fishing Communities in India: Case Studies of Orissa and Maharashtra. Food and Agriculture Organization of the United Nations.

World Bank (2008). *Finance for All: Policies and Pitfalls in Expanding Access.* Washington: World Bank Policy Research Report.

Yunusa, A., Micheal, E. T., & Joseph, A. D. (2018). Contributions of cooperative societies to economic development in Kogi State, Nigeria. *GPH-International Journal of Business Management, 1*(1), 01–18.

Chapter 12

Collective Approach for Green Entrepreneurship: A Case Study

Sneha Kumari[*,§], K.K. Tripathy[†,‖], and Vidya Patkar[‡,¶]

[*]*Symbiosis School of Economics, Symbiosis International (Deemed University), Pune, Maharashtra, India*

[†]*Officer on Special Duty in the Ministry of Cooperation, Government of India, New Delhi, India*

[‡]*Symbiosis Institute of Geoinformatics, Symbiosis International (Deemed University), Pune, Maharashtra, India*

[§]*snehakumari1201@gmail.com*

[‖]*tripathy123@rediffmail.com*

[¶]*drvidyapatkar@gmail.com*

Abstract

Green entrepreneurship aims at addressing environmental or social problems through the implementation of innovative entrepreneurial ideas. One such approach to green entrepreneurship is to explore and implement innovative practices for sustainable waste management. This chapter aims to carry out an in-depth study on the green entrepreneurship of converting wastes into renewable energy for sustainable development. The chapter follows a case study approach to explore rural management practices for the reuse of wastes through the adoption of improved technologies.

This chapter describes alternative innovative practices and approaches of sustainable waste management drawn from a case study conducted at

Thikekarwadi Gram Panchayat at Pune District in Maharashtra and explores the inherent economic benefits on the adoption of such approaches by the rural populace. The study is beneficial for the green transformation of waste and sustaining the environment.

Keywords: waste management, reduce, recycle, reuse, green transformation, sustainable, agriculture, triple bottom line, green entrepreneurship

1. Introduction

Over the past two decades, entrepreneurship has received wide attention in the global academic sphere and has become a matter of recurrent academic research. Sustainable entrepreneurship and green entrepreneurship largely conform to the norms prescribed within the framework of triple bottom line (TBL). Green entrepreneurship refers to addressing environmental or social problems through entrepreneurial ideas. One such approach of green entrepreneurship is waste management innovative practices for attaining sustainable development. These wastes if left unused can have a hazardous impact on human and animal health and the environment. The concept of green entrepreneurship deals with economic, social, and environmental parameters, where there is a strong link between the entrepreneur and the environment (Dixon & Clifford, 2007). Green entrepreneurship encourages the setting up of profit-seeking commercial enterprises, whose business ideas are realised considering environmental and social objectives. There is a high demand for managing wastes of a country through the promotion and propagation of green entrepreneurship. Many organisations have now started customising and innovating their business strategy in which the focus is not only on profit realisation and the welfare of the society but also on assuring a net positive impact on the natural environment during the process of actualisation of their entrepreneurial ideas. Environmental activities such as waste minimisation, pollution control, and recycling, are the major concerns of green entrepreneurship (Ndubisi & Nair, 2017). This leads to different alternatives for the green transformation of wastes. Green entrepreneurs are capable of bringing in green value-added systems and process models.

The green entrepreneurs are those who start the business based on TBL considering people, planet, and process (Silajdzic *et al.*, 2013). There is a value given for green products and services. Green entrepreneurs are economic actors who transform innovative ideas into reality (Farinelli *et al.*, 2011). Their businesses have a positive impact on sustainability.

1.1 Green entrepreneurship and triple bottom line

TBL is a concept coined by John Elkington in 1994 to ensure enterprise-led sustainable development. The TBL is confined to social, economic, and environmental parameters (Kumari & Patil, 2019; Kumari *et al.*, 2020). The concept has been further developed to 3Ps, i.e. people, planet, and process. The revised model of sustainable entrepreneurship comprises social, economic, environmental, and cultural parameters (Majid & Koe, 2012). The economic dimensions deal with the optimum utilisation of resources and the flow of money. The social dimensions include contributions towards society, such as job creation, product development, and human rights. The ecological dimension includes environmental protection. The cultural dimension includes social equity and environmental responsibility. In his report, Elkington (1994) has discussed that the TBL is driven by market, value, transparency, life cycle technology, partnership, time, and corporate governance. Green entrepreneurship has linked these drivers to achieve sustainable development goals, i.e. economic, social, and environmental measures (Slaper & Hall, 2011).

The study enables us to answer the following research question: What is the role of green entrepreneurship in the TBL?

Driven by this research question, the study has framed the objectives and adopted a case study approach.

The research aims to explore green entrepreneurship based on reducing, reusing, and recycling wastes and their role in the TBL.

The study discusses a case of green transformation analysing major focus areas followed by conclusions, limitations, and future research directions.

2. Research Methodology

The study is based on primary and secondary data. It adopts a case study method to analyse green entrepreneurship in waste management in the global era. The study has explored several practices that have been in use and their contribution towards sustainable development of a particular locality. It has come up with alternative uses of wastes through a case study conducted at Thikekarwadi Gram Panchayat (GP) of Pune District in Maharashtra. The study has discussed the concept of green entrepreneurship based on the TBL using a case of green practice in Thikekarwadi Village in Pune District. The study has outlined several approaches for sustainable waste management.

Basic information about the entrepreneur setup, management, and scale of benefits have been discussed.

3. Result and Discussion

This section discusses a case study on green entrepreneurship where different sources of waste management are discussed in detail.

3.1 Case study on green entrepreneurship towards reduce, recycle, and reuse

To proceed with the research, a case study of biogas as a source of renewable energy has been explored. Biogas technology, having the required potential to short-circuit the "energy transition" technology, is a useful green energy generation system to accomplish several socio-economic end uses of a community. Biogas is a type of biofuel that is naturally

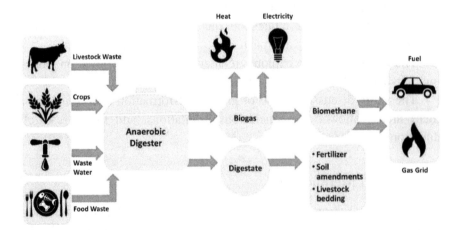

Figure 1.   Biogas and its use.

Source: https://www.eesi.org/papers/view/fact-sheet-biogasconverting-waste-to-energy (Graphic by Sara Tanigawa, EESI).

Figure 2. Biogas plant connecting villages at Thikekarwadi Village.
Photo credit: Dr. Santosh Sahane, CEO & Founder Forecast Agrotech Innovations Pvt. Ltd., Pune, India.

produced from the decomposition of organic waste (Figure 1). When organic matter such as food scraps and animal waste breakdown in an anaerobic environment (an environment absent of oxygen), they release a blend of gases, primarily methane and carbon dioxide. Because this decomposition occurs in an anaerobic environment, the production process of biogas is also known as anaerobic digestion. It was found that the surveyed GP has generated adequate awareness among the villagers on the benefits of setting up of a biogas plant with the connecting village households becoming the principal stakeholders in completing the process of local green waste management (Figure 2).

The approach followed by the surveyed GP has registered a significant contribution in the TBL emphasising the economic, social, and environmental parameters of development. Such a set up cares for the 3Ps: people, planet, and process. The green activity of managing the village waste through biogas plants has become a good source of income and employment for the villagers. The various products of such biogas plants are cooking gas, electricity, bio-fertiliser, and manures, which are locally used and have inherent commercial value. The waste-to-useful-resources approach has had a positive contribution towards the society and environment through feasible, easy-to-handle, and participatory waste management intermediations to bring in socially, commercially, and environmentally useful products from disused wastes for sustaining the global arena.

3.2 Types of wastes generated and their utilisation through green entrepreneurship

Different types of wastes generated by human activities are fruit and vegetable waste, food waste, animal waste, etc. This case study is confined to the green management of food and agriculture wastes produced by the community. The biogas plants are cost-effective and significant sources for the conversion of wastes into valuable resources for community use. The biogas plant has the potential to create biogas, phosphate-rich organic manure (PROM), and other elements. Figure 3 shows the biogas generation potential per ton. The figure depicts that the biogas generation potential is maximum (100 cum) from poultry litter. The biogas generation potential for vegetable and fruit waste is around 60 cum. The total biogas generation potential is highest from vegetable and fruit waste, as depicted in Figure 4. Fruit and vegetable waste generates a total of 8.2 million cum biogas per day from 60 cum biogas generation potential per ton. Figure 5 shows that the total compressed biogas generation is the highest from poultry litter followed by vegetable and fruit waste. The waste also results in the generation of PROM, which is useful for agriculture. Figure 6 shows that fruit and vegetable waste generates 13,700 tons of PROM per day. This manure if applied to the soil helps in increasing the soil fertility and improving the crop yield.

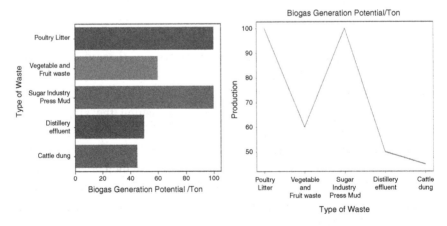

Figure 3. Biogas generation potential per ton (cum).

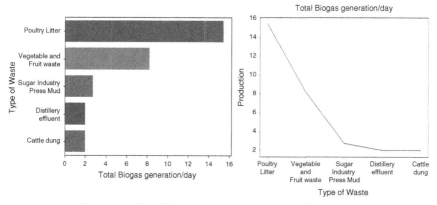

Figure 4.   Total biogas generation per day (million cum).

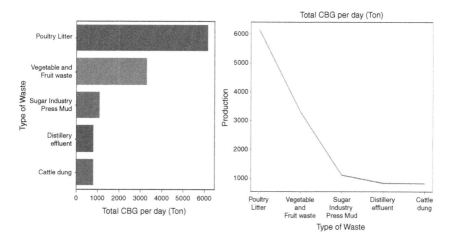

Figure 5.   Total compressed biogas generation per day (ton).

Figure 7 shows a comparison between the biogas generated and the biogas potential per ton. It can be observed that the biogas generation potential is maximum in the case of sugar industry press mud followed by fruit and vegetable waste. The total compressed biogas and PROM generated is the highest from poultry litter followed by fruits and vegetable waste. It is thus observed that fruit and vegetable waste is a good source of all the three resources: biogas generation, total compressed biogas, and PROM, as compared to other sources of wastes.

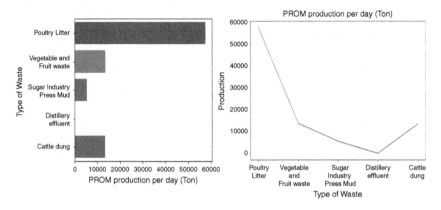

Figure 6.   Phosphate-rich organic manure production per day (ton).

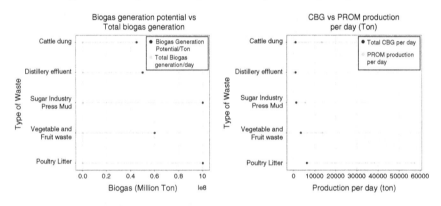

Figure 7.   Comparison of different types of wastes.

3.3 Individual household biogas plant with slurry filter

The surveyed GP has also initiated the construction and operation of individual household biogas plants. The individual household biogas plant set up is a prefabricated, easy-to-install structure. The plant is molded with high-density, rust- and leak-proof polythene, which is manufactured by the Sintex Group and approved by the Ministry of New and Renewable Energy. One cum per day of biogas is sufficient for a family of three to four members, and each plant has the potential to save one LPG cylinder or 17 L of kerosene or 150–200 kg firewood per month. Each user gets excellent organic manure, which is helpful for the productivity of the soil. The manure so generated from a biogas plant can replace 2 tons of single super phosphate per year.

3.4 Food waste crushing and dung mixing

The 200 cum biogas per day plant at the location processes 4 ton mixed waste, including dung, kitchen waste, and vegetable waste. The biogas was supplied to around 35 households through pipelines, and there is a provision for connecting another 40 households. The biogas so generated has been estimated to be around 12 kW power and is being used by the school and the community for street lighting, lighting in temple, and GP office.

Biogas slurry gets converted into PROM and the residual liquid is sold as a liquid fertiliser in five- and fifty-litre cans for addition to soil through drip fertigation. These are permanent sources of income to the inhabitants of the GP. The yield of crops, grams, vegetables, flowering plant, and orchard plants obtained with PROM is observed to be higher than that obtained with synthetic phosphatic fertilisers, such as single super phosphate or diammonium phosphate. PROM is derived from 100% cow dung waste. Organic acid secreted by cow dung converts rock phosphate into a soluble form. The phosphorus content of PROM is around 16.5% (as soluble P_2O_5) and is directly assimilable by plants. It is a sustainable conversion of biodigested sludge into PROM. Figure 8 shows the process of the production of PROM. The biogas plant has generated employment and revenue from waste. Bioslurry generated is a probiotic microbial-derived bioactivator used as a fertiliser for fish ponds, bioslurry as applicable to the soil for remediation (Figure 9). Bioslurry is applied to the soil in the form of drip irrigation or fertigation. It also provides a viable solution to nutrient depletion of many agricultural arable lands in developing countries like India.

3.5 Analysis of the case study

Table 1 presents the analysis of the case in the form of basic business information followed by facts and a TBL.

Figure 8.   Processing of manure into PROM. *Photo credit*: Dr. Santosh Sahane, CEO & Founder Forecast Agrotech Innovations Pvt. Ltd., Pune, India.

Figure 9.   Slurry management and preparation of bioslurry. *Photo credit*: Dr. Santosh Sahane, CEO & Founder Forecast Agrotech Innovations Pvt. Ltd., Pune, India.

Table 1.   Analysis of the case study.

Parameters	Case Study Analysis
Business description	Thikekarwadi GP in Maharashtra
Date of incorporation	17 July 2015
Overall motivation	Wastes are easily available in the country free of cost and generate revenue when converted to resources. Reduce, reuse, and recycle can add a green value system.
Number of employees	3–4
Starting point	GP
Strengths	A total of 120 households with around 400 cattle and vegetable cultivation in 300-acre land round the year
Challenges and constraints	The setup requires a leadership approach or someone who takes the lead. There is a need to create more green entrepreneurs. The setup also needs an open space which is difficult to get in an urban area.
Social impacts	Green entrepreneurship results in electricity generation, fertilisers production, and minimisation of foul smell and other hazardous effects of waste on human and animal health
Environmental impacts	Green entrepreneurship results in controlling environment pollution
Economic impacts	The generated electricity and fertilisers, as well as the byproducts from wastes generates revenue. The waste is converted to resources.
Scale of benefits	Green entrepreneurship is an approach based on TBL, achieving economic, social, and environmental sustainability
Facts	Biogas is supplied to around 35 households through pipelines. Around 12 kW power is generated and utilised by school authorities, community for street lighting and managing temple, GP office as and when required. Biogas slurry gets converted into PROM and the liquid left out is sold as liquid fertiliser.
Strengths	A lot of household and vegetable wastes are generated in the country. So, input for such businesses is not an issue.

(Continued)

Table 1:   (*Continued*)

Parameters	Case Study Analysis
Weakness	There is a need to create awareness and common linkage for transferring the household wastes to a commonplace. The setup needs an open space for functioning.
Lessons and recommendations	Green entrepreneurship is an approach for controlling the environment adversity while taking care of social aspects and economic benefits. The system can result in green value-added systems and processes.

4. Conclusion and Future Research Direction

Green entrepreneurship brings about appropriate development opportunities for emerging economies. Green entrepreneurs are expected to meet environmental, economic, and social aspects of the TBL. There is an acute need to focus on managing sustainably the ever-increasing wastes generated by households. A proper waste management policy can address the issues of collection, segregation, and processing of huge magnitude of wastes for sustainable development. Literature review on the current situation in developing countries suggests that a lack of timely and effective initiatives has restricted the potential growth of green entrepreneurship in India. This case study discusses the networking of households of villages for successfully implementing a green value-added economic process of waste management, resulting in reducing the waste without compromising the principles of the TBL. Though the concept of biogas is not new, community participation and stakeholder contribution in green entrepreneurship have remained one of the under-researched areas. There is a paucity of human action for promoting and implementing innovative practices of linking the villages together to create a culture of green entrepreneurship,

In this context, we observed that with increasing environmental concerns, green transformation is an emerging concept in developing countries. This has opened up future research directions to explore successive factors, to create awareness and application of technology for reduction of wastes, the role of leadership, industrial network, transparency of material flow in the industry and policy in the context of green transformation (Kumari, 2017). The study is limited to the management of food and agriculture waste using a case study analysis. The study can be extended by deriving a model linking the drivers for sustainable entrepreneurship models for environmental sustainability.

5. Managerial Implications

Waste management is the need of the hour. Green waste management through community enterprises ensures community participation for sustainable development. The major problem in waste management is the lack of willingness towards innovative practices. There is a need for proper training and awareness to setup green entrepreneurship based on the TBL. The study can be beneficial to entrepreneurs, practitioners, and policymakers to link green entrepreneurs for achieving the TBL.

References

Dixon, S.E.A. and Clifford, A. (2007), Ecopreneurship — a new approach to managing the triple bottom line, *Journal of Organizational Change Management*, 20(3), 326–345.

Elkington, J. (1994). Enter the triple bottom line. In A. Henriques and J. Richardson (eds.), *The Triple Bottom Line: Does it All Add Up?*, London: Routledge, pp. 23–38.

Farinelli, F., Bottini, M., Akkoyunlu, S., & Aerni, P. (2011). Green entrepreneurship: The missing link towards a greener economy. *ATDF Journal*, 8(3/4), 42–48.

Kumari, S. (2017). Review on developing a conceptual framework for technology adoption towards sustainability in agro based industry. *SAMVAD*, 13, 14–19.

Kumari, S. & Jeble, S. (2020). Waste management through industrial symbiosis: Case study approach. *Latin American Journal of Management for Sustainable Development*, 5(1), 37–46.

Kumari, S. and Patil, Y.B. (2019), Enablers of sustainable industrial ecosystem: framework and future research directions, *Management of Environmental Quality*, 30(1), 61–86.

Kumari, S., Kumbhar, V., & Patil, Y. (2017). Measuring the impact of technology trends and forecasts in sugar industry towards sustainable health-care services. *Indian Journal of Public Health Research & Development*, 8(4), 939–946.

Kumari, S., Patil, Y., & Rao, P. (2020). An approach to sustainable watershed management: Case studies on enhancing sustainability with challenges of water in Western Maharashtra. In Information Resources Management Association, USA (ed.), *Waste Management: Concepts, Methodologies, Tools, and Applications*, Hershey, PA: IGI Global, pp. 286–305.

Majid, I. A. & Koe, W. L. (2012). Sustainable entrepreneurship (SE): A revised model based on triple bottom line (TBL). *International Journal of Academic Research in Business and Social Sciences*, 2(6), 293.

Naik, S., Bhandari, J., Pati, S., Bhandari, D., Acharya, M. K., Mane, M. K., Kudale, A., & Kumari, S. (2019). Developing a model to study the influence of resource based and social capital theory on performance of sugar cooperative factory: A case study approach. *SAMVAD*, *19*, 20–33.

Ndubisi, N. O. & Nair, S. R. (2009). Green entrepreneurship (GE) and green value added (GVA): A conceptual framework. *International Journal of Entrepreneurship*, *13*, 21.

Silajdžić, I., Kurtagić, S. M., & Vučijak, B. (2015). Green entrepreneurship in transition economies: A case study of Bosnia and Herzegovina. *Journal of Cleaner Production*, *88*, 376–384.

Slaper, T. F. & Hall, T. J. (2011). The triple bottom line: What is it and how does it work. *Indiana Business Review*, *86*(1), 4–8.

Chapter 13

Viability Analysis of Primary Agricultural Cooperative Society: A Case in Pune, India

Madhuri Chaure

Global Business School & Research Centre, Pune, India

madhuri.chaure@dpu.edu.in

Abstract

Primary agricultural cooperative societies (PACSs) are the bases of cooperative credit structure in India. The cooperative credit structure functioning in Maharashtra state has three tiers. The main function of the PACSs is to provide short- and medium-term credit to its members. PACSs play a vital role in the socio-economic development of its members. Finance is the key to all types of activities. The efficient management of any society depends on the efficient management of finance. PACSs being financial intermediaries provide financial service with the objective of growth and profit. In the era of globalisation, PACSs face a different type of challenge which raises questions about the viability and sustainability of PACSs. A low resource base has been a major constraint in the effective functioning of PACSs. Financial stability has a direct bearing on the deposit mobilisation and overdue reduction. Limited resources result in low business activity. Limited resources, an increase in nonperforming asset, low recovery, overdue, lack of finance and lack of diversification have affected the viability of primary agricultural societies. Besides providing agriculture credit, some PACSs in Pune District are engaged in diversified activities. The PACSs that have diversified their business are more viable and sustain better than non-diversified societies. This chapter reports the viability analysis of selected PACSs in the Pune District. Multi-stage sampling technique was used. The primary and secondary data were mixed together. Primary data were collected with the help of specially designed schedules by conducting interviews, and secondary data were collected from different published sources and annual reports of PACSs. The study concludes that, as a result of the diversification, Talegoan Dhamdhere PACS in Shirur Block is potentially viable as compared to the Bhairawnath Kasarsai PACS in Mulshi Block of Pune District.

Keywords: primary agricultural cooperative society, viability, assets, liability, financial ratio

1. Introduction

Cooperative credits societies have engaged in assembling rural savings and motivating agricultural investment. Cooperative credit is based on the principles of mutual help and thrift; it is motivated by service rather than profit and is managed on democratic lines.

Primary agricultural cooperative societies (PACSs) are the crux of the cooperative movement in India. They are the keystone of the cooperative credit structure for a large number of cooperative institutes in India. They are known by different names, such as PACSs, service cooperative banks, farmers service societies (FSSs), large-sized Adivashi multipurpose societies (LAMPSs), and multipurpose service cooperatives societies (MPSCSs), while these organisations are generally known as PACSs in India. The key purpose of cooperative credit societies is to provide short and medium-term credit, supply of agricultural inputs, and marketing of agricultural produce. The whole concept of credit societies advancing only loans in cash has now made way to the concept of a service cooperative society, which is expected to provide not only cash loans but also the necessary supplies, such as seeds, fertilisers, and insecticides, the distribution of essential consumer commodities, storage facilities, etc. In some states, PACSs are providing non-financial services to their members, they are known as MPCSs. In Maharashtra, they are known as "Vividh Karyakari Seva Sahakari Societies" or VIKAS societies. In some parts of the country, efforts are now being made to transform many of the credit societies, which historically have been the most important cooperative organisations, into multipurpose societies.

The cooperative movement in Maharashtra had played a remarkable role in the socio-economic development of the state. In the last four decades, the progress of the cooperative movement in Maharashtra showed an increasing trend. The PACSs in Maharashtra has created a spirit of competition and encouraging environment in the rural as well as urban areas. They help to support economic activities and increase the social participation of their members. The PACS continues to be the major source of agricultural credit to the farmers in rural areas.

In the process of liberalisation, a number of private banks are coming up, hence the PACSs have to resort to new marketing strategies. Many secretarial and monetary problems are appearing in the process of quantitative and qualitative development of the cooperative credit system. For the development of the agricultural and allied sectors, timely and adequate finance is required; however, nowadays the PACSs are unable to provide sufficient and timely finance to their members as a consequence of lack of funds.

The increasing incidence of overdue and consequent rise in NPAs have crippled their financial solvency, productivity, and thus the profitability of credit cooperatives. Viability is increasingly hassled and the prudential standard is made applicable to cooperatives. With these new expectations, perhaps, the cooperatives may have to get an altogether new look in the coming century. In the changing economic setting, it is required to make them relevant by rationalisation of the cooperative structure and joining together their functioning with the demands of its clientele. So, there is a need to adopt various diversified activities by PACSs to make them viable and competitive, which would be helpful for rural development. The present study was carried out in the Pune District of the Maharashtra State. The Pune District Central Cooperative Bank occupies a prime position in the rural development of the Pune District. There are 13 blocks in the Pune District, and distributed throughout these blocks are 1,282 PACSs, which are affiliated to Pune District Central Cooperative Bank and working efficiently. Yashavantha Dongre and M. V. Narayana Swamy (1999) carried out a study on "Performance Evaluation Model for Primary Agricultural Credit Societies" and stated that the primary task of any cooperative is to serve the economic needs of its members. The financial stability of these societies has a direct bearing on the extent of mobilisation of deposit and collection of loans before they become overdue. Hence, a comprehensive study of these societies is required to identify financial strengths and weaknesses in their operation.

In this regard, an attempt was made to examine the organisational, operational, and financial health of the PACSs in Pune District affiliated to Pune District Central Cooperative Bank.

2. Research Methodology

The study was carried out in the Pune District of Maharashtra State and mostly concerns the financial assessment of two selected PACSs associated with Pune District Central Cooperative Bank. These two societies from different talukas of the district, among which Shirur and Mulshi were randomly selected based on the number of PACSs that are present per block, i.e. Shirur Block with more than 100 and Mulshi Block with less than 100. The study uses both primary and secondary data. To achieve the objective of the study, the necessary primary data were obtained with the help of specially designed schedules by conducting interviews and discussions with members, farmers, and officials of PACSs and Pune District Cooperative Bank in a field visit. The secondary data of PACSs on various resources, membership, share capital, deposit mobilisation borrowing, working capital, loan operations, income, business strategies, etc. were gathered from the official records, including the annual reports/balance sheets of the respective PACS in the Pune District during 2014–2018. In order to estimate the viability of select societies, the following financial ratios have been worked out (Table 1).

3. Findings of the Study

In this section, the organisational, operational, and financial health of the selected PACSs from Pune District is discussed. In addition, the performance of two PACSs associated with Pune District Central Cooperative Bank has been estimated for the last five years.

Table 1. Financial ratio and their computations.

S. No.	Ratios	Formula
1	Current Ratio	$\text{Current Ratio} = \dfrac{\text{Current Assets}}{\text{Current Liabilities}}$
2	Current Liability Ratio	$\text{Current Liability Ratio} = \dfrac{\text{Current Liabilities}}{\text{Owners Equity}}$
3	Current Assets to Fixed Assets Ratio	$\text{Current Assets to Fixed Assets Ratio} = \dfrac{\text{Current Assets}}{\text{Fixed Assets}}$
4	Debt-equity Ratio	$\text{Debt-equity Ratio} = \dfrac{\text{Long Term Debt}}{\text{Equity}}$
5	Debt-assets Ratio	$\text{Debt-assets Ratio} = \dfrac{\text{Current Liabilities Term Liabilities}}{\text{Total Assets}}$
6	Fixed Ratio	$\text{Fixed Ratio} = \dfrac{\text{Fixed Assets}}{\text{Term Liabilities}}$
7	Return on Assets	$\text{Return on Assets} = \dfrac{\text{Net Profit After Taxes}}{\text{Total Assets}} \times 100$
8	Return on Equity	$\text{Return on Equity} = \dfrac{\text{Net Income After Taxes}}{\text{Total Assets}} \times 100$
9	Owners' Equity to Total Assets	$\text{Owners' Equity to Total Assets} = \dfrac{\text{Owners Equity}}{\text{Total Assets}}$
10	Marginal Efficiency of Capital	$\text{Marginal Efficiency of Capital} = \dfrac{\text{Profit}}{\text{Working Capital}} \times 100$
11	Net Profit to Total Income	$\text{Net Profit to Total Income} = \dfrac{\text{Profit}}{\text{Total Income}} \times 100$

3.1 Organisational structure of PACS

Performance indicator of the two selected cooperative credit societies under study is shown in Table 1.

It is noticed that the number of board members in the two PACSs is the same, i.e. 13 (Table 2). The total membership in the PACS shows much

Table 2. Organisational structure of the selected PACSs.

| S.No. | Name of the PACS | Year of Establishment | Area of Operation | Membership | | Facilities | | | | |
				Board Members	Total Members	Manpower	Other	Audit Class	Diversified Activities
1	Talegoan Dhamdhere	1913	Talegoan Dhamdhere	13	2000	Secretaries: 1, Assistants: 2; Total: 3	(i) Good infrastructure facility (ii) Computer facility	A	Photocopy centre, rented warehouses, and shops
2	Bhairawnath Kasarsai	1990	Kasarsai	13	289	Secretaries: 1	(i) No infrastructure (ii) No IT facility	C	No diversified activities

difference. The membership in Bhairawnath Kasarsai PACS is only 289, whereas it is 2000 for Talegoan Dhamdhere PACS. In the case of infrastructure, it is observed that Talegoan Dhamdhere PACS has good infrastructure and computerisation, whereas Bhairawnath Kasarsai PACS doesn't. The lack of manpower is the main problem afflicting cooperative credit societies in Maharashtra. During the study, it was observed that a single secretary was handling more than three PACSs. As seen in Table 2, three persons, i.e. one secretary and two assistants were working in Talegoan Dhamdhere PACS and only one secretary was handling the operations of Bhairawnath Kasarsai PACS. Talegoan Dhamdhere PACS had diversified their business by running a photocopy centre and renting out warehouses and shops, while Bhairawnath Kasarsai PACS was not doing any diversified activities. Based on the performance of the PACSs, Talegoan Dhamdhere PACS was continuously securing "A" audit class and Bhairawnath Kasarsai PACS securing "C" audit class.

Table 3. Average annual asset and liability positions of selected PACSs for the years from 2013–2014 to 2017–2018.

S. No.	Assets/Liabilities	Talegoan Dhamdhere		Bhairawnath Kasarsai	
		Annual Average	CGR (%)	Annual Average	CGR (%)
	Assets				
1	Current Assets	67,751,373.73	−3.30**	3,336,007.6	−3.44**
2	Fixed Assets	2,527,084.6	3.88***	17,281	20.7***
3	Other Assets	16,179,239.2	3.63**	237,994.6	40.57***
4	Total Assets	76,476,417.16	−3.06**	4,696,146.62	−5.02***
	Liabilities				
1	Current Liabilities	38,732,378.48	1.74*	1,424,536.4	29.64***
2	Term Liabilities	19,806,798.75	−10.09***	886,914.8	24.1***
3	Total Liabilities	76,476,417.16	−3.06**	4,696,146.6	−5.02**
	Profit	4,942,766.118	−1.11NS	126,922.12	21.08***

Note: *, **, *** represent the significance of the growth rate at the level of 10%, 5%, and 1% levels of significance, respectively.

3.2 Portfolio structure of PACS

Portfolio structures of two the selected societies for the last five years were examined to investigate various financial ratios, which are based on assets and liabilities of the societies. The average annual asset and liability positions of both the societies with their growth rates for the last five years are given in Table 3.

Table 3 lists compound growth rate in a current, fixed, and miscellaneous, total assets and liabilities, and profit of the selected PACSs in Pune District. It was observed that the fixed assets of both the societies were increasing positively and significant at 1% level, whereas the current assets of both the societies were decreasing and significant at the 5% level. It was found that current liabilities of both the societies were increasing, and highly significant at the 1% level in the case of Bhairawnath Kasarsai as compared to Talegoan Dhamdhere PACS. As regards to the liability position of the select PACSs, it was observed that there was fast and extensive expansion in liability of the Bhairawnath Kasarsai society as compared to the Talegoan Dhamdhere society. To find out the allegation of the altering structure in various assets and liability positions of selected societies during the selected period, a supplementary financial analysis of the societies is needed and it is presented in the next section.

3.3 Financial ratio analysis

To evaluate the viability, operational and financial efficiency of the societies was estimated with the help of financial ratios. In this study, different financial ratios, such as liquidity, profitability, and financial leverage ratios, for the selected societies were estimated and are presented in Table 4.

The above table indicates the financial performance of Talegoan Dhamdhere and Bhairwanath Kasarsai PACSs. Working capital measures the efficiency and short-term financial health of the company. It was observed that the working capital of the selected societies was maintained properly over the period. The current ratio shows an increasing trend. The current ratio of both societies is more than one, which means that the societies are able to maintain proper liquidity to meet current liabilities. The current liability ratio of Talegoan Dhamdhere society was more than

Table 4.   Average financial ratio of selected societies for the last five years.

S. No.	Financial Ratio	Talegoan Dhamdhere	Bhairawnath Kasarsai
1	Working Capital	29,018,995.1	1,911,471.222
2	Current Ratio	1.78	3.96
3	Current Liability Ratio	0.50	0.28
4	Current Assets to Fixed Assets Ratio	26.97	19.70
5	Current Liability Ratio	50%	28%
6	Debt-equity Ratio	4.60	1.04
7	Debt-assets Ratio	0.76	0.48
8	Fixed Ratio	0.08	0.01
9	Return on Assets	0.06	0.02
10	Return on Equity	0.39	0.05
11	Owners' Equity to Total Assets	0.16	0.47
12	Marginal Efficiency of Capital	0.17	7.19
13	Net Profit to Total Income	49%	5%

that of Bhairwanath Kasarsai. On the other hand, current assets to fixed assets ratio is more in the case of the Talegoan Dhamdhere primary society as compared to the Bhairwanath Kasarsai society.

The rate of return on assets and return on equity have been considered to obtain profitability ratio in this study. In general, an increase in profitability ratio is considered a good sign for the financial health of the society. However, this increase could also be dangerous if the society relies too heavily on debt. Both the ratios, return on assets (0.06) and return on equity (0.39), were higher in the case of Talegoan Dhamdhere PACS as compared to Bhairwanath Kasarsai PACS. The marginal efficiency of capital, which is the percentage of profit expected from a given investment on a capital asset, was 0.17 in the case of Talegoan Dhamdhere PACS and 7.19 in case of Bhairwanath Kasarsai PACS.

A similar trend was obtained through net profit to total income percentage: It was 49% in the case of Talegoan Dhamdhere PACS and 5% in the case of Bhairwanath Kasarsai PACS. The net profit to total income percentage is higher in the case of Talegoan Dhamdhere PACS but concurrent higher expenditures results in decreased profitability. Overall, the Talegoan Dhamdhere society is potentially viable and functioning well, whereas the Bhairwanath Kasarsai primary agriculture society is not viable.

4. Conclusions

On the whole, the analysis performed in the study raised numerous doubts about the efficient functioning of the PACSs in the Pune District of Maharashtra State. The viability analysis of primary agriculture societies in Pune District shows that the Talegoan Dhamdhere PACS from Shirur Block is diversified, potentially viable, and functioning well, whereas the Bhairwanath Kasarsai PACS is not diversified and not viable. It can be concluded that many administrative and financial problems emerge during the qualitative and quantitative development of a cooperative credit society. The various problems include too low a resource base, high dependency on refinancing agencies, low recovery levels, huge accumulated losses, increase in NPAs, lack of diversification, lack of professionalism, more government and vested interest interference, and various types of organisational weakness. The PACSs in Pune District were additionally faced with major problems, which were the absence of infrastructure and computerisation, insufficient manpower, and lack of IT facility and diversification. The loan waiver schemes affected the recovery of the loan by the PACSs. The members are not ready to repay loans within the stipulated period. The low loan recovery increased NPA of many PACSs and was responsible for the loss of business. The study found that such PACSs are not viable and need to diversify for their sustainability. For smooth functioning and viability, PACSs need to adopt diversification activities along with their credit business. Revival and diversification could be a possible solution but not the sole remedy for the viability and sustainability of PACSs. It ought to be supported by HRD interventions. Proper monitoring and evaluation of the operation of the PACS is essential to confirm their efficient functioning.

References

Kannapiran, P. (2010). Financial performance of Nilgiris district Central Co-operative Bank Ltd. *Co-operative Perspective, 45*(2), 53–58.

Khazan, C. (2016). Viability Analysis of the Wadala Primary Agriculture Cooperative Service society ltd. Wadala. Success story, C-PEC,BIRD.Oct.

Kulandaiswamy, V. & Murugesan, P. (2004). Performance of PACS — An empirical evaluation. *Indian Co-operative Review, 42*(2), 121–130.

Mohit, K. & Mehta, V. P. (2018). Performance and Prospects of Primary Agricultural Credit Societies (PACS) in Haryana during 2000-01 to 2014-15. *International Journal of Current Microbiology and Applied Sciences, 7*(4), 20–32.

Pujari, A., Suhag, A., & Malik, D. P. (2009). An evaluation of primary agricultural co-operative societies in Karnataka state. *Indian Co-operative Review, 46*(4), 275–285.

Ravi Varma, S. & Rajender Naidu, R. (2009). The performance evaluation of primary agricultural co-operative societies — A micro level study. *Indian Co-operative Review, 46*(4), 296–304.

Shah, D. (2007). Measuring viability of PACS during reform period in Maharashtra: A case study. *Journal of Rural Development*, NIRD, *23*(4), 435–450.

Yashavantha, D. & Narayana Swamy, M. V. (1999). Performance evaluation model for primary agricultural credit societies. *Vikalpa: The Journal for Decision Makers, Indian Institute of Management Ahmadabad, 24*(1), 45–53.

Yashoda. (2017). Role of Primary Agricultural Co-Operative Society (PACS) in agricultural development in India. *Global Journal of Management and Business Research: C Finance, 17*(3), 18–22.

Index